Management Information Systems

8th Edition

Terry Lucey

M.Soc.Sc., F.C.M.A., F.C.C.A., J.Dip.M.A.

Terry Lucey has been an accountant and consultant in industry and has had over twenty years' examining and teaching experience at all levels of professional studies and for diploma and degree courses in business studies. He was previously Head of Department of Business Studies at the University of Wolverhampton, and is now a consultant and Visiting Fellow at Aston Business School, Aston University.

Among his other published works are: *Investment Appraisal: Evaluating Risk and Uncertainty*; *Accounting and Computer Systems* (co-author); *Quantitative Techniques*; *A First Course in Management Accounting*; *Management Accounting*; *Business Administration* and *Costing*.

continuum
LONDON • NEW YORK

Acknowledgements

Examination Questions

The author would like to express thanks to the following for giving permission to reproduce past examination questions.

Chartered Association of Certified Accountants (ACCA)
Chartered Institute of Management Accountants (CIMA)
Chartered Institute of Public Finance and Accountancy (CIPFA)
Institute of Chartered Secretaries and Administrators (ICSA)
Chartered Institute of Bankers (CIB)
Chartered Institute of Marketing (CIM)
Institute of Administrative Management (IAM)

A CIP catalogue record for this book is available from the British Library

First Edition 1976
Second Edition 1978
Third Edition 1979
Fourth Edition 1981
Reprinted 1982, 1984
Fifth Edition 1987
Reprinted 1989, 1990
Sixth Edition 1991
Reprinted 1991, 1992, 1993, 1994
Seventh Edition 1996
Eighth Edition 1997
Reprinted 1998, 1999 (twice), 2000, 2002

ISBN   0 8264 5407 0

Typeset by Elizabeth Bennett and Jane Conway

Printed by Martins the Printers Ltd, Berwick upon Tweed

Formerly published by DP Publications.

Continuum
The Tower Building, 11 York Road, London, SE1 7NX
370 Lexington Avenue, New York, NY 10017-6550

Contents

Preface

Aims of the book

This new edition has the same objectives as the previous editions, namely to provide a thorough coverage of the principles, application and design of management information systems in both public and private sector organisations. It is aimed at both the *producers* of information, for example, accountants, systems analysts, computer specialists, operational researchers and so on, and the *users* of information who are management at all levels. The book is particularly relevant for:

a) students preparing themselves for Professional Examinations which include the study of information systems. Examples include: the Chartered Association of Certified Accountants; the Institute of Chartered Accountants; the Chartered Institute of Management Accountants; the Chartered Institute of Public Finance and Accountancy; the Chartered Institute of Bankers; the Institute of Administrative Management; the British Computer Society; the Chartered Institute of Secretaries and Administrators; the Institute of Accounting Technicians.

b) students on BTEC, diploma and degree courses in Business Studies and Accountancy where the study of information systems is part of the curriculum.

c) Students on Systems Analysis and Computer Science diploma and degree courses.

d) Students on Management Courses who need to understand the principles of information systems design.

e) Managers and others in industry, commerce, local authorities and public corporations who wish to gain a working knowledge of management information systems.

Scope of the book

This edition, the eighth in twenty years, contains numerous detailed revisions and extensions of coverage. There are many more current examples and new material on; Business Process Re-engineering, Organisational Culture, Soft-System Methodology, the World Wide Web and Data Mining. There are Assignments, Cases and a selection of Examination Questions from the latest professional examinations which can be used to aid assessment and revision.

Over the years the response to this book has been gratifying and it is hoped that this enlarged and revised edition will continue to fulfil the needs of students, lecturers and practitioners.

I would like to thank everybody who contributed comments on the earlier editions and suggestions for improvement, which I have endeavoured to include wherever possible.

Approach

The book has been written in a standardised format with headed paragraphs, end of chapter summaries and review questions at the end of chapters.

To gain genuine understanding of any technical subject constant reinforcement of knowledge and practice in answering problems is vital. Special attention has been given to this and, at suitable stages, the book includes several Assessment and Revision sections. These contain:

- assignments for individual or group activity;
- mini-cases with tasks to be accomplished;
- examination questions (with and without answers);
- suggestions for further reading.

Most of the examination questions used have been drawn from past professional examinations and are cross-referenced accordingly. To ensure full coverage of the book's contents occasionally it has been necessary to develop other questions and mini-cases of an equivalent standard.

Note for lecturers

This book is suitable both for topic based teaching or student centred learning using the questions without answers, assignments and cases provided in the Assessment and Revision sections.

A Lecturers' Supplement is available free to lecturers adopting this book as a course text. The supplement contains:

- guidance notes on the cases;
- answers to the questions in the book;
- OHP masters of key diagrams from the book.

T. Lucey
March 1997

1 Management Information Systems – an Overview

Objectives

After you have studied this chapter you will:

- have had an introduction to the book as a whole;
- know that the book takes a decision focus to management information systems;
- understand that it is the user who determines what is information not the producer;
- know the main knowledge requirements for MIS design;
- know how change is affecting organisations.

What is a Management Information System (MIS)?

There is no universally accepted definition of an MIS and those that exist reflect the emphasis – and prejudices! – of the particular writer. The term MIS has become almost synonymous with computer based data processing and indeed many books with MIS in the title turn out to be exclusively concerned with topics such as systems analysis, file design and the various other technical facets of computer based systems. This emphasis results in a production-orientated definition of MIS of which the following by Kelly is a typical example:

> 'Management Information System: The combination of human and computer-based resources that results in the collection, storage, retrieval, communication and use of data for the purpose of efficient management of operations and for business planning.'

This book does *not* take a production-orientated view and emphasises that the means of producing the information – whether by computer or manual methods – is a secondary consideration compared with the importance of ensuring that the correct problems are addressed and that relevant information is available when, where, and in the form required to be usable by management. Then, and only then, should the means of producing the information be considered.

This book takes a *decision focus* to the design and operation of MIS which means that the information system is viewed as a means of processing data, i.e. the routine facts and figures of the organisation, into information which is then used for decision making. It is changes in decision behaviour which distinguish data from information. Figure 1/1 summarises this approach.

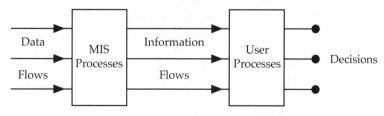

Figure 1/1 Decision focus of MIS

This means that MIS are qualitatively different from data processing systems and that management involvement and interaction between information specialists and management is the key feature of successful MIS design.

Having regard to the emphasis of this book an MIS can be defined as:

> A system to convert data from internal and external sources into information and to communicate that information, in an appropriate form, to managers at all levels in all functions to enable them to make timely and effective decisions for planning, directing and controlling the activities for which they are responsible.

Note the emphasis in the definition is on the use of information not on how it is produced.

Problems with MIS

There is abundant evidence from numerous surveys both in the UK and the USA that existing MIS, often using advanced computer equipment, have had relatively little success in providing management with the information it needs. The typical reasons discovered for this include the following:

- lack of management involvement with the design of the MIS;
- narrow and/or inappropriate emphasis of the computer system;
- undue concentration on low level data processing applications particularly in the accounting area;
- lack of management knowledge of computers;
- poor appreciation by information specialists of management's true information requirements and of organisational problems;
- lack of top management support

To be successful an MIS must be designed and operated with due regard to organisation and behavioural principles as well as technical factors. Management must be informed enough to make an effective contribution to systems design and information specialists (systems analysts, accountants, operations researchers and others) must become more aware of managerial functions and needs so that, jointly, more effective MIS are developed.

Management do not always know what information they need and information specialists often do not know enough about management to be able to produce relevant information for the managers they serve. An example given by Professor Kaplan graphically illustrates this point.

He reported that a group of American industrialists visiting Japan found that their counterparts were regularly supplied with information on the proportion of products which pass through the factory without re-working or rectification. They found that a typical percentage of products that needed no re-working was 92%. The American managers found that this information was not available to them in their factories at home but on investigation it was found that their ratio was 8%. They then worked on this factor for 6 months at which point the ratio had moved up to 66% and, more importantly, productivity was 25% higher.

There is no doubt that better communication between management and information specialists, plus a wider knowledge by both groups of MIS principles would greatly facilitate the task of developing relevant and appropriate information systems. There is, unfortunately, no simple checklist of essential features which, if followed, will automatically produce the perfect MIS. What is required is an awareness and understanding of key principles and function so that the design, implementation and operation of the MIS is the result of informed decisions and judgements rather than haphazard development without regard to real organisational requirements.

Knowledge Requirements for MIS

By their nature, MIS draw upon a wide and growing range of concepts and techniques and Figure 1/2 shows the major areas of knowledge which are considered to be the most important in the development and operation of MIS.

Figure 1/2 has been drawn not only to show the various areas of knowledge, which are each developed in subsequent chapters of the book, but also to show that inter-relationships exist between all the areas. This point is stressed because the knowledge areas are not self-contained, independent entities but interact with, and complement, each other. The understanding of these interactions and cross relationships makes the task of designing MIS much more difficult but conversely, enhances the likelihood of designing relevant information systems which make a positive contribution to the organisation.

It will be seen that encircling the core of the diagram is an area entitled 'Behavioural Factors'. This attempts to show in a diagrammatic form the all pervasive influence and importance of behavioural considerations in the design and operation of MIS. Even within areas which are conventionally deemed to be purely quantitative, the reactions, motivations, aspirations and capabilities of the people involved must be considered.

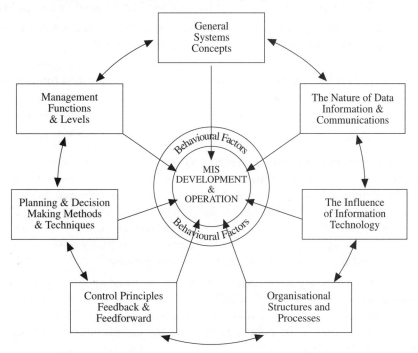

Figure 1/2 Knowledge requirements for the development and operation of MIS

An example is the accounting technique of Budgetary Control which is often regarded by accountants as a neutral, technical process but which is viewed by the personnel affected as anything but neutral. Properly designed, such systems may have beneficial motivating effects but all too often are seen by the managers and staff as unwanted impositions which cause resentment and dysfunctional behaviour, i.e. behaviour which does not contribute to organisational objectives. Because of the overall importance of behavioural considerations they are dealt with throughout the book in context with the topic under consideration.

Each of the knowledge areas shown on Figure 1/2 is introduced in the following paragraphs.

The Nature of Data, Information and Communications

The processing of data into information and communicating the resulting information to the user is the very essence of MIS. Data is the term for collections of facts and figures; hours worked, invoice values, part numbers, usage rates, items received etc. These basic facts are stored, analysed, compared, calculated and generally worked on to produce messages in the form required by the user, i.e. the manager, which is then termed *information*.

This outline of the process is simple and readily understandable but further study will show that information is a more complex and ambiguous concept than so far indicated. From the viewpoint of developing relevant MIS, rather than the routine production of standardised reports, consideration must be given to the source of the information, the means by which it is communicated and, most important of all, the meaning attached to the message received and the use made of it. This final link in the communication chain is clearly of critical importance to both the information system designer and user and again emphasises the pervasive nature of human and behavioural factors in MIS.

A theme which is developed in this book is that the value of information can only come from the results of decisions and actions based on the information.

> In summary, data incur costs, information – which is properly communicated and acted upon – can create value.

General System Concepts

Many of the concepts of General Systems Theory (GST) have direct applicability to organisations and MIS. GST emphasises that not only is it necessary to examine and analyse the individual parts of the system or organisation – known as the *reductionist approach* – but also it is vital that the system is viewed as a totality where the whole is greater than the sum of the parts – known as the *holistic approach*. Systems are composed of sub-systems, or expressed in commercial terms, organisations consist of departments and sections, and these parts interact and are interdependent.

Accordingly it is necessary to consider these inter-relationships otherwise the system or organisation as a whole will not function efficiently and will be slower to adapt to changing conditons, which is a primary requisite to survival. The reductionist approach ignores these vital inter-relationships by treating the individual parts as self contained entities – which they are not.

A simple organisational example of this would be if a stock control system in a firm was to be analysed in order to make it more efficient and it was decided that no attempt was to be made to consider the linkages which exist between the production control system, the replenishment system and the stock control system itself. In such circumstances even if the stock control system operated at peak efficiency, the overall effect would be less than optimal and a condition of sub-optimality would occur.

Organisation Processes and Structures

Organisations are artificially contrived structures with procedures and objectives which should, and usually do, adapt to changes in the environment. MIS exist in organisations in order to help them achieve objectives, to plan and control their processes and operations, to help deal with uncertainty and to help in adapting to change or, indeed, initiating change. Accordingly it is important for information system designers to be aware of the various influences on organisation design. These range from earlier mechanistic concepts, largely stemming from the 'scientific management' movement in the early part of this century, to more modern ideas which recognise the social and behavioural characteristics of the members of the organisation and the need for adaptation and change to deal with ever more rapidly changing conditions.

Management Functions and Levels

As already stated, the value of information derives from the actions management take as a result of using the information. It follows that information specialists need to know what type of tasks and functions management have to perform so that they are able to produce relevant – therefore usable – information.

The functions of management can be grouped into five areas: planning, decision making, organising and co-ordinating, leadership and motivation, and control.

Obviously the emphasis given to each area varies from manager to manager and is especially dependent upon the level of the manager in the organisation.

In broad terms, three levels of management can be seen in all organisations. Top or strategic management, middle or tactical management and junior or operational management.

There are clear differences in information requirements between a manager at the operational or transactional level such as, say, a transport supervisor and a manager at the strategic or top level such as, for example, the marketing director. At the highest level, structured, formal MIS may actually be counter productive, for at these levels informal MIS and external influences become increasingly important.

Another factor which affects the tasks a manager has to perform, and hence his information requirements, is the extent of functional authority within the organisation. Functional authority is that which is exercised by specialist managers and staff throughout the various departments and units of the organisation. Possibly the most common example of this is the Personnel Department which has functional responsibility for many personnel and industrial relation activities throughout the whole organisation.

Whilst each of the five functional areas, which in total constitute the task of management, need relevant information, three particular areas – planning, decision making and control – make heavy demands on the organisation's MIS and thus are given special attention in this book.

The Nature of Planning and Decision Making and the Techniques Available

Planning and decision making have rightly been called the primary management tasks and these tasks occur at every level of management although, naturally, the type of planning and decision making will vary between the levels.

Planning is the process of deciding in advance what is to be done and how it is to be done. The planning process results in plans which are pre-determined courses of action that reflect organisational objectives and the plans are implemented by decisions and action. Thus, effective planning and decision making are inextricably linked, for without decisions and actions the planning process is a sterile exercise.

In order to provide appropriate information, MIS designers must be aware of the types of decisions made at the various levels of organisation. A useful, broad classification is that given by H.A. Simon who classified decision making into *programmed* and *non-programmed* areas.

Programmed decisions are those that are routine and repetitive and where the decision rules are known. Conversely, non-programmed decisions are novel and unstructured and the nature of the problem and decision rules are complex and little understood. It follows from these brief descriptions that radically different information and procedures are required for the different decision types, which has obvious implications for MIS design.

To create value from information, changes in decision behaviour must result and consequently there must be a decision focus to the MIS. This means that the MIS must be designed with due regard to the types of decision, how decisions are taken, how the decision maker relates to the organisation, the nature of the organisation, its environments and so on. Acceptance and understanding of this emphasis by both managers and information specialists is the primary requisite to effective MIS design. Managers, and the MIS which supports them, must distinguish between *effectiveness* and *efficiency*.

- Effectiveness means doing the right thing i.e. producing the desired results.
- Efficiency is a measurement of the use of resources to achieve results.

Thus an organisation may be producing the *wrong* output efficiently and is thus an ineffective organisation. Good management concentrates on *what* must be done before considering *how* it should be done and the MIS should help them do this.

Control Principles – Feedback and Feedforward

Control has already been mentioned as one of the main management tasks. Much of the lower and middle management effort, and consequently much of the routine output of MIS, is concerned with control activities. Control is the process of ensuring that operations proceed according to plan and at the most basic level this is done by comparing the actual results or output of the system against a target and using any differences found to adjust the input side of the system so as to bring activities in line with the target. In practice the target may be termed a norm, a budget, a standard, a performance or stock level and so on.

The procedure outlined above, i.e. input – process – output – monitor and compare – adjustment, requires what is known as a *feedback control loop* and such a loop is a common feature of many aspects of MIS, for example, stock control, budgetary control, production control and so on. It will be realised that the basic system described is relatively mechanistic and is therefore not necessarily suitable for all facets of the organisation's activities. For example, there is the implicit assumption that the target or plan does not change and that conditions in the next control cycle will be similar to those in the past. Clearly, in volatile and uncertain conditions these assumptions are hardly likely to be correct.

Where a self regulating feedback system is not able to control a process adequately it may be feasible to use *feedforward*. This is where monitoring at some early stage of a system or process may indicate that an adjustment should be made at a later stage of the process, prior to the final output. Feedforward is not an automatic process and requires management intervention for it to operate successfully and consequently, it does not have the degree of 'automatic' control inherent in a feedback system.

The Influence of Information Technology (IT)

IT is a general expression covering computers, telecommunications and electronics and there is little doubt that IT is having a profound influence on all aspects of life, including organisations and MIS. Much of the expenditure on computers and IT incurred by organisations to date has been on relatively routine data processing applications, particularly in the accounting area, and in operational control systems such as stock control.

Of course these are vital tasks but of themselves they do not constitute management information systems. These traditional data processing systems, which are often highly sophisticated and complex, perform the essential role of processing the day-to-day transactions and provide much of the data from which management information can be prepared. The rapid growth of technology and the dramatically falling cost of computing capability means that more and more aspects of managerial planning and decision making can be assisted by information technology provided, of course, that the information system is developed in accordance with properly defined objectives and principles.

Although there are many overlaps and inter-relationships, it is possible to distinguish three types of systems using information technology:

a) **Data Processing** (or **transaction processing**). These are computer and electronics based systems for recording, processing and reporting on the day-to-day activities of the organisation. Examples include; ledger keeping, payroll, barcode readers, automatic teller machines.

b) **Office Support Systems**. These systems provide day-to-day assistance with the functions of the office. Examples include; word processing, electronic mail, telephones, fax.

c) **End User Systems**. These systems seek to provide management with direct assistance with their work. Examples include; Decision Support Systems, Expert Systems, Executive Information Systems.

Contrary to the impression given by some consultants and computer manufacturers the mere fact of using IT does not of itself automatically bring benefits. If IT is misapplied or installed without sufficient analysis of the real management or organisational problems then no benefits will be gained and money will be wasted. Examples abound; the £48m computer system developed by the Government for use by the Training and Enterprise Councils (TECs) was unused because it did not meet the TEC's needs, the TAURUS system for computerising the Stock Exchange was finally abandoned in 1992 at a cost of £400m because it could not meet the Stock Exchange's requirements, the reversion to manual systems by the manufacturers of Parker Knoll furniture and so on.

The Parker Knoll example is of particular interest because it is an example of de-automation producing dramatic efficiency gains. Parker used to monitor the movements of 1700 parts on an inventory control network with 15 shop-floor computer terminals. These have been replaced by a basic manual card system (adapted from the Japanese KANBAN system) whereby a card is placed in each pile of stocks. When stocks fall sufficiently for the card to appear, staff arrange for a further batch to be made. The firm is also replacing modern high technology machine tools by older models. Although the high technology machines were faster and could do several different jobs, set-up times were in hours rather than the minutes required for the older machines. The result of these changes has been a production increase of 20%, fewer mistakes, and lead times reduced from 12 weeks to under 3 days.

The key moral from this example is that automating inefficient methods, as Parker did previously, does not produce benefits. The methods and systems must be right before any attempt is made to automate them and no IT system should be installed unless it is demonstrably better than the best manual method. The proper, planned use of IT can, of course, be highly beneficial but benefits do not automatically accrue.

Changes Affecting Organisations

A common feature of the environment in which all types of organisation operate is the presence of an apparently ever-accelerating rate of change. Management, and the information systems that support them, have to learn to deal with change and to adapt their operations and systems and the organisations themselves in order to survive and prosper.

Typical of the changes taking place are the following:

- *More competition:* All types of organisations face greater competitive pressures. These may be Tesco competing with Sainsbury, Asda and Waitrose or it may be competition from the new discount stores from abroad such as Lidl, Aldi, Netto and others. There are similar pressures in the public sector. For example, Trust Hospitals compete for business from fund holders and health authorities, Local Authorities must implement Compulsory Competitive Tendering for an ever-increasing proportion of the services they provide, Government Agencies have to be competitive in pricing and cost control in order to meet targets and so on.

- *Faster pace:* The faster pace of society and business is apparent in many ways. New models of all types of manufactured goods have shorter life cycles, this in turn means that product development must also be speeded up. The knowledge and training that people have rapidly becomes obsolete because of changing requirements. Existing work patterns and practices need to be updated more or less continuously to keep pace, current information rapidly becomes out of date, technology seems to change month by month and so on.

- *Increased globalisation:* Because of lower trade barriers, faster transport and communications, and the easier flow of capital, effectively there is a world market in manufactured and agricultural products and raw materials such as oil, coal, iron ore etc. In addition, banking and financial services operate on an international scale.

The effect of these developments is that there is increased competition for virtually every product, commodity or service. There is a further problem with the global marketplace; that of volatility. Currencies, markets and political environments change continually and often unpredictably. The global marketplace has caused dramatic changes in the location of certain types of manufacturing businesses. Many Western firms have set up manufacturing plants in various parts of Asia and China to take advantage of lower labour and overhead costs with obvious consequences for domestic manufacturers.

The process is not just one way. For example, Japanese, Korean and American firms have established factories in the UK making cars, televisions, computers and domestic appliances in order to secure an entry into the lucrative European market. This inward investment has several advantages for the UK. Firstly there are the direct employment and financial effects of the new factories. In addition there are indirect but arguably more important benefits arising from the introduction of more efficient management practices, and higher quality and productivity standards which permeate through to domestic manufacturers.

Foreign investment by multi-nationals (i.e. firms which own and control production and/or service facilities outside their home countries) takes place according to a world-wide corporate strategy which considers; markets, relative costs and revenues, taxation, and political factors. Multi-nationals operate *process specialisation* whenever possible. This means that processes are specialised within particular factories spread throughout the world. For example, a car manufacturer may locate labour-intensive processes in lower wage countries with the final stages of manufacture located nearer the intended market. Ford Motors are following this policy and have announced that production will be planned globally based on just five centres.

The Drive for Productivity and Quality

Increased competition and more discerning consumers has meant that all types of organisation are striving for greater productivity, whilst maintaining or enhancing quality. This applies to both service and manufacturing organisations. In manufacturing the greatest stimulus has been from the Japanese. The Japanese have developed a total quality approach with the target of zero defects. This has been accompanied by lean production methods which have dramatically increased productivity. A key feature of *lean production* is the use of *Just-in-Time (JIT) systems.*

The aim of JIT systems is to produce the required items, of high quality, exactly at the time they are required. There is the pursuit of excellence at all stages with a climate of continuous improvement. The key elements of JIT are:

- a move towards zero inventory
- elimination of non-value added activities
- an emphasis on perfect quality i.e. zero defects
- short set-ups
- a move towards a batch size of one

- 100% on time deliveries
- a constant drive for improvement
- Demand-pull manufacture

The application of efficient production techniques such as JIT and the use of computers and robots (known as Advanced Manufacturing Technology – AMT) have enabled some manufacturing companies throughout the world to become very successful. Collectively these are known as *World Class Manufacturers*.

The drive for productivity is also apparent in numerous service industries. Improved methods and the use of Information Technology have enabled banks and building societies to increase business yet at the same time to reduce the number of staff, whilst British Telecom have reduced staff in each of the years since privatisation even though more services are now offered and turnover has increased. The same movement can also be seen in the privatised utilities for electricity, gas and water.

Changing Employment Patterns

A long term seeming inexorable change in employment is taking place in Britain and other developed countries. There are now many more part-time workers or workers on temporary contracts. More women are employed than men and organisations are seeking to gain flexibility and lower costs by shrinking their core work-force of full-time employees and employing sufficient part-time or temporary workers to cope with fluctuations in demand. In many firms just-in-time inventory management is now accompanied by just-in-time labour.

In addition, changes in manufacturing techniques, the growth in the use of technology and other changes in the work place have increased demand for skilled/educated personnel at the expense of the unskilled. This means that many unskilled workers are now effectively unemployable even in boom times. Although a number of these changes no doubt benefit the individual organisation when considered in isolation there are wider, social costs. These include; greater stress and insecurity, a growing gap in incomes between those in work and those unemployed, a sense of alienation from society by the long-term unemployed, poorer health, possible increase in crime etc.

Key Point Summary

- The book adopts a decision focus to MIS with an emphasis on the user's requirements for relevant information not on the means of production.
- There are wide ranging knowledge requirements for MIS including; the nature of data and information, general systems concepts, organisation principles, planning and decision making, control principles, management functions, and the use of information technology.
- There is an all pervasive influence of behavioural factors on the design and operation of MIS
- Management and MIS must concentrate on *what* before *how*.
- Coping with change is the primary task of management and the MIS which support them.
- Areas of change include; greater competition, faster pace, new technologies and methods, globalisation, employment patterns.

Self Review Questions

1. Define a MIS.
2. What problems have been found from surveys of MIS?
3. What are the main areas of knowledge required for MIS design?
4. Distinguish between data and information.
5. What is the reductionist approach?
6. What is the holistic approach?
7. What is the role of MIS in organisations?
8. Into what groups can management functions be grouped?
9. What is planning?
10. Distinguish between programmed and non-programmed decisions.
11. What are feedback and feedforward?
12. What are the three major areas in which IT is influencing information systems?
13. What major internal and external changes are taking place with which organisations have to deal?

2 Information, Data and Communication

Objectives

After you have studied this chapter you will:

- understand the importance of information to management;
- be able to distinguish between data and information;
- know how data are transformed into information;
- understand how information creates value;
- be able to define the characteristics of good information;
- have had an introduction to the problems of perception;
- know the outline of communication systems;
- be able to define a MIS;
- understand the importance of informal channels of communication.

Information and Management

In all but the smallest organisations management rarely observe operations directly. They attempt to make decisions, prepare plans and control activities by using what information they can obtain from formal sources – for example the organisation's MIS – or from informal means, such as face to face conversations, telephone calls, through social contacts and so on.

Management are faced by an accelerating rate of change, an ever more complex environment and at higher levels, by considerable uncertainty.

Ideally, the manager should be able to define the type of information he requires and the MIS should be able to supply it. In practice, of course, it does not happen like this and managers have to use whatever information is available, from whatever source. As Peter Drucker has said:

'The manager will never be able to get all the facts he should have. Most decisions have to be based on incomplete knowledge – either because the information is not available or it would cost too much in time and money to get it. There is nothing more treacherous or alas, more common, than the attempt to make precise decisions on the basis of coarse and incomplete information.'

In spite of the difficulties of producing it, managers need *relevant information* to assist them to plan, to control, and to make decisions. Relevant information is information which:

(a) increases knowledge

(b) reduces uncertainty

(c) is usable for the intended purpose

A worthwhile extension to the well known adage that 'management get things done through people', would be that, 'management get things done through people, by using relevant information'.

Although all managers need information they do not all need the same type of information. The type of information required is dependent on many factors including; the level of management, the task in hand, confidentiality, urgency etc. These and other factors are developed in this and following chapters.

Information Classifications

Information has many characteristics and can be classified in numerous ways. The following gives some examples.

Information Classifications

Information may be classified in many ways including:

By Source: e.g. internal, external, primary, secondary, Government etc

By Nature: e.g. quantitative, qualitative, formal, informal etc

By Level: e.g. strategic, tactical, operational etc

By Time: e.g. historical, present, future

By frequency: e.g. continuous (real time), hourly, daily, monthly, annually etc

By Use: e.g. planning, control, decision making etc

By Form: e.g. written, aural, visual, sensory etc

By Occurrence: e.g. at planned intervals, occasional, on demand etc

By Type: e.g. detailed, summarised, aggregated, abstracted etc

The various classifications shown above, and others, are developed in detail throughout the book.

Data and Information Defined

The terms 'data' and 'information' are used interchangeably in everyday speech as meaning the same thing. However, for managers and information specialists the terms have distinct meanings:

(a) Data are facts, events, transactions and so on which have been recorded. They are the input raw materials from which information is produced.

(b) Information is data that have been processed in such a way as to be useful to the recipient.

In general terms basic data are processed in some way to form information but the mere act of processing data does not itself produce information. This is an important distinction which is developed later.

Data Characteristics

Data are facts obtained by reading, observation, counting, measuring, weighing etc which are then recorded. Frequently they are called *raw or basic data* and are often records of the day to day transactions of the organisation. For example; the date, amount and other details of an invoice or cheque, payroll details of pay, National Insurance and tax for a person, the output for a machine or shift, the number of vehicles passing a road monitoring point and so on.

Data are derived from both external and internal sources and whilst most external data are in readily usable and concrete forms – for example, bank statements, purchase invoices – internal activities require appropriate measuring and recording systems so that facts can be captured. Data may be produced as an automatic by-product of some routine but essential operation such as the production of an invoice or alternatively a special counting or measuring procedure must be introduced and the results recorded. Much of cost accounting, stock control, production control and similar systems would fall into this latter category.

Frequently, considerable attention is given to the methods of processing data whilst the *quality* of the source data is mistakenly taken for granted. If the source data are flawed any resulting information will be worthless. The following are practical examples of source data inaccuracies.

A control panel manufacturer found that labour time booking was routinely done from memory at the end of the day with the result that job times were often incorrect and no idle time was ever recorded. (The job times were the basis of estimating, job costing and invoicing.)

The weigh-bridge clerk at a sand and gravel quarry estimated stocks by sighting scratch marks on the window frame with the piles of material. (The stock figures were used for production planning and profit calculations.)

In order to meet quotas, interviewers working for an opinion survey company just filled in the questionnaires themselves without actually interviewing people. (The opinions recorded in the questionnaires were used to decide marketing plans for a new product.)

The pool of data available to an organisation, from both external and internal sources, is effectively limitless. This abundance causes problems and means that organisations have to be selective in the data they collect. Also they must continually monitor their data gathering procedures to ensure that they continue to meet the organisation's specific needs. The data gathered and the means employed naturally vary from business to business depending on the organisation's requirements. For example, few organisations record all incoming telephone calls but this is done routinely by stockbrokers and others in financial service industries because so much business is carried out by telephone.

What is Information?

The concept of information in an organisational sense is more complex and difficult than the frequent use of this common word would suggest. Information is data that have been interpreted and understood by the recipient of the message. It will be noted that the *user* not just the sender is involved in the transformation of data into information. There is a process of thought and understanding involved and it follows that a given message can have difference meanings to different people. It also follows that data which have been analysed, summarised or processed in some other fashion to produce a message or report which is conventionally deemed to be 'management information' only becomes information if it is understood by the recipient. It is the *user* who determines whether a report contains information or just processed data. Accordingly it is vital for the producers of reports and messages of all types to be aware of the user's requirements, education, position in the organisation, familiarity (or otherwise) with language and numeracy and the context in which the message will be used in order to increase the likelihood of information being derived from the message.

In summary, information is knowledge and understanding that is usable by the recipient. It reduces uncertainty and has surprise value. It must tell the recipient something not already known which could not be predicted. If a message or report does not have these attributes, *as far as the recipient* is concerned, it contains merely data not information. This is a crucial point not always fully appreciated by information specialists.

The point has been well put by Finlay.

> Without an efficient means of filtering and aggregating data, a manager could be ... *data rich yet information poor.*

A report in 1996 by Reuters called 'Dying for Information' graphically confirms the above point! This report drew on interviews with 1300 managers in the UK and elsewhere. It found that half already complained of information overload and expected the problem to get worse in the next few years. The survey found that the information (more correctly, data) overload caused mental stress and physical illness and a general feeling of not being able to cope. All in all a depressing story which provides clear evidence that badly designed MIS are all too common.

The Functions Performed by Information

In addition to the general function of improving knowledge, information assists management in several ways including:

- *The reduction of uncertainty:* uncertainty exists where there is less than perfect knowledge. Rarely, if ever, is there perfect knowledge but relevant information helps to reduce the unknown. This is particularly relevant in planning and decision making.

- *As an aid to monitoring and control:* by providing information about performance and the extent of deviations from planned levels of performance, management are better able to control operation.

- *As a means of communication:* managers need to know about developments, plans, forecasts, impending changes and so on.

- *As a memory supplement:* by having historical information about performance, transactions, results of past actions and decisions available for reference, personal memories are supplemented.

- *As an aid to simplification* by reducing uncertainty and enhancing understanding, problems and situations are simplified and become more manageable.

These and other functions of information are developed in the chapters which follow especially regarding information for planning, decision-making and control.

Information Systems in Outline

Having differentiated between data and information and recognised the key role of the user we can now describe, in outline, a model which is applicable to *all* information systems; whether manual or computerised. This is shown in Figure 2/1.

The Value of Information

Information has no value in itself; its value derives from the value of the change in decision behaviour caused by the information being available minus the cost of producing the information. There is a tendency to assume that more information, earlier or more up to date information, more accurate information etc is all better information. It may be better information but only if it improves the resulting decisions, otherwise it has no value.

It will be seen that, once again, the user is all important. Data capture, handling, recording and processing – by whatever means – incur costs and do not produce value. It is only when data are communicated and understood by the recipient and are thus transformed into information, that value may arise – providing that the information is used to improve decision making.

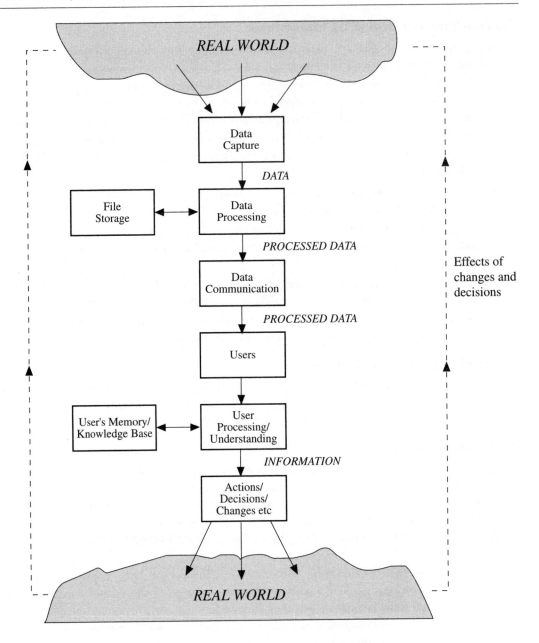

Figure 2/1 Information systems in outline

A typical relationship between costs and values is shown in Figure 2/2.

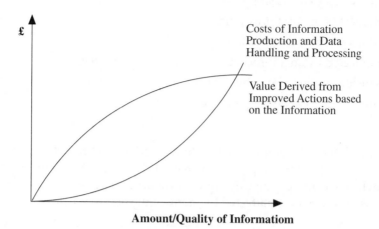

Figure 2/2 Information – cost and value

To ensure that information does have value means considering both the *user* and the *problem* or *decision* being dealt with. This is summarised below:

Appropriateness/Relevance of information for problem	Understanding by user	Value of Information
None	None	None (still data)
High	None	None (still data)
None	Some	None
Some	Good	Moderate
High	Good	High
Critical	Good	Maximum

It should be apparent at this stage that the primary objective of an information specialist, the sender of a message, is to achieve understanding by the recipient of the message and through that understanding to produce alterations in decision behaviour in order to create value. To do this, the information specialist must consider the characteristics which make information relevant, the way information is communicated and how the manager perceives and understands information.

Characteristics of Good Information

Good information is that which is used and which creates value. Experience and research shows that good information has numerous qualities as follows:

Good information is

(a) *relevant* for its purpose

(b) sufficiently *accurate* for its purpose

(c) *complete* enough for the problem

(d) from a source in which the user has *confidence*

(e) communicated to the *right person*

(f) communicated in *time* for its purpose

(g) that which contains the *right level of detail*

(h) communicated by an appropriate *channel of communication*

(i) that which is *understandable* by the user

The various qualities are developed below.

Relevance

In effect this is the over-riding quality. Information must be relevant to the problem being considered. Too often reports, messages, tabulations and so on contain irrelevant parts which make understanding more difficult and cause frustration to the user. Relevance is of course much affected by many of the qualities below.

Accuracy

Information should be sufficiently accurate for it to be relied upon by the manager and for the purpose for which it is intended. There is no such thing as absolute accuracy and raising the level of accuracy increases cost but does not necessarily increase the value of information. The level of accuracy must be related to the decision level involved.

At operational levels information may need to be accurate to the nearest penny, £, kilogram or minute. A sales invoice, for example, will be accurate to the penny. On the other hand a Sales Manager at the tactical level will probably be best suited to information rounded to the nearest £100 whilst at the strategic level roundings to the nearest ten thousand pounds or higher are common.

Accuracy should not be confused with precision. Information may be inaccurate but precise or vice versa. See Figure 2/3.

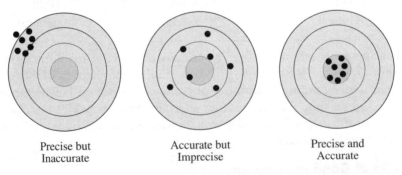

| Precise but | Accurate but | Precise and |
| Inaccurate | Imprecise | Accurate |

Figure 2/3 The distinction between accuracy and precision

Completeness

Ideally *all* the information required for a decision should be available. In the real world of course, this never happens. What is required is that the information is complete in respect of the key elements of the problem. This means that there must be close liaison between information providers and users to ensure that the key factors are identified.

For example, a supermarket chain in making a strategic decision whether or not to place a new superstore on the outskirts of a town would identify such things as population density, road access, presence of competitors and so on as key factors in the decision and would not try to include every detail about the town in their initial analysis.

Confidence in the Source

For information to have value it must be used. For it to be used managers must have confidence in the source. Confidence is enhanced when:

(a) the source has been reliable in the past

(b) there is good communication between the information producer and the manager.

For example when the manager has been consulted over the content, format and timing of reports and there is frank discussion over possible uncertainties and inaccuracies, confidence will be increased. Especially at strategic levels, management will cross check information from various sources to increase confidence in the message.

Communication to the Right Person

Each manager has a defined sphere of activity and responsibility and should receive information to help him carry out his designated tasks. In practice this is not always as easy as it sounds. It is quite common for information to be supplied to the wrong level in the organisation. A superior may not pass it on to the person who needs it whilst a subordinate may hold on to information in an attempt to make himself seem indispensable.

Information suppliers need to analyse the key decision points in an organisation in order to direct information exactly where it is required.

Timing

Good information is that which is communicated in time to be used. To an extent, the need for speed can conflict with the need for accuracy although modern processing methods can produce accurate information very rapidly. Delays in data gathering, processing or communication can transform potentially vital information into worthless waste paper.

The timing of regularly produced information is also important. Information should be produced at a frequency which is related to the type of decision or activity involved. Too often reports are produced routinely at quite arbitrary intervals – daily, weekly, monthly and so on – without regard to the time cycle of the activity involved. At operational levels this may mean a requirement for information to be available virtually continuously – say on a V.D.U. screen – but at other levels much longer intervals are likely to be appropriate which should not be determined merely by the conventions of the calendar.

Detail

Information should contain the least amount of detail consistent with effective decision making. Every superfluous character means extra storage, more processing, extra assimilation and possibly poorer decisions. The level of detail should vary with the level in the organisation; the higher the level the greater the degree of compression and summarisation. Sometimes information, particularly at lower levels, has to be very detailed to be useful, but the general rule of as little as possible consistent with effective use, must always apply. Because of the need to be concise and to direct attention to where it is needed *exception reporting* is frequently used for control information.

Exception reporting is a 'system of reporting which focuses attention on those items where performance differs significantly from standard or budget'.

An example of exception reporting is the accounting technique of budgetary control in which actual expenditure, item by item, is compared with budgeted or expected expenditure. Minor differences would be considered acceptable but where the differences exceed established tolerance levels this would be highlighted. These exceptions are thus brought to the manager's attention saving his time.

The layout of a typical budgetary control report is shown in Figure 2/4.

BUDGETARY CONTROL REPORT NO ....

BUDGET CENTRE ....   DATE PREPARED ....

BUDGET HOLDER ....   BUDGETED ACTIVITY LEVEL ....

BUDGET RELATIONSHIP   UP.............   ACTUAL ACTIVITY LEVEL ....
                            DOWN...........

ACCOUNTING PERIOD ....

BUDGETTED ITEM		CURRENT PERIOD			YEAR TO DATE			TREND OF VARIANCE	SIGNIFICANT?	COMMENTS
CODE	DESCRIPTION	BUDGET	ACTUAL	VARIANCE	BUDGET	ACTUAL	VARIANCE			

Figure 2/4 Typical budgetary control report

Exception reporting is only appropriate in relatively well structured situations i.e. where a plan exists and it is required to keep performance in line with the plan. It is thus more applicable to lower and middle management rather than to top, or strategic, management.

Users of information of whatever level, must not be overloaded with unnecessary information. The information system must act as a selective filter; summarising, highlighting, editing, combining as appropriate.

Communication Methods

Various channels of communication are used by organisations. These include:

Face-to-face communications

- Interviews
- formal meetings
- informal contacts
- talks and discussion groups
- video telephones

Written communications

- external mail by letter
- internal mail by memoranda
- booklets and manuals
- reports
- statements and tabulations
- company, magazines, newsletters and bulletins
- notice boards
- fax

Visual communications

- films and slides
- videos
- charts
- posters

Oral communications

- telephone
- public address systems

Electronic communications

- video displays using electronic mail (E mail)
- Data transmission networks
- Electronic Data exchange (i.e. computer to computer)
- Telex
- Pagers

Channels of Communication

To be usable by the manager, information must be transmitted by means of a communication process. Communication involves the interchange of facts, thoughts, value judgements and opinions and the communication process may take many forms; face-to-face conversations, telephone calls, informal and formal meetings, conferences, memoranda, letters, reports, tabulations, V.D.U. transmissions and so on.

Whatever the process, good communication results where the sender and receiver are in accord over the meaning of a particular message. Although this sounds like a modest objective, it is proving to be, in Peter Drucker's words 'as elusive as the Unicorn'.

The channel of communication should be selected having regard to such things as; the nature and purpose of the information, the speed required and, above all, the requirements of the user. The typical output of formal information systems is a printed report or tabulation. These have their uses, of course, but there is research evidence that many managers, specially at senior levels, obtain most of their information aurally. They use written reports merely to confirm or reinforce information they already have.

The main principles of communication systems are given later in the chapter.

Understandability

Understandability is what transforms data into information. If the information is not understood it cannot be used and thus cannot add value. Many factors affect understandability including:

(a) *Preferences of the user.* Some people prefer information in the form of pictures and graphs, others prefer narrative. Some are happy with statistical and numeric presentations whilst others do not understand them. Research shows that some people absorb concrete facts in detail whilst others evaluate situations as a whole with little regard for factual detail. This variability means that the same message will inevitably receive many interpretations.

(b) *Remembered knowledge.* Although the working of memory is not well understood there is no doubt that the extent of remembered knowledge, including technical knowledge, influences understanding. Understanding is thus a result of the association of memory and the received message.

(c) *Environmental factors.* As well as the individual characteristics mentioned above a number of environmental factors influence understanding. These include; group pressures, the time available, trust in the information system and so on.

(d) *Language.* Information is conveyed by means of signals or messages. These may be in a code (for example, mathematical notation) or in a natural language, such as English or Spanish. Natural languages are very rich in the range of information they can accommodate but are inherently ambiguous. Mathematical notation or programming languages can be very precise but lack the capacity to cope with a wide range of concepts. (Language and perception is of great importance to information specialists and is developed further below).

Characteristics of Good Information – Conclusion

It will be seen from the above that many things need to be right before information can be considered as good. Note particularly how many of the factors relate to social and behavioural characteristics. It is not sufficient merely to consider the technical aspects of data capture and processing; these are only one aspect of information systems.

Perception

From the viewpoint of MIS this can be defined as the understanding a person gains from the communication of a message in written or verbal form, or from observing a situation. As the main outputs of MIS are messages and reports, what the managers understand from them is of critical importance to information specialists. The central point to understand about this process is that it is the *manager,* as the recipient, who communicates, *not* the provider of the message. The provider of the message can only make it more likely – or less likely – that the recipient understands the meaning of a message.

The process of perception is individual and varies from time to time. People attach meanings to messages and situations in accordance with their attitudes, experiences and value systems. In general people see and understand what they want to see and understand. For example:

A study gave an identical management case study to a group of managers who were from different functional areas, sales, production, accounting etc. They were asked to identify what they thought to be the major problem facing the company. Most of the managers identified the problem as one related to their own function, over 80% of the sales executives thought that sales were the major problem whereas under 30% of non-sales people thought that sales were the problem.

The significance of this for information providers is that they must know what the recipient expects to see and hear. They must become familiar with the language, terminology and experience backgrounds of the recipients otherwise true communication will not take place.

Language and Perception

Much of the output of information systems uses language so the way this is perceived is of importance to information specialists. Much of our thought is verbalised so that our behaviour, and that of others with whom we wish to communicate, is likely to be influenced by how we verbalise a situation and not purely by what we see. Words, whether in spoken or written form, often label too small a part of the picture or imply relationships which are inappropriate. There is a tendency of language to lead us into oversimplifying complex problems, particularly relating to behavioural matters, and consequently of finding solutions more by verbal habit than by reference to the facts.

The English language has a tendency to force things into one of two verbal categories: right/wrong, black/white and so on. Subtle graduations of value and emphasis are much more difficult to achieve. Some of these problems can be overcome by the use of numeric or mathematical or probability concepts which act as an extension of ordinary language by assigning a scale of measures linking the two extremes.

Although not always practicable, the most reliable way of ensuring that a word is taken to have the same meaning by both the sender and receiver of a message is to show or demonstrate the object, action or property being named. This is the reason why samples are required when purchasing and why demonstrations and exhibitions are held. Many abstract words and concepts cannot be supported in this way even though they may represent matters of critical importance to the manager concerned. For example, how can you demonstrate or show a sample of, say; marginal cost, good labour relations, the potential demand for a product?

Technical Terms

When technical terms and abstract words are used it is necessary for the information specialist to ensure that mutually agreed and acceptable definitions exist otherwise misunderstandings will occur and true communication cannot take place. As an example, consider the possible ways a common word such as 'profit' could be interpreted. It might be; net profit before or after tax, gross profit, taxable profit, profit before or after head office charges, inflation adjusted profit etc. And profit would normally be considered a more concrete concept than say, employee morale!

Technical terminology, or jargon, is often used within the same organisation, profession or group. It can be a useful shorthand way of communicating between 'insiders' but the danger is that the habit persists even when communicating to non-specialists. As an example, the following is an extract from a letter in *The Independent* newspaper commenting on an earlier article by a cancer specialist...

> One of the biggest obstacles to good communication from doctor to patient/potential research subject is the language the doctor uses.
>
> Many technical words, common as the definite article to doctors of 20 years' experience, can be double Dutch to any lay person – or worse, make only partial and therefore misleading sense.
>
> Mr Arnold's piece contains the following words, accompanied by no definition or explanation, which I would find unacceptable in any letter to a patient explaining her

situation: aggressive treatment; local, regional and metastatic; primary breast cancer; tumour; malignant ulcer; silicone implant; external prosthesis; mastectomy; pathologist; readily accessible modes; radiotherapy; chemotherapy; hormone therapy.

Of course, many people will recognise most of these words – but will not be able to define them exactly, nor give their full significance in the context of Mr Arnold's information.

The study of language and perception is a vast, specialised field well beyond the scope of this book, but it is hoped that the above brief section will at least cause readers to think more carefully about the way they express their ideas and the meaning of the words they use.

Numeric Data and Perception

Much of the output of an organisation's MIS is in the form of numerical data, for example; sales forecasts, production statistics, all forms of accounting statements, statistical analyses of all types and so on. Many people are mesmerised by figures and although they may challenge or query a normal, written report they are inclined to accept on trust a numeric statement, particularly if some form of sophisticated statistical manipulation has been employed. The ready availability of computing power has tended to exacerbate this problem as it has become all too easy to classify and analyse large volumes of data without regard to its meaning or quality.

Most people are poor intuitive statisticians. They are unable to relate the past occurrence of events with the likelihood of recurrence. For example, the incidence of deaths from accidents is greatly over-estimated. In fact deaths from disease are about 20 times greater than from accidents.

In general people tend to place a higher probability on events that

- are understood by the individual
- are favourable to the individual
- are most recent
- have received most publicity

Management's ability to deal with numeric data and how they perceive it is of obvious importance to information specialists.

Problems with Numeric Data

Because of the frequent use of numeric data in MIS it is important that the common causes of misuse of statistical and numeric data are understood by both the suppliers and users of the data. These include:

(a) Incorrect definition or conception of the problem which may result in the failure to include or collect data concerning important variables.

(b) Inadequacy of original data caused by poor or incomplete measuring and/or classifying techniques. This is a frequent problem in business and commercial organisations which could be, but seldom is, recognised by expressing results with a given range of accuracy. As an example, stock valuations cannot by their nature be exact figures yet this is the normal assumption in accounting statements. A few percentage points variation in the valuation – which is all too likely – could cause dramatic fluctuations in the profit figure, yet conventionally this possibility is ignored.

(c) Subjective errors caused by the inclusion in the computations of assumptions, value judgements and guesswork without making it clear to the recipient of the processed data that the results are not based entirely on objective, verifiable facts.

(d) Analysis by inappropriate techniques and methods. To be able to use successfully a particular quantitative, statistical or accounting technique, it is vital that the underlying assumptions and limitations are clearly understood because no method or technique is universally applicable.

(e) Poor presentation of results. As with language, numeric and statistical data must be presented in a manner appropriate to the manager who will receive them. This requires a detailed knowledge by the information specialist of the manager's level of numeracy and the purpose for which the data are required so that the format, style and amount of technical content can be tailored to suit.

(f) Inaccuracy and misconception. Nothing destroys a manager's confidence in the information source more swiftly than for him to find errors in the calculations. Well organised procedures, perhaps computer based, and the incorporation of checks will help to avoid this problem. Misconceptions of what the data and statistics refer to are usually caused by poor or non-existent definitions of the terminology used. This problem is especially pronounced when the information supplier is a specialist in statistics or quantitative methods who may assume that certain terms are self-evident. For example, would we all understand the same thing if terms such as 'exponential smoothing', 'statistically significant' or 'EOQ model' appeared in a report without being precisely defined in context?

Graphs, Charts and Diagrams

Graphs, charts and other forms of visual presentations are useful devices for highlighting trends, summarising information and showing comparisons. They are based on numeric data and often appear as a supplement to more detailed reports.

Graphs and charts will be found useful for:

- Highlighting simple impressions from masses of data
- Analysing relationships between variables e.g. Advertising and Sales
- Comparing changes in patterns over time e.g. rejection rates, service times, interest rates
- Detecting subtle trend changes e.g. customer purchasing patterns, price/cost fluctuations
- Providing overall summaries e.g. sales per month or per region, output levels.

Graphs and charts would not generally be used for the presentation of specific data items or trends and relationships based on a small amount of data. Properly used they can increase the impact and understandability of numeric reports.

Communication Systems

Communication at its most basic level involves three elements – the source, the message and the destination – and these three components are always present regardless of the size or sophistication of the system. A general outline of features common to all practical communication systems is shown in Figure 2/5 together with the example of sending a letter.

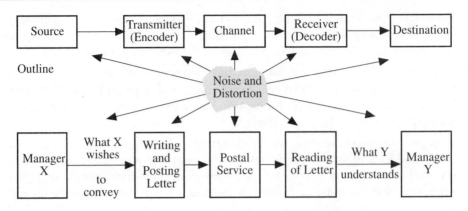

Outline

Sending a Letter

Figure 2/5 Communication systems

Brief explanations follow of the terminology used.

- *Encoding*: all messages originate in a person's mind and the process of encoding is the way that the message is written down or spoken in order to be able to communicate with another person. Variation in word connotation by different people can alter the meaning of a message and voice emphasis and/or facial expressions and/or gestures all play a part in the encoding process when conversation is used. It will be realised that the way we convey meaning by the written word, figures, diagrams, and speech is an individual, often idiosyncratic process.

- *Channel*: the means by which the information is carried, e.g. the internal mail system, external postal services, telephone and telecommunication networks, television, radio, satellite links and so on. Channels are not perfect because distortion, losses and delays may occur. Care must be taken by the MIS designer to ensure that the correct type of channel is used having regard to such matters as urgency, sensitivity, need for security and accuracy, type of information, cost effectiveness.

- *Noise*: the term used in communication theory for anything which causes the message at the receiver to be different from the message that went into the transmitter. For example, poor or illegible writing, accents, bad form design, poor picture quality, loss or damage, actual physical noise etc.

- *Decoding*: this is the process of achieving understanding from the message. In general, people read, see and hear what they want to read, see and hear so that decoding is an individual process. Different people are likely to derive different meanings from the same message, influenced by their experience, attitudes and value systems.

Numerous methods are used to ensure that messages are properly received and understood, particularly if they contain urgent or important items.

Examples include:

(a) repetition of important words or figures

(b) confirmatory letters or fax messages following meetings or telephone calls

(c) multiple copies of the message

(d) repeated V.D.U. screening at intervals.

Most communication systems deal readily with *hard communications* i.e. where there is some tangible record of the information. For example; letters, memoranda, tape/disc recordings etc. Where information is in a less concrete form, such as the tone of voice, body language, facial expression, it is known as *soft communication*. For obvious reasons these nuances are difficult to transmit through formal channels although these less tangible characteristics provide assistance in interpreting or judging the quality of a message and are thus important in making information more useful.

MIS Definition

By this stage there should be an awareness of the distinction between data and information, the characteristics which make information usable by the manager and the way that information can create value. With this background it is a useful point to re-emphasise what is meant by a management information system:

> It is a system using formalised procedures to provide management at all levels in all functions with appropriate information, based on data from both internal and external sources, to enable them to make timely and effective decisions for planning, directing and controlling the activities for which they are responsible.

It will be noted from this definition that the emphasis is on the uses to which the information is put and that no mention is made of the means by which the information is processed. This emphasis is correct for it is the end use of the information which is important and not the intermediate processing stage.

An MIS is usually efficient at providing regular formal information from routine transaction data, for example, relating to stock movements, sales, production and so on. However, the MIS may be rather rigid and less able to deal with relatively unpredictable information, especially from outside the organisation or that required by strategic management. Also, formal systems are poor at providing the behavioural context of information i.e. the less tangible characteristics mentioned earlier. Fortunately there is another information system in every organisation which helps to overcome these problems; the *informal system*.

The Informal System

Informal communication takes place at all levels from discussions, telephone calls, meetings, observation and so on. The informal network, often called the grapevine, is flexible and can convey nuances which are lost in formal communications.

Informal networks are speedier and can cater for local problems more readily than formal MIS. There is research evidence that at higher levels of management informal channels, particularly concerned with external information, are of greater importance than the formal MIS. The information specialist is prone to exaggerate the importance of written information compared to face-to-face conversation even though research evidence confirms its importance.

Studies by Mintzberg, and Ives and Olson found that as much as 80% of a chief executive's time was spent in verbal communication.

The formal and informal channels should not be viewed as competitors but as complementary facets of the total information network in the organisation.

Information in Organisations

So far information has been viewed in a neutral objective manner but it is not always treated thus in organisations. People in organisations jockey for positions, protect territories and seek to dominate others and information is used to help these aims as well as the more obviously beneficial purposes discussed in this chapter.

In general, the possession of information gives power so people wishing to retain or enhance status and position sometimes restrict access to information which they possess. Examples include the specialist department that refuses to distribute information before a meeting, the use of 'confidential' and 'restricted access' filters etc. Sometimes the total pool of information is restricted in some way, causing bias and distortion. Undesirable facts or those which refute a popular viewpoint may be downplayed or suppressed. For example a computer department which wishes to upgrade equipment may only give cursory attention to the resulting benefits to the organisation, which may be slight, and instead concentrate purely on the capabilities of the new equipment they desire.

Information specialists must be aware of these potential problems and must seek to ensure that the information produced, communicated and used is that which benefits the *organisation as a whole*, not some sectional interest.

Key Point Summary

- Information increases knowledge, reduces uncertainty, adds value when used
- Data are facts which have been recorded
- Information is processed data which is understood by the user
- The value of information comes from its use
- Good information is: relevant, accurate, in time to be used, sent to the right person and is understandable
- Communication systems include a source, a message and the destination
- Perception is the understanding a person receives from a message
- Unexplained jargon is a barrier to understanding
- A Management Information System provides managers at all levels with appropriate information for planning, control and decision making
- Both formal and informal sources are important and should complement one another.

Self Review Questions

1. What is relevant information for a manager?
2. Distinguish between data and information.
3. How is data transformed into information?
4. How does information become valuable?
5. What are the characteristics of relevant information?
6. What is good communication?

7. What are the elements in a communication system?
8. Define: encoding, channel, noise, decoding.
9. Why is perception of importance?
10. What are some of the problems with using language?
11. What are the common causes of problems when numeric data are used?
12. Define a management information system.
13. What are formal and informal sources of information?

3 Systems Concepts – Structure and Elements

Objectives

After you have studied this chapter you will:

- be able to define a system;
- know the main features of the Systems Approach;
- understand the key systems terminology;
- be able to distinguish between open and closed systems;
- understand the importance of the environment;
- know the benefits and costs of decoupling;
- be able to define: deterministic, probablistic, and self-organising systems.

What is the Systems Approach?

The systems approach is a method or framework which helps us to analyse and explore the operation and interactions which exist in the systems around us.

There are many definitions of the term 'system'. A comprehensive one is that used by the Open University:

> 'A system is an assembly of parts where:
> 1. The parts or components are connected together in an organised way.
> 2. The parts or components are affected by being in the system (and are changed by leaving it).
> 3. The assembly does something.
> 4. The assembly has been identified by a person as being of special interest.'

This definition contains the essential elements of *parts*, *relationships* and *objectives*. It is very broad and can apply to any of the systems around us; examples of which are:

- the railway system

- a hospital
- an accounting system
- a manufacturing company
- an information system
- a Local Authority
- a central heating system.

In effect, any arrangement which involves the handling, processing or manipulation of resources of whatever type can be represented as a system. However, because of its intended readership this book concentrates on the systems approach applied to organisations and their problems so that we are only concerned with systems which exist to meet objectives.

Thus a typical manufacturing company or service organisation can be viewed as a system whereby people grouped into sections and departments, process inputs to produce outputs of goods and/or services in order to fulfil the objectives of the organisation.

Features of the Systems Approach

The systems approach has many facets of which the following are the most important:

- all systems are composed of inter-related parts or sub-systems and the system can only be explained as a whole. This is known as *holism* or *synergy*. Holism states that any whole is more than the sum of its individual parts. When the appropriate parts are combined properties appear from the whole which the parts alone do not possess. These are known as *emergent properties*.

  Examples of emergent properties
  - *Taste* is a property of water not the constituent hydrogen and oxygen atoms.
  - *Growth* is a property arising from the combination of seeds and soil.
  - *Obsolescence* is likely to arise from consideration of financial, technical and personnel factors. A machine may still work but may be too expensive or dangerous to run or may no longer be required for current production.

- systems are *hierarchical* in that the parts of sub-systems are made up of other smaller parts. For example, the accounting systems of an organisation may be a sub-system of the information system which is itself a sub-system of the planning system, which is a sub-system of the organisation as a whole.

  Progressing down the hierarchy increases the detail but reduces the area whilst moving upwards provides a successively broader view.

- the parts of a system cannot be altered without affecting other parts. Many organisational problems stem from ignoring this principle. For example, a departmental procedure or form might be changed without considering the ripple effects on the other departments affected, with dire consequences.

- the sub-systems should work towards the goal of their higher systems and not pursue their own objectives independently. Where sub-systems do pursue their own objectives to the detriment of higher objectives, then a condition of *sub-optimality* is said to exist and in general MIS designers seek to avoid sub-optimality wherever possible.

Sub-optimality example

A production manager may seek to minimise production costs by producing regular quantities each period. This may result in orders being lost at certain times and excessive stocks at others. If the savings in production costs are less than the lost sales contribution or the extra stock-holding costs then there is sub-optimality as far as the business as a whole is concerned.

- organisational systems contain both *hard* and *soft* properties. Hard properties are those that can be assessed in some objective way. Examples are; the number of components in a storage bin, the amount of PAYE tax a person will pay with a tax code of 250, the size of a product and so on.

  The soft aspects of a system are a matter of individual values or taste. They cannot be assessed by any objective standard or measuring process. Examples are; the appearance of a product, the suitability of a person for a job, any problem containing a political element and so on.

Because of their importance, these points are developed in detail later in this and the next chapter.

The systems approach – also known as *systems thinking* or *General Systems Theory (GST)* – does not provide a ready made list of answers to organisation problems. Instead it recognises that organisations, as one example of a system, are complex entities with multiple relationships and helps to avoid taking a narrow, mechanistic view of their problems.

Systems Elements

Before discussing the classifications of systems and other system properties, it is necessary to explain certain key features of systems; namely the transformation process, boundaries, environment.

The Transformation Process

All systems are composed of the same basic elements; inputs, processes and outputs as shown in Figure 3/1.

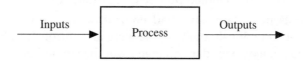

Figure 3/1 The transformation process

Systems theory gives a much more embracing meaning to the terms inputs and outputs than would normally be considered. For example, the inputs to a Production System include; raw materials, labour (skills, quantity), equipment and plant facilities, job specifications, standards of all types, maintenance facilities, power supplies etc. A similar, almost endless list could be given for the output side of the system.

Fortunately it is not usually necessary (or possible) to consider all possible inputs and outputs. The usual procedure when analysing systems is,

(a) to choose those outputs with which we are concerned – these are usually those outputs most relevant to the system objectives

and

(b) to choose those inputs for examination and control which are considered to have significant effects on the outputs considered important.

Thus in planning a Production process certain input and outputs would be considered more relevant than others, as shown in Figure 3/2.

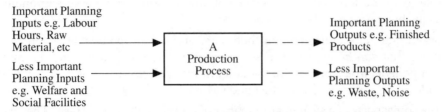

Figure 3/2 Production process – important and less important elements

In all systems other than physical or mechanical ones, the transformation process is controlled by information. In the simplest case, information on the *output* of the system is used as a basis for *control* of the *input* of the system. This is known as *feedback* or *information feedback*. This outline is developed in detail later in the book.

System Boundaries

The features which define the extent of a system are its boundaries. In mechanical, physical and biological systems the boundaries are readily identifiable as they tend to arise naturally. With any form of social organisation, boundaries are not obvious and often change to meet differing demands. In social organisations there are many transfers across boundaries of ideas, people, materials and information.

Within organisations, boundaries are determined by management and vary from organisation. For example, in one organisation the Sales Department may be responsible for invoicing whereas in another, invoicing may be within the boundary of the Accounting Department.

Boundary alterations are an inevitable consequence of organisations adapting to change which is essential if they are to survive. Changes at the margin of interacting systems can be a source of friction if not handled properly. For example:

Since 1991 schools in Britain have had control of their own budgets for salaries, expenses, books etc. Previously the budgets were all controlled by the Local Education Authority. This is a major boundary change from the single Local Authority system to the numerous individual school systems. It is an imposed boundary change which has caused considerable friction. A classic 'soft' problem.

Throughout the 1990s more and more functions and departments of the Civil Service have been transformed into quasi-independent operating agencies. Examples include the Benefits Agency, the Ordnance Survey, Drivers' Licensing and so on. The theoretical boundary is that Agencies are responsible operations and politicians are responsible for policy. However as the well publicised problems with the Prisons' Agency demonstrate there is no clear boundary between operations and policy and politicians cannot resist crossing the boundary to interfere with day-to-day affairs.

The Environment of Systems

In the widest sense, a system's environment is all those elements not in the system. However, this is a very broad notion and more appropriately for our purposes the environment can be defined as those external elements whose changes in attitudes, behaviour or properties affect the state of the system *and* those external elements which are changed by the system's behaviour. In effect, this means that the relevant environment of any system comprises those elements with which it has some connection or relationship.

The environment is diverse and is rarely static. Figure 3/3 is an attempt to show some of the influences in the environment which may affect the organisation or be affected by the organisation's actions or outputs.

Although some factors in the environment cannot be controlled, for example, the weather, organisations do attempt to influence their environment. For example.

* Charities lobby MPs and the Government in an attempt to change legislation or to alter funding levels.
* Commercial companies advertise their products to create and maintain demand.
* Local Authorities vigorously promote their towns and areas in an attempt to gain inwards investment by a Japanese and domestic manufacturers.

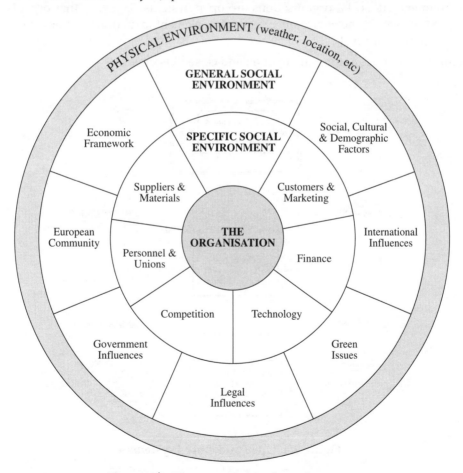

Figure 3/3 The organisation's environment

The ideas of boundaries and environments lead to the distinction between *closed systems* and *open systems*.

Closed Systems and Open Systems

A *closed system* is one that is isolated from its environment. Closed systems are self contained so that the external environment does not influence the behaviour of the system, nor does the system influence its environment. The idea can only strictly be applied to mechanical and physical systems as all social systems have some interaction with their environment. Nevertheless, within organisations, attempts are made to limit or prescribe the exchanges with the environment for particular sub-systems.

An example of this is the Production sub-system of an organisation where arrangements are usually made to limit exchanges with the external environment so that operations can flow as smoothly as possible. The Production Control system, the Sales and Distribution system, the Personnel system and so on act as buffers between Production and the outside world. There are of course, exchanges between these internal systems but in a controlled and relatively predictable fashion.

An *open system* is a system which interacts with its environment. It receives inputs and influences from the environment and, in turn, passes back outputs and influences to the environment. *All* social organisations are open systems. The way that organisations adapt to changes in the environment is the key element in an organisations success and indeed its very survival.

Figure 3/4 provides a summary of open and closed systems.

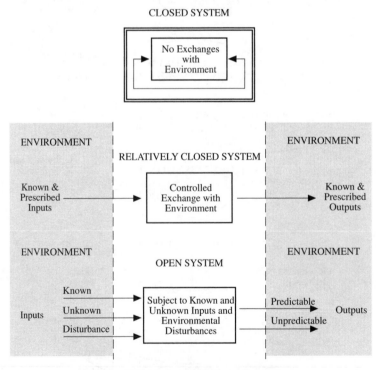

Figure 3/4 Open and closed systems

Organisations as open systems attempt to monitor and anticipate environmental disturbances. However, some disturbances are so great or unexpected that the existence of the organisation is threatened. The disturbances may arise from virtually any source; changes in market conditions, technology, the law, conflict and so on. For example:

- The collapse of the world price of tin, in the early 1990s caused Rio Tinto Zinc to close the last remaining tin mine in the UK.

- From 1994 firms offering investment advice and selling financial plans must meet new, stringent requirements and be registered with the Personal Investment Authority. This has meant that some firms have had to cease this type of trading as they are unable to conform to the new legislative requirements.

- The outbreak of civil war in 1992 in what was Yugoslavia caused the collapse of several travel agencies which specialised in providing holidays in that area.

- Traditional high street banks and building societies will shortly have to contend with strong competition from 'virtual' banks. Virtual banks will offer interactive television in the home and automated kiosks in public places. Apart from the technological changes it provides the opportunity for telecommunications and utilities companies to enter the banking field. This is already happening to an extent with AT & T in America and British Telecom in the UK who act as bankers for companies such as Interflora who use their networks. These developments constitute a major change in the environment for traditional financial institutions.

In summary, closed systems are designed for efficiency; open systems for survival.

Systems and Adaptability

To be successful and to remain in existence organisations must be flexible and adapt to change. This means change not only in the organisation's relationship with the external environment but also in their internal methods and structures. Successful organisations are characterised by their internal openness and their readiness to accept that yesterday's methods and products are very unlikely to be suitable for tomorrow. Recognising the need for change, initiating change and managing change successfully are the hallmarks of good quality management. Organisations do not automatically adjust to change.

Adaptation only occurs as a result of management decisions and action. Ways of managing change successfully are dealt with in the chapters on management which follow.

Successful change is change that is planned and considered. This means that the effects on the organisation as a whole must be considered when making a change to part of the organisation. It will be recalled that a key element of the systems approach is that changes in *parts* of a system affect the system as a *whole*. Thus, to make successful changes one must be aware of the interactions which exist in the organisation.

Systems theory recognises that open systems can achieve their objectives in a variety of ways using varying inputs, processes and methods. This is known as *equifinality*.

Shared and Overlapping Sub-Systems

Sub-systems can belong to more than one system and there is a need to recognise this overlap and to design operations and processes accordingly. The recognition of overlap is particularly important when changes are made in one of the systems which share the same sub-system.

An example of a shared sub-system is shown on Figure 3/5.

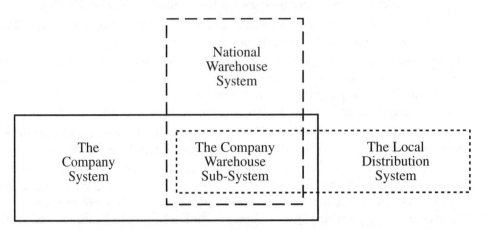

Figure 3/5 Sub-system overlaps

Overlap is often an efficient and economical arrangement. For example a central purchasing sub-system used by various companies in a group may be able to obtain greater discounts and may aid the standardisation of parts and materials. A centralised computer facility may be shared by all departments within an organisation with a reduction in overall costs. However such overlaps are likely to increase communication difficulties and may have longer response times. Because of the need to co-ordinate activities and to obtain numerous approvals for change, such structures may be less flexible in rapidly changing conditions.

Katz and Kahn, two American researchers into organisations as open systems, identified five sub-systems within organisations.

These can be summarised as follows:

- *Production or Technical Sub-Systems*. These deal with the basic tasks of the organisation i.e. the production of goods or the provision of services.
- *Supportive Sub-Systems*. These maintain the relationships between the Production Sub-System and the external environment i.e. the procurement of inputs and the disposal of outputs.
- *Maintenance Sub-Systems*. These provide the rules, rewards and roles of those who work in the organisation.
- *Adoptive Sub-Systems*. Whereas the above three sub-systems are concerned with the present organisation the adaptive sub-system is concerned with the future i.e. new markets, new products, new methods etc.
- *Managerial Sub-Systems*. These consist of the controlling and co-ordinating activities which govern all the sub-systems which make up the total system. These include; co-ordination decision making, planning and control.

Interconnections

Since each sub-system has many inputs and outputs, many interconnections may exist within the same system. For example a system containing 4 sub-systems has a possible 6 interconnections as shown in Figure 3/6.

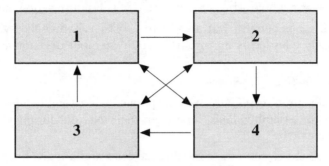

Figure 3/6 Sub-system interconnections

The number of interconnections rise rapidly as the number of sub-systems rise. In general the number of interconnections is

$$\frac{n(n-1)}{2}$$

Thus in a system containing 30 sub-systems the possible number of interconnections is 435.

Fortunately not all sub-systems interconnect with all others but in spite of this, very large numbers of interconnections exist in most organisations and these can cause difficulties steps are taken to reduce the numbers. One of the more usual ways is by *decoupling*.

Decoupling

If the sub-systems (departments, processes etc) are tightly connected close coordination between them is vital. This implies a high degree of integration which may be difficult to achieve. Resources and facilities need to be finely balanced, parts and documentation need to be available exactly when required and there needs to be a good flow of accurate information to keep the system going.

One solution is to *decouple* or loosen the connection so that the two systems can operate with a degree of independence. Some ways of decoupling are:

- Stocks of work-in-progress decouple one stage of production from the next.
- Some slack capacity in a department enables it to respond to an urgent request from a department it services.
- Standard specifications and standardised procedures allows one department to communicate with others secure in the knowledge that real communication will be possible.

Decoupling, both in a physical and information sense, allows sub-systems more independence in planning and control. It is likely that with some decoupling the organisation is better able to deal with unexpected disturbances.

Two major costs are involved with decoupling:

(a) The cost of the decoupling mechanism itself e.g. the cost of carrying stocks, the cost of the slack capacity and so on, and

(b) the possibility that the sub-systems may act in their own interests and not that of the organisation as a whole: This is the problem of sub-optimisation mentioned earlier.

Thus decoupling has benefits but also incurs costs. Whether the systems should be tightly or loosely coupled is an important management decision with far-reaching consequences.

The Japanese Just-in-Time (JIT) System

Japanese manufacturers, especially of cars, operate their assembly lines with virtually no stocks of parts for assembly. Parts flow from their external suppliers to the assembly point 'just in time' to be used.

Suppliers are located close to the assembly factories and are given long-term contracts which define product specifications, quality and delivery requirements in great detail.

In system terms, the Japanese have coupled their system more tightly and thus reduced stocks, which are an expensive decoupling mechanism. The tight coupling increases the need for co-ordination with their suppliers and for first class information flows.

Deterministic, Probablistic and Self-Organising Systems

In considering how systems and sub-systems behave it is also possible to classify them according to their predictive behaviour thus.

Deterministic Systems

These are predictable systems where the output can be predicted from the input. Examples include; a computer program, a machine producing a component.

Probablistic or Stochastic Systems

These are where some conditions of the system can be predicted from the previous state but only in terms of probable behaviour and there is always a certain degree of error attached to the prediction of what the system will do. For example in an inventory control system the *average* demand or the *average* stock may be predicted, but the exact *value* of these factors cannot be predicted.

Most industrial and business systems are regarded as probablistic and it is to these that most control effort is directed.

Self Organising Systems

Self organising systems are those which adapt and react to inputs or stimuli. The method of adaptation is uncertain and the same inputs do not always produce the same responses. Social groups and organisations are within this category.

The Information-Processing System

To conclude this chapter on systems, Figure 3/7 outlines a typical information processing system in terms of inputs – processes – outputs.

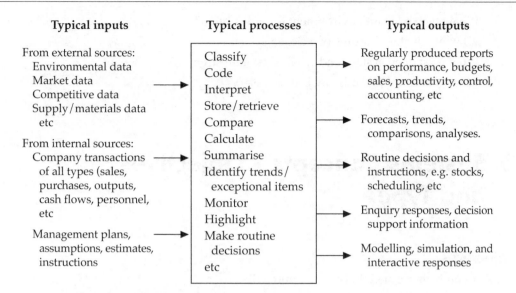

Typical inputs	Typical processes	Typical outputs
From external sources: Environmental data Market data Competitive data Supply/materials data etc From internal sources: Company transactions of all types (sales, purchases, outputs, cash flows, personnel, etc Management plans, assumptions, estimates, instructions	Classify Code Interpret Store/retrieve Compare Calculate Summarise Identify trends/ exceptional items Monitor Highlight Make routine decisions etc	Regularly produced reports on performance, budgets, sales, productivity, control, accounting, etc Forecasts, trends, comparisons, analyses. Routine decisions and instructions, e.g. stocks, scheduling, etc Enquiry responses, decision support information Modelling, simulation, and interactive responses

Figure 3/7 A typical information-processing system

Key Point Summary

- The systems view is that the whole is greater than the sum of the individual parts.
- Parts or sub-systems cannot be altered without other parts.
- All system definitions contain the essential elements of *parts*, *relationships* and *objectives*.
- All systems comprise: inputs, processes and outputs.
- The constraints or features which define a system are its boundaries and many practical problems are concerned with alterations in boundaries.
- The environment of a system includes those elements with which it has some connection or relationship.
- Closed systems have rigid boundaries and do not have any changes with their environment.
- Open systems have a dynamic relationship within their environment which is vital to ensure adaptability.
- Sub-systems can belong to more than one system.
- The number of inter-connections between sub-systems increases rapidly as the number of sub-systems increases.
- Decoupling allows more flexibility and independence but incurs costs.

Self Review Questions

1. What are the key features of the systems' approach?
2. What is sub-optimality?
3. Give several alternative definitions of a system.
4. What is the transformation process?
5. What is a boundary and an interface?

6. What is the relevant environment for any system?
7. What are the key features of a closed system?
8. What is an open system and what is its main strength?
9. What is decoupling and why is it necessary?

4 Systems Concepts – Objectives and Types

Objectives

After you have studied this chapter you will:

- understand the importance of objective setting.
- know that 'what' comes before 'how'.
- understand the factors which constrain organisations.
- be able to summarise the hard and soft characteristics of problems.
- be able to distinguish between hard uncertainty and soft issues.
- know what is a socio-technical system.

Purpose and Objectives

The primary purpose of any organisation is to satisfy the needs of its clients or market. This applies whether it is a profit orientated organisation such as a manufacturer of breakfast cereals or a not-for-profit organisation, such as the Social Services department of a local authority.

The purpose of the organisation reflects the long term nature and characteristics of the organisation and this purpose is expressed in its *objectives*. Objectives express the direction and level of achievement expected from the organisation as a whole and, at lower levels, from the individual parts, sections and departments which make up the organisation.

The systems approach is objective orientated and thus can be of value as a way of studying organisational problems. The approach is a top-down one where objectives are clarified first before considering how they are to be achieved.

> *What* must be done must be decided *before* considering *how* it should be done.

The alternative bottom-up approach starts from a detailed analysis of the workings of particular parts of the system. This latter approach tends to produce solutions which find better ways of organising unnecessary activities or cheaper ways of producing unwanted products. Although objective setting is of primary importance there are many problems. Some of the more important ones are dealt with below including; personal and organisational objectives, conflicting objectives and constraints.

Personal and Organisational Objectives

Organisational objectives are for the most part non-personal yet they are developed and implemented by people. The needs of individuals are important bases of their motivation. Individuals have goals and if they are to accept organisational objectives they must feel that working towards the achievement of the organisational objectives will satisfy, or at least not conflict with, their own personal objectives. Attention to these factors by management will help to ensure a dynamic, motivated work force rather than a grudging 'work to rule' attitude.

Multiple Objectives

Organisations, especially large ones, are diverse and complex and operate in an uncertain and changing environment. They have to meet many, often competing, demands from their clients or customers, their employees, their social environmental responsibilities, their shareholders (where appropriate) and so on. In such circumstances it is simplistic to think that there can be a single, overriding objective. As a consequence, organisations have to develop a series of objectives to cope with their various responsibilities. Take, for example, the objectives of Sainsbury's plc.

Sainsbury's plc objectives

- To discharge the responsibility as leaders in our trade by acting with complete integrity, by carrying out our work to the highest standards and by contributing to the public good and to the quality of life in the community.

- To provide unrivalled value to our customers in the quality of goods we sell, in the competitiveness of our prices and in the range of choice we offer.

- In our stores, to achieve the highest standards of cleanliness and hygiene, efficiency of operation, convenience and customer service, and thereby create as attractive and friendly a shopping environment as possible.

- To offer our staff outstanding opportunities in terms of personal career development and in remuneration relative to other companies in the same market, practising always a concern for the welfare of every individual.

- To generate sufficient profit to finance continual improvement and growth of the business whilst providing our shareholders with an excellent return on their investment.

Note the balancing of the needs of the various stakeholders; the customers, staff and shareholders, with the needs of the community as a whole. Note also that part of the first objective relating to the public good and quality of life in the community. This is an area of *social responsibility* which is taken seriously by most leading organisations.

Conflicting Objectives

In general, all systems have conflicting objectives so that some form of compromise is necessary. For example, there may be conflicting requirements of low initial capital costs, low operating costs (best served by more capital expenditure), high safety standards (in conflict with capital and operating costs) and so on.

At lower levels in organisations it is sometimes possible to define an overall measure which summarises the efficiency with which that part of the organisation meets its objectives. For example, the production sub-system of a company might summarise its objectives by using as a measure 'cost per unit of good output produced'. In many organisations this type of simple, overall target is not practicable. For example, is it feasible to think in terms of a single economic criterion for a hospital, a local authority, a school?

Indeed concentration on single numeric targets for complex organisations can lead to unexpected and adverse effects. An example is the ranking of schools by examination (GCSE and A level) results, the so called League Tables. This has led to some schools not entering pupils for public examinations where they think that they would lower their League Table position and or neglecting other aspects of the wider educational process particularly relating to less able or difficult children.

Constraints

Constraints are the limitations, shortages or difficulties which restrict the capacity of the organisation to achieve its objectives. Constraints represent the problems management have to overcome, or learn to live with, if the organisation is to operate successfully. Identification of constraints is thus essential if the organisation is to meet its objectives. Constraints may take many forms:

Because of the reluctance of teachers to work in inner-city areas Tower Hamlets and other London Boroughs are experiencing great difficulty in meeting their objective of providing good education for all children. They are attempting to remove this constraint by offering assistance with housing and transport and even by recruiting teachers from abroad.

A property company had difficulty in obtaining planning permission for a site it owned because of objections by local residents. They largely met these objectives by re-planning the development and re-routing the access roads.

Organisations are continually trying to overcome constraints and to adapt to disturbances from their environment. An essential factor in this process is the flow of information into and around the organisation. Internal information is of great value in monitoring, controlling and improving operations but to ensure adaptation and survival, information about the environment is essential. This latter point is of such importance that it is worth stressing. To cope with change and to deal with threats and opportunities from the environment, *external information* is of paramount importance.

Hard and Soft Properties

The systems approach to organisational problems emphasises the need to consider both hard and soft properties.

Hard properties are those that can be defined, measured or assessed in an objective way whereas soft properties are more imprecise and are matters of individual values and tastes.

Figure 4/1 summarises the main soft and hard characteristics.

Most problems contain both hard and soft features. For example, an organisation is thinking of re-locating its offices from London to Newcastle. This has hard (i.e. measurable) effects (what will be the saving in office rent?) and also soft effects (what will be the impact on morale and family life caused by the disruption?).

However, at operational levels certain problems can effectively be considered as hard. For example:

A typical hard system is an inventory control system for an engineering component. The structure of the system is well known and relatively standardised, quantitative decision methods are suitable for setting re-order levels, ordering quantities and other key elements. The system can be judged by readily acceptable quantitative measures, for example, the rate of stocks held in relation to sales, number of orders placed and so on. In short the system is structured and relatively mechanistic.

Figure 4/1 Hard and soft properties

On the other hand 'soft' systems are characterised by more vagueness and irrationality. Objectives are hard to define and are subject to change and argument, decision making is more uncertain, measures of performance must often be formed in qualitative terms, and above all, the systems must include recognition of human behaviour with all its attendant conflicts, aspirations and irrationalities. To a greater or lesser degree it will be apparent that *any* system in an organisation contains soft system elements because of the presence of people. Because individuals pursue personal goals as well as those of the organisation some sub-optimality is present in all organisations.

Hard Uncertainty and Softness

Care must be taken to distinguish between uncertainty applied to hard properties and the idea of soft issues.

Aspects of a system which are measurable in some objective way are hard whether or not they are accurate or certain. For example, the sales of a company for last year can be calculated and are known with certainty (i.e. they are a hard property). Next year's sales cannot be known with certainty but it is possible to make estimates which will have various levels of certainty attached to them. For example:

There is a 20% chance that sales will be between £1m and £2m.

There is a 50% chance that sales will be between £2m and £3.5m.

There is a 30% chance that sales will be above £3.5m.

This is known as probabilistic or stochastic measurements. Although we are not *certain* what next year's sales will be, sales are a hard factor that can be measured objectively. There are many examples of hard uncertainty:

- Actuarial calculations in insurance companies.
- Forecasts of electricity demand on the National Grid.
- Population and morbidity forecasts.

Soft systems are thus those which incorporate and depend on some facet of human nature. The behaviour of people, their reactions, their objectives and their motivations cannot be predicted with certainty but nevertheless are of critical importance in developing and using information systems. Because of this it is necessary to examine the behavioural aspects of information systems as well as the technical and structural elements. Checkland has developed a way of describing soft systems, known as Soft System Methodology (SSM) which is used in system design. SSM is described in detail in Chapter 14, together with other tools used for defining information systems.

People in Organisations

Organisational problems contain hard and soft issues to varying degrees and the importance of the soft system's viewpoint is that it avoids thinking about solving problems in a machine-like or mechanistic way. There may be a yearning for systems to behave in a controllable and predictable fashion but, where people are involved, they will not. Often managers see situations in a narrow fashion and solve the more obvious 'hard' problems, for example about technology changes, when the real problem is about the human interactions involved.

For example, the 1994 Signalmen's strike which caused major disruption to virtually the entire railway network had its roots in the introduction of new computer assisted signalling technology. The management wished to view this introduction as a 'hard' problem concerning the new equipment and economics whereas the staff and the RMT union saw it quite differently as being concerned with the people affected, that is very much a 'soft' system problem.

The interactions of people and organisations have also been studied from other viewpoints. One idea developed was that of socio-technical systems.

Socio-Technical Systems

This view of organisations was developed by Trist and the Tavistock Institute and arose from consideration that any production system requires both a *technological organisation*, i.e. the equipment, processes, methods etc and a *work organisation* relating to those who carry out the necessary tasks to each other, i.e. the social system. Based on this view an organisation is not just a technical or social system but it is the structuring of human activities round various technologies.

The technologies involved determine the technical sub-systems and vary widely. Consider, for example, the differing skills, procedures, machinery, equipment and the layout of facilities required in an electronics company, a car manufacturer, a hospital or a computer bureau.

In addition to the technical sub-system, every organisation has a social sub-system which consists of the aspirations, expectations, interactions and value systems of the members. The two sub-systems – the technical and the social – cannot be looked at separately but must both be considered as inter-relating within the organisation. Sociotechnical theory suggests that the organisation consists of four inter-related elements – tasks, people, structure and technology as shown in Figure 4/2.

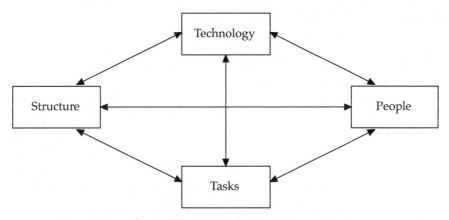

Figure 4/2 Socio-technical view of organisations

More traditional approaches to organisations and their problems have tended to concentrate on one or other of the sub-systems with little or no recognition of the other. For example the production engineering/management science approach to organisational problems concentrated on the economic-technical sub-system and on fairly mechanistic techniques for quantifying decision making, control and of planning production. The human relations and behavioural schools concentrated on the social sub-system and considered motivation, aspirations, group dynamics and other related factors with scant regard to the technologies involved. The socio-technical view considers each of the primary sub-systems *and* their inter-relationships and effects on each other and thus makes a genuine attempt at a comprehensive understanding of the systems we call organisations.

Key Point Summary

- The systems approach is objective orientated.
- The approach is a top-down one where *what* comes before *how*.
- Objectives are often in conflict and some compromise is usually necessary.
- Management have to overcome constraints which hinder the fulfilment of objectives
- Hard issues are measurable, clearly defined with known solution techniques.

- Soft issues are fuzzy, involve values and opinions and do not necessarily have a right solution.
- Hard system may include uncertainty.
- Sub-optimality is inevitable with soft systems.
- Socio-technical systems is a term for organisations structured round technologies.

Self Review Questions

1. In what sequence should objectives be set?
2. What is the top-down approach?
3. Why do organisations have multiple objectives?
4. Give examples of conflicting objectives.
5. What are typical constraints faced by a manufacturer and a hospital?
6. Distinguish between hard and soft properties.
7. What type of problem can be considered totally hard?
8. Describe hard uncertainty and distinguish between it and softness.
9. What is a socio-technical system?

Assessment and revision section

Assignments

1. Find out all you can about a specific real management decision. For example; what are the objectives of the decision maker, what are the rules for making the decision (if any)? What information is required for making the decision and so on.

2. Within an organisation familiar to you list 10 items of source data. Are the source data always accurate and on time? How could the position be improved? What is the effect of inaccuracies? How are the source data collected?

3. An example is given in the text of writing containing unexplained technical jargon. Find other examples:

   (a) which are acceptable because of the target readership.

   (b) which you consider to be unacceptable.

4. Define the inputs, processes and outputs for the following systems

   (a) A college system

   (b) An accounting system

   (c) A heating system

   (d) A police force

5. The objectives of Sainsburys are given in the text. Find other examples for:

   (a) a not-for-profit organisation such as a college, local authority, a charity etc.

   (b) a profit seeking organisation

   How are the needs of the various stakeholders reflected in the objectives?

6. An organisation is contemplating changing its existing manual systems to a computer based system using terminals throughout the organisation.

   Analyse the hard and soft issues involved.

7. Find examples of sub-systems (e.g. departments) which are closely coupled. What information flows are necessary to maintain the coupling?

8. In an organisation known to you try to find an example of information not at present available which would add value to the organisation. How could the information be produced? Why is it not produced at present?

Mini-Case 1 – Problems of Communication

X plc is a large business producing a range of branded products. It has a number of divisions covering similar brands, including frozen food, canned products, and bakery products. Each division is a profit centre headed by a managing director reporting to the chairman.

The bakery division has a number of factories, each of which manufactures a major product line. In each factory several production managers report to the works manager.

The sales department provides a demand schedule to the production planners, who then schedule the week's production. The production schedule is sent to the sales department after approval by the works manager.

The maintenance engineers supply production planning with a list of work to the done on the production machinery. This work is also scheduled to avoid interfering with production. There is considerable annoyance in the sales department because the agreed production is never fully delivered.

One of the salesmen is seriously concerned about losing an important customer. He has obtained an order for pies and cakes. He wants to make absolutely certain that these are delivered on time. Fortunately, he is friendly with both the production managers responsible for manufacturing these lines. He telephones John, in charge of pie production, to see whether there is a problem and is assured that production of pies is on schedule. He passes this information on to the customer. He also telephones James, in charge of cake production, who informs him that there is a gap in the schedule, so that the order for cakes will be delivered early.

When the time comes to deliver, neither order is ready. The customer cancels all his orders and an investigation is ordered by the managing director.

It appears that the pie machine broke down. The operator said that he knew that it was bound to break down shortly. John furiously complains to the works manager, Peter, that the operators always say 'I knew it would' when the machines break down. When challenged why they did not pass on their knowledge, they claim they did, but neither John nor the maintenance engineer admits to having been informed.

The investigation showed that the gap in the schedule for the cake machine had been reserved for an experimental run arranged between the managing director, the development director and production planning. 'How are we to keep our promises if there is always interference from the top?' asked Peter, but when the managing director pointed out that delivery dates were often not met even when there was no interference, Peter decided to investigate production planning.

Mary, the manager in charge of production planning, blamed most of the problems on not being informed about changes in specification and other factors affecting output, such as machines or raw materials not being available. Store keepers and maintenance engineers all protested that they always try to let Mary know, but have difficulty in making contact with her.

You are required to analyse the problems that occur in the above situation from the point of view of communication.

CIMA

Mini-Case 2 – Information Requirements in a Service Industry

Corinth Hotels plc is a successful hotel group with a chain of hotels throughout the UK. As part of an expansion and diversification programme the group has acquired a travel and holiday booking company and proposes to expand its operations to include road, rail and air travel booking and all types of holidays at home and abroad.

The directors of Corinth are anxious that the new business is operated as efficiently as possible and that all necessary information is available so that informed planning and decision making can take place and current activities can be monitored and controlled.

Task 1 Describe what external information the new business should try to gather and how this would help planning and decision making.

Task 2 Give details of what information would help to monitor and control the new business.

Task 3 Describe, in outline, the managerial and reporting relationships between the management of the new business and the Board of Corinth Hotels plc.

Examination Questions (with Answers)

A1. It is generally accepted that effective management is impossible without information.

You are required to:

(a) define information;

(b) discuss the characteristics of information that assists the key management functions of planning, control and decision making; and

(c) describe how to assess whether it is worthwhile producing more information for use in a particular decision.

CIMA

A2. The quality of management information is directly related to its timing.

(a) Discuss this statement, with particular reference to:

   i.   the different purposes for which the information may be required; and

   ii. the relative merits of speed versus accuracy in each case.

(b) Explain in what ways the timing of information flows should be taken into account when designing information systems.

CIMA

A3. Using general theory as the basis of your approach, identify and describe the main functional elements which must be identified within a business system, together with their related information requirements.

ACCA

A4. Traditional theory considers an organisation to be a closed system whereas modern theory considers it to be an open system. (Kast and Rosenzweig 'The Modern View – a Systems Approach'). Comment on this difference and identify the implications.

CIPFA

A5. The production plan for a company, which was agreed by the board of directors after consideration of all factors, calls for 10,000 units each of products X, Y and Z, to be produced each week. However, to obtain longer production runs and lower production costs per unit, the production manager decided to produce 30,000 units of each product every third week.

Discuss the conflict of system goals inherent in this situation, in the context of the systems approach.

CIMA

A6. The primary task of any systems investigation is the establishment of the objectives of the area being studied.

Explain what is meant by the above statement and discuss the problems involved in establishing relevant objectives.

CIMA

A7. Explain
   (a) the concept of *open systems*;
   (b) how the concept is used in organisation theory.

CIMA

A8. (a) Distinguish between data and information.
   (b) Why do organisations expend resources in the collection of information?
   (c) What features should the output from a system possess to provide useful information?

IAM

A9. Name three major barriers to communication in an organisation and say how they might be overcome.

ACCA

Examination Questions (without Answers)

B1. (a) What are the barriers to effective communication which may occur between two people working in the same department.
   (b) What can be done to reduce or eliminate such barriers?

CIMA

B2. It is generally stated that reports produced by a management information system may be classified into four types.
   What are these four types and what is the purpose of each?

CIPFA

B3. A group consists of three different-sized factories each of which produces varying quantities of a mix of five products and uses the same raw material which is in short supply.

In order to optimise its own production facilities, each factory prepares a production plan, using a Linear Programming model, in order to utilise its allocation of raw material from group headquarters.

As an exercise, a young systems analyst at group headquarters entered the various production constraints of all the factories into a single LP model and found that an overall production plan emerged which differed from the earlier three individual plans and produced a higher total contribution.

You are required to discuss:
   (a) the systems problems inherent in the above situation; and
   (b) ways in which the problems can be avoided in the future.

CIMA

B4. You are required to define briefly the following terms, within the context of management information systems and data processing, and provide a commercial or accounting example of each:
   (a) system boundary;
   (b) decoupling;
   (c) sub-optimality;
   (d) negative feedback;
   (e) probablistic system.

CIMA

B5.   The managing director of GH Ltd, a manufacturing company, is learning about information and systems theory.

You are required, as management accountant in the company,

(a) to identify and comment on each of the factors which give information its value when used in management reports;

(b) to explain the concepts of subsystem coupling and decoupling, using just-in-time (JIT) and conventional stores/stock control systems as examples.

CIMA

Additional reading

1.   Checkland, *Systems Thinking, Systems Practice*, Wiley
2.   Drucker, *Management, Tasks, Responsibilities and Practice*, Heinemann
3.   *Systems Behaviour*, Open University
4.   Johnson, Kast and Rosenweig, *Theory and Management of Systems*, Wiley
5.   Parker and Case, *Management Information Systems*, McGraw-Hill
6.   Beer, *Diagnosing the System for Organisations*, John Wiley
7.   Avison, *Information Systems Development*, Blackwell

5 Organisations: Scientific Management and the Classical School

Objectives

After you have studied this chapter you will:

- be able to define an organisation.
- understand the main influences which have contributed to our knowledge of organisations.
- be able to explain the main principles of Taylorism or Scientific Management.
- understand the benefits and drawbacks of Scientific Management.
- know the contribution made by the Classical School.
- understand Fayol's approach to management.
- be able to define bureaucracy.
- understand the main Classical principles.

What are Organisations?

An organisation is a group created and maintained to achieve specific objectives. It may be a hospital with objectives dealing with health care, it may be a local authority with objectives concerned with providing services to the local community, it might be a commercial company with objectives including earning profits, providing a return for shareholders and so on.

Modern economies consist of countless organisations so their efficiency and performance is of critical importance. As a consequence the types of organisations, their structures, methods of management used, the relationships with other organisations and so on have been extensively studied and researched.

There is no universally accepted definition of an organisation but the following are examples from well known management writers.

'Organisations are systems of interdependent human beings' *Pugh*
'Organisations are intricate human strategies designed to achieve certain objectives' *Argyris*
'An organisation is a system of cooperative human activities' *Barnard*

Although there will probably never be a universally accepted definition, the following features describing organisations would be accepted by most people;

Organisations are:

(a) goal orientated i.e. people with a purpose.

(b) social systems i.e. people working in groups.

(c) technical systems i.e. people using knowledge, techniques and machines.

(d) the integration of structured activities i.e. people co-ordinating their efforts.

Note particularly, the emphasis in definitions on 'people' and that organisations are more than just groups of people. There may be a group of people in a disco or a club but they do not have a structure or a common purpose nor do they coordinate with each other. They are a group but not an organisation.

Organisational Complexity

It has to be recognised that the study of organisations, the way they work, the way they are organised and their effectiveness, is complicated. It is complicated because organisational effectiveness is influenced by a wide variety of factors which interact with each other. Figure 5/1 tries to summarise the key factors that contribute to organisational effectiveness. The double-headed arrows between the boxes are a diagrammatic attempt to emphasise that there are inter-actions between all factors. The title of each box is but a summary heading for yet more factors. As an example within Individual Staff Attributes there are such things are; experience, personality, age, motivation and so on.

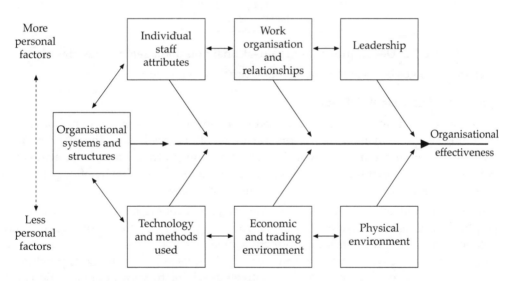

Figure 5/1 Factors influencing organisational effectiveness

Influences on Organisations

The modern view of organisations describes them in terms of open systems, their responses to external and internal influences and the way they achieve their objectives. However, this is a view which has evolved from earlier ideas which have had, and still have, considerable influence on the structure and operation of today's organisations. Figure 5/2 shows in broad chronological sequence the three main schools of thought which have contributed to an understanding of the nature of organisations and their management.

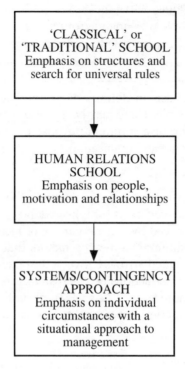

Figure 5/2 Development of organisational and management theories

Each of the stages is developed in the paragraphs which follow.

Traditional or Classical School

Traditional organisational theory is based on contributions from a number of sources including scientific management (from Taylor, Gantt, Gilbreth and others), administrative management theorists (Fayol, Urwick, Brech and others) and from academics, notably Weber who, unlike the other contributors to the classical view of organisations, was not a practising manager, but an academic sociologist.

Whilst not completely ignoring the behavioural aspects of organisations, the traditional emphasis was on the structure of organisations, the management of structure and detailed analysis and control of production methods. All organisations were treated similarly and there was a search for universal principles which could be applied to any organisation and, on the whole, took a relatively mechanistic view of organisations with a tendency to treat them as *closed systems* i.e. systems which do not interact with their environment.

Scientific Management or 'Taylorism'

At the turn of the century Frederick Winslow Taylor introduced the concept of 'scientific management'. This developed from his experiments in improving labour-productivity at the Bethlehem Steel Works, USA. He was committed to improving the efficiency of working methods and realised that this could only be done by detailed analysis, timing , and the elimination of unnecessary movement, i.e. the substitution of fact for opinion.

Taylor's pioneering work was refined and developed by other workers such as Frank and Lilian Gilbreth and H. Gantt and their approach has evolved into the technique known today as Work Study which is used throughout the world.

Scientific management has four main principles:

(a) Develop the best or ideal method of doing a task and determine 'scientifically' a standard.

(b) Select the best man for the task and train him in the best way to achieve the task.

(c) Combine the scientific method with the selected and trained men.

(d) Take all responsibility for planning and preparing work away from the worker and give it to management. The worker's only responsibility is for the actual job performance.

Scientific management was based on strong financial incentives but undoubtedly the most far reaching principle was that management should take over work organisation. This reduced the scope for individual workers and this fragmentation of work effect – or de-skilling – still has strong repercussions today, nearly a century later.

A number of recent managerial developments, for example, job enrichment and group assembly methods have been designed to counteract the frustrations caused by the legacy of the worst aspects of scientific management.

Scientific management was applied to lower level routine and repetitive tasks and said nothing about higher level planning and decision making in the organisation. Taylor's heavy emphasis on financial incentives, rationality and the need for close supervision of 'unwilling' workers has had strong and lasting influences on management thinking and practice. The attitudes and approaches adopted by the Scientific Management movement are still clearly discernible today in many organisations.

Benefits and Drawbacks of Scientific Management

The major benefits and drawbacks of Taylorism can be summarised as follows:

Benefits

- The improvement in working methods resulted in enormous gains in productivity.
- The measurement and analysis of tasks provided factual information on which to base improvements in methods and equipment.
- It provided a rational basis for piecework and incentive schemes which became more widely used.
- There were considerable improvements in working conditions.
- Management became more involved with production activities and were thus encouraged to show positive leadership.

Drawbacks

- Jobs became more boring and repetitive.
- Planning, design and control became divorced from performance thus de-skilling tasks.

- Workers become virtual adjuncts to machines with management having a monopoly of knowledge and control.

- De-skilling, excessive specialisation, repetition and so on cause workers to become alienated and frustrated. This has become an increasing problem with generally rising education standards and personal expectations.

Classical School – Departmental Approaches

A number of earlier management thinkers notably Fayol, Urwick, Brech and others developed a top down view of organisations which contrasted with the factory floor emphasis of Taylor. Fayol and others described organisations based upon the grouping of various activities into departments. They looked at the organisation as a large machine and tried to develop universal laws or principles which governed the machine's activities.

The general problem addressed by them was; how are tasks organised into individual jobs, how are jobs organised into administrative units and how are these combined into departments? The result of this analysis was the structuring of departments within an organisation; each department containing a set of tasks to be performed by the people in that department.

As an example a common departmental organisation on a functional basis might have the following divisions:

- *Finance.* Activities associated with providing funds and ensuring their effective use.
- *Production.* The provision and maintenance of equipment to convert raw materials into finished products and the control of the production process.
- *Marketing.* Including sales, distribution, promotion.
- *Supply.* The procurement of raw materials and other inputs for production and administration.
- *Personnel.* Providing and training the people for the organisation.
- *Research and Development.* The development of new products and processes and the modification of existing products and processes.

Of the classical management thinkers Henri Fayol was the first and undoubtedly the most influential.

Henri Fayol

Fayol was a successful French industrialist (1841–1925) who also thought deeply about the management and structure of organisations. Fayol's original definition of management has become a classic and has served as the basis of more modern ones.

Fayol's definition of management:

'To manage is to forecast and plan, to organise, to command, to co-ordinate and to control'.

Some modern variations are:

'Managing is an operational process initially best dissected by analysing the managerial functions [of]: planning, organising, staffing, directing and leading and controlling'.

or

> '[Management is] a social process entailing responsibility for the effective and economical planning and regulation of the operations of the organisation in the fulfillment of a given purpose or task involving
>
> (a) judgement and decision in determining plans and in using data to control performance and progress against plans and,
>
> (b) the guidance, integration, motivation and supervision of the personnel compromising the enterprise and carrying out its operations'

There are common themes throughout these definitions and it should be noted how more modern attitudes to people at work are reflected in the change of Fayol's original phrase, 'to command' into 'directing and leading' and 'guidance, integrating and motivating'.

Fayol's Principles of Management

Based on his experience Fayol derived fourteen general principles of management which had served him well in his career. These are shown in Figure 5/3 together with a brief explanation of each.

Fayol's General Principles formed the basis of later works by writers such as Urwick and Brech. These writers amended and refined Fayol's ideas but still adopted a largely prescriptive approach with an emphasis on the structural nature of organisations.

A contemporary of Fayols, Max Weber (1864–1920), a German Sociologist, also studied formal organisation structures and developed a concept which he termed *bureaucracy* which remains of fundamental importance.

Bureaucracy and Organisations

Although the term bureaucracy has popularly acquired the sense of inefficiency, officialdom and 'red tape', it was first coined by Weber to describe a particular organisational form which exists to some extent in every large scale enterprise whether in the private or public sector.

In Weber's view the bureaucratic organisation was a logical, rational organisation which was technically superior to all other forms.

The key elements in the 'ideal' bureaucratic type of organisation were as follows:

(a) A well defined hierarchy of legitimate authority.

(b) A division of labour based on functional specialisation.

(c) A clear statement of the rights and duties of personnel.

(d) Rules and procedures in writing should exist to deal with all decisions and situations.

(e) Promotion and selection based on technical competence.

In Weber's view a depersonalised form of organisation, such as outlined above, would minimise the effect of human unpredictability. Weber concentrated on the structural aspects of organisations and in consequence took a rather mechanistic and impersonal standpoint.

A number of problems and weaknesses have identified with the bureaucratic model of which the following are the most important:

- Adaptability and the ability to change are made more difficult because of standardised rules, procedures and rigid structures.
- Innovation, creativity and initiative tend to be discouraged.
- Rules tend to become important in their own right rather than as a means of promoting efficiency.
- Control systems are rigid and frequently out of date.
- Decision making is slow and cumbersome.

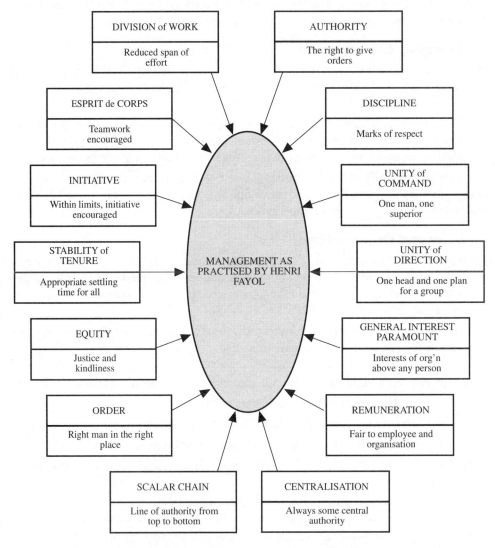

Figure 5/3 Fayol's principles of management

However, in spite of these and other deficiencies, as organisations grow in size and/or complexity the need increases for some form of systematic organisation, which experience shows inevitability incorporates a number of Weber's bureaucratic elements.

The Main Traditional 'Principles'

The traditional approach to organisational problems and structures sought to discover or prescribe basic principles which could universally apply to any organisations. Although it is generally recognised today that there are few, if any, principles which can be applied equally to all organisations, the principles developed from the classical approach have, for generations, had strong and pervasive influences on management thinking and consequently on the structure of organisations. The main organisational principles developed from the traditional or classical movement are as follows:

- the scalar or hierarchical principle;
- span of control;
- unity of command;
- specialisation and division of labour;
- the principle of correspondence.

Each of these principles is discussed in the following paragraphs.

The Scalar or Hierarchical Principle

Hierarchy appears to be a natural order of nature which applies to organisations. This was recognised by classical organisation theory in the statement of the scalar principle which refers to the vertical division of authority and responsibility within the organisation. This states that there should be a flow of authority and responsibility, in an unbroken chain, from the top to the bottom of the organisation. This flow reflects the hierarchical nature of the organisation and the way that duties have been assigned to the sub-units of the organisation i.e. the departments and sections. The vertical flow of authority is known as *line authority* and the managers who exercise it are known as *line managers*.

Span of Control

The span of control or span of supervision, means the number of subordinates a supervisor can supervise effectively.

At higher levels the span should be small but at lower levels, where activities are more repetitive, the span may be larger. Various numbers of subordinates were specified as appropriate, ranging from 3 to 6 but it must be recognised that these numbers are quite arbitrary. Implicit in the span of control concept is the need for a superior to co-ordinate the activities of subordinates which would be generally recognised as a primary management function.

Unity of Command

Essentially this is a re-statement of the hierarchical, scalar principle and means that a subordinate should receive orders from only one superior, i.e. one boss. The vertical, downward flow of authority, as espoused by classical organisational theory, has a militaristic appearance in relation to modern, complex organisations where technological, financial, legal and other implications make it necessary to diffuse authority across the hierarchy as well as vertically downwards.

Specialisation and Division of Labour

Division of labour means that work is sub-divided into small tasks or areas. By working at their narrow task people gain more skill and proficiency and become specialists. The classical school was by no means the first to recognise the gains in efficiency that could be made, from specialisation. Indeed, it is arguable that this is a process which has been evident throughout history, but they were extremely influential in emphasising its importance in organisations.

Specialisation applies not only to production workers on the shop floor but to every level in the organisation, including management. In modern organisations there are very few people indeed who are not specialists in some form or another.

The Principle of Correspondence

This states that authority should be commensurate with responsibility.

> Authority is the right to give an instruction or to carry out a task and responsibility is the obligation to carry out the task satisfactorily.

The classical theorists saw authority solely in terms of formal authority i.e. that specified and imposed by the organisation. This makes for status conscious, authoritarian organisations where upward communication is reduced and personal initiative is stifled.

Nowadays it is recognised that authority is more likely to be acceptable to subordinates when superiors are respected personally and technically. Military style authority is replaced by the concept of teamwork in which the superior works with, rather than being placed over, subordinates.

Classical Theories in Retrospect

Although the classical theorists did not ignore people and their needs their concentration undoubtedly was on structures, authority and control. The search for universal principles produced too much emphasis on what ought to be and thus investigations into actual behaviour, its causes and consequences, were limited.

In spite of many modern criticisms, a number of the classical principles have become almost universally adopted. Examples include; the scalar chain of authority, the matching of authority and responsibility, clear definition of jobs and so on. Others such as unity of command, style of leadership and so on may well have suited earlier, paternalistic organisations but appear to have little place in modern society.

> The contribution of the classical theorists can be summarised thus:
> - they introduced the idea that management was a suitable subject for intellectual analysis.
> - they provided a foundation of ideas on which subsequent theorists have built.
> - criticism of their work has stimulated empirical studies of actual organisational behaviour.

Modern views on organisations have become markedly less rigid than the classical approach. Perhaps the following quotation from William Ouchi, author of Theory Z, represents the ultimate expression of the modern viewpoint:

'My ideal of a completely efficient and perfectly integrated organisation is one that has no organisational chart, no divisions, no visible structure at all. In a sense, a basketball team that plays well fits this description, although on a small scale. The problem facing a basketball team is huge in its complexity, and the speed with which problems occur is great. Yet an effective team solves these problems with no formal reporting relationships and a minimum of specialisation of positions and tasks'.

Key Point Summary

- Organisations have been variously described but there is general agreement that they combine both social and technical systems in which efforts are co-ordinated to achieve specified objectives.
- The main theoretical approaches to organisations include: Scientific management, the departmental approach, the human relations school and the systems/contingency school.
- Scientific management was a production orientated rational approach to organisations pioneered by Taylor.
- Fayol and others adopted a 'top-down' view of organisations.
- Line relationships are those in the direct chain of command.
- Bureaucracy, as defined by Weber, was an ideal, rational view of organisations with clearly defined tasks and relationships.
- The main traditional principles of organisations include the scalar principle, unity of command, span of control and specialisation.

Self Review Questions

1. What is an organisation?
2. What are the three main schools that have contributed to our understanding of organisations?
3. What is Scientific management?
4. What was the approach to organisations adopted by Fayol and others?
5. What is Fayol's definition of management?
6. What are the features of Weber's bureaucratic form of organisation?
7. What are the main traditional 'principles' of management applied to organisations?
8. What is the consequence of task specialisation?

6 Organisations: Human Relations School and the Contingency Approach

Objectives

After you have studied this chapter you will:

- understand the contribution of the Human Relations School to organisation theory.
- appreciate the importance of motivation in organisations.
- be able to describe Maslow's hierarchy of needs.
- understand McGregor's Theory X and Theory Y.
- be able to distinguish between motivators and hygiene factors.
- understand the reasoning behind the contingency approach to organisations.
- be able to describe the features of key studies such as those conducted by Lawrence and Lorsch, Burns and Stalker, and Woodward.

Human Relations School

The problems of organisations have also been studied from a human relations or behavioural viewpoint which to some extent was a reaction against the more mechanistic and impersonal bias of the classical school. The undoubted pioneers in this area were Mayo, Roethlisberger and Dickson who conducted the famous 'Hawthorne Experiments' at the Hawthorne, Illinois plant of Western Electric. Initially the studies were carried out to see the effects on productivity of such factors as heat, lighting, fatigue and layout. As such these studies were in the tradition of the scientific management movement, at least initially. But as the study progressed it became clear that efficiency was being influenced by factors beyond the physical working environment and as a result of the emphasis of the study changed to an examination of the motives and attitudes of individual workers, the characteristics of the work group and the relationship of the individual to the group.

The research found that worker performance could be favourably influenced by social factors in the work environment and by changes in attitudes of supervisors. The Hawthorne studies clearly showed that people do not pursue financial ends blindly nor can their behaviour be predicted and governed in the way that Taylor and his colleagues assumed i.e. virtually as adjuncts to machines with predictable responses. Although the methodology of the Hawthorne Experiments has been criticised in recent years the study remains a major landmark in the study of organisations from a behavioural viewpoint.

Concepts of the Human Relations School

Mayo and the other early workers in the human relations field studied the role of individuals, informal groups, inter-group relationships and the formal relationships within the organisation. They developed a number of concepts of which the following are the most important.

(a) People are not only motivated by financial factors but by a variety of social and psychological factors as well.

(b) An organisation is a social system as well as a technical/economic system.

(c) Informal work groups have important roles in determining the attitudes and performances of individuals.

(d) Management requires social skills as well as technical ones.

(e) Traditional 'authoritarian' leadership patterns should be modified substantially to consider psychological and social factors and should become more 'democratic' in nature.

(f) Participation in work organisation, planning and policy formulation is an important element in organisations. This meant establishing effective communications between the various levels in the hierarchy to ensure a free flow of information.

Following Mayo's pioneering work, the study of people and their motivations continued to dominate the minds of researchers and practising managers alike. It was soon apparent that motivation was influenced by many more factors than assumed by the classical theorists.

Motivation in Organisations

For our purposes motivation can be explained as the driving force or commitment people have for doing things. A motive is a need or desire within a person to achieve some goal or objective and understanding human motivations is a complex matter with no precise answers. Although the causes of motivation are imperfectly understood, the results of having motivated people in an organisation are obvious and highly beneficial. As a consequence managers have to try to understand the conditions and influences that motivate people so that they can manage, organise activities and create an organisational atmosphere that encourages positive motivational effects. Early management theory took a somewhat mechanistic view of human motivation assuming that:

(a) individual goals were consistent with, or sublimated to, organisational goals.

(b) individuals responded positively to authority, and

(c) that people were motivated solely by monetary reward.

Experience and behavioural research has shown that these early views are incomplete and simplistic and that people are much more complex than suggested by the early management theorists. Numerous theories have been advanced to explain motivation and how and why people are motivated. A possible classification of the various approaches is into *content* and *process* theories.

- *Content theories* are based on the assumption that people have a set of needs or desired outcomes and that they pursue actions to achieve their wants. Two important content theories, developed by Maslow and by Herzberg are outlined in this chapter.

- *Process theories* concentrate on the ways outcomes become desirable and are pursued by people. Two examples of process theories, Vroom's expectancy theory and Handy's Motivational Calculus are also dealt with in this chapter.

Before examining the various motivational theories it will be useful to consider the classification developed by Professor Schein of the assumptions about motivation.

Schein's Classification of Motivational Assumptions

Professor Schein reviewed the assumptions about people that were implicit in the then current ideas about what factors and conditions motivate people at work. His four-way classification, which follows a rough historical sequence, is summarised below:

(a) *Rational-Economic man*

Assumptions: Man is primarily motivated by economic needs. He has to be manipulated, controlled and financially motivated by the organisation.

These views stemmed from the Industrial revolution and were important assumptions behind the 'Scientific Management' movement of Taylor and others. Schein says that these assumptions ultimately categorise people into two groups; the untrustworthy, money-motivated majority (McGregor's Theory X people – described later) and the self-motivated, more trustworthy elite who must assume responsibility for the management of others.

(b) *Social man*

Assumptions: Man is essentially a social animal and gains his basic sense of identity through relationships with others.

This categorisation is based on Mayo's conclusions from the Hawthorne Experiment described earlier. The effect of these assumptions is that management is only effective to the extent it can mobilise and rely on these social relationships. Issues of leadership and group behaviour are therefore paramount.

(c) *Self-actualising man*

Assumptions: Man is primarily self-motivated and self-controlled. Man needs self-fulfillment, challenge, responsibility and a sense of pride in his work.

This concept is based on Maslow's hierarchy of human needs and is closely allied to McGregor's Theory Y view – both explained later. The concept of self-actualising man means that managers should seek to provide demanding, challenging work and to provide for genuine delegation of responsibility and greater autonomy. Research studies have supported the concept of self-actualising man especially for professional and managerial grades, although it is less clear whether it applies to lower grade or less skilled workers.

(d) *Complex man*

Assumptions: Man is variable. He has many motives which are arranged any one time in a hierarchy but the hierarchy may change from time to time and from situation to situation.

The result of this view is that managers need to adapt and vary their behaviour in accordance with the motivational needs of particular individuals and groups and the task in hand. Schein sees the relationship between the individual and the organisation as 'interactive and interdependence'.

It is apparent from the above that there are numerous views about how to explain human behaviour at work. The following paragraphs expand some of the categories given above and outline the more important findings of the major contributors to the theory of motivation.

Maslow's Hierarchy of Needs

Abraham Maslow was an American psychologist who developed the theory that people are motivated by a desire to satisfy specific groups of needs and that they tend to satisfy their needs progressively, starting with basic physiological needs and moving up the hierarchy.

Maslow's hierarchy of needs is shown in Figure 6/1.

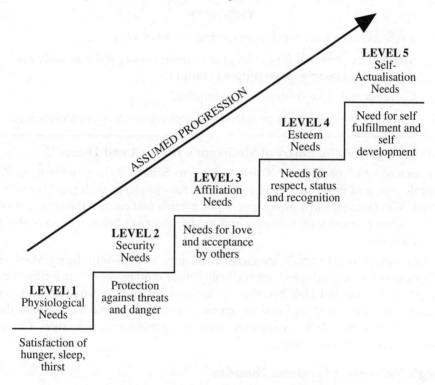

Figure 6/1 Maslow's hierarchy of needs

According to Maslow when one need is more or less satisfied another, higher level need becomes dominant. The consequence of this is that when a need is satisfied it ceases to be a motivator.

In a general sense Maslow's theories have intuitive appeal. A starving man is obviously dominated by the need for food, to him esteem and status are unimportant. However, above this primitive level, difficulties appear. There is doubt whether people do in fact move progressively up the hierarchy and whether higher levels can ever be considered as truly satisfied. For example, it is likely that the need for esteem and status requires continual reinforcement. Although the research evidence in support of Maslow's hierarchy is inconclusive his theories have been influential in the study of motivation.

McGregor's Theory X and Theory Y

McGregor evolved two sets of propositions and assumptions about the nature and behaviour of people in organisations. He termed these two sets 'Theory X' and 'Theory Y', the key elements of which are shown in Figure 6/2.

THEORY X

1. The average man is inherently lazy.
2. He lacks ambition, dislikes responsibility and must be led.
3. He is resistant to change and is indifferent to organisational needs.
4. Coercion and close control are required.

THEORY Y

1. To the average man, work is as natural as rest or play.
2. Motivation, potential for development, imagination and ingenuity are present in all people given proper conditions.
3. Coercion and close control are not required.
4. Given proper conditions people will accept and seek out responsibility.

Figure 6/2 Summary of McGregor's Theory X and Theory Y

The characteristics of Theory X are similar to Schein's classification of Rational-Economic man and there are clear implications for management if the Theory X view is adopted. Management must direct, persuade, punish and control the activities of people and management must seek to coerce and modify people's behaviour to fit the needs of the organisation.

The assumptions of Theory Y are close to Maslow's 'Self-Actualising Man' (Schein's third category) and, if adopted, considerably alter management's priorities and tasks. Management's essential task becomes to harness the inherent qualities of people by arranging conditions and methods of operations so that people can achieve their own goals best by directing their own efforts towards organisational objectives. Co-operation rather than coercion is required.

Herzberg's Motivation-Hygiene Theories

A further influential insight into motivation was provided by the researches of Frederick Herzberg. He concluded that certain factors led to job satisfaction, which he termed *motivators* and certain factors could lead to dissatisfaction, termed *hygiene factors*. The major factors found in the two groups are summarised in Figure 6/3.

HYGIENE FACTORS (leading to dissatisfaction)	MOTIVATORS (leading to satisfaction)
Policies & Administration Supervision Working Conditions Money Job Security Status Relationships with Peers and Subordinates	Achievement Recognition Responsibility Growth & Development Growth

Figure 6/3 Herzberg's Hygiene Factors and Motivators

It will be seen that the motivators are related to the *content* of the job whilst the hygiene factors are more related to the *environment* of the work and not intrinsic to the job itself.

Hygiene factors and motivators are not opposites. Hygiene factors, even if provided for, do not themselves induce job satisfaction; they merely prevent dissatisfaction. Motivators must be present to promote positive satisfaction. A production analogy is that hygiene factors are necessary to maintain production but motivators are needed to increase output.

Although there are some differences between Maslow's and Herzberg's approaches they both tend to assert that the individual's performance in a job is influenced by basic needs (necessary for maintaining performance) and higher order-needs (needed to improve performance). Hertzberg's work has led to much of the modern interest in the design of the job and to what is called 'job enrichment' i.e. where the task is enriched with motivators such as responsibility and recognition.

Other Investigations into Motivation

There have been numerous other contributions towards the understanding of motivation and of course investigations still continue. Another American, Rensis Likert, found from his researches that successful managers built their success on tightly knit groups of staff whose co-operation had been obtained by close attention to a range of lower and higher order motivational factors. Participation was encouraged and supportive relationships within and between groups were fostered. These features led to full commitment to the organisation's goals and high performance levels.

Researchers who attempted to study the *process* of motivation were Vroom and Lawler who developed a set of ideas which has been named Expectancy Theory. The main part of the theory relates to how a person perceives the relationship between two factors:

- the value placed on a particular outcome, called *valence*, and
- the strength of a person's expectation that behaving in a certain way will produce the desired outcome, called *expectancy*.

This can be summarised thus:

Expectancy × Valence = Strength of motivation

This theory really only states what is intuitively obvious i.e. if a person desires something strongly and thinks that a certain action will achieve the desired effect then they will be strongly motivated to do it.

Handy's Motivational Calculus

Another of the process theories of motivation has been developed by Professor Charles Handy. He suggests that for any individual decision there is a conscious or unconscious assessment of three factors, which he terms the *motivational calculus*. The factors are:

- the individual's *needs*
- the desired *results*
- the *E Factors* (i.e. effort, emotion, energy, expenditure and excitement in achieving desired results).

This can be summarised as shown in Figure 6/4.

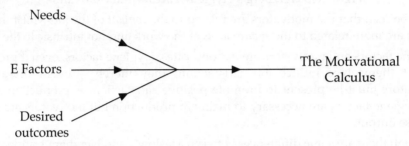

Figure 6/4 Professor Handy's movitational calculus

Professor Handy suggests motivation in organisation is increased when intended results are made clear and when there is feedback on performance. Also he suggests that individuals are more committed to specific goals which they have helped to set themselves.

Although the two 'process' theories outlined above (Vroom's and Handy's) have differences, they both emphasise that motivation is dependent on a form of calculation whereby a person weighs up the potential rewards and the effort required to achieve those rewards.

Human Relations and Motivation – A Conclusion

The preceding paragraphs have outlined (very briefly) some of the ideas developed by researchers into motivation and human relationships in the workplace. All have contributed to the understanding of the human factor at work yet none provides a complete answer and probably no research ever will. Consideration of the various theories and assumptions on which a manager subscribes will colour his views about the way to manage and the ways to deal with people.

Assumptions that man is rational-economic will lead to a bargaining approach and to a preoccupation with the intrinsic conditions of work. Believers in self-actualising or psychological man, will be more concerned with providing the right type of work in the right climate in order to create opportunities for the individual to develop and realise his talents.

Systems/Contingency Approach

Historically, organisational theory developed from two main sources. The Classical School with its somewhat mechanistic emphasis on structures which could be imposed on people and the human relations school whose laudable concentration on the needs of the individual to an extent obscured study of the organisation as a whole. Modern workers have built upon earlier ideas in an attempt to provide a more comprehensive view of behaviour in organisations. One influential approach has been that using Systems Theory. Systems Theorists see organisations as complex social systems that interact with their environment and which must respond to numerous interdependent variables of which the following are the most important:

- People
- Tasks
- Technology
- Organisation Structure
- Environment

Whilst earlier approaches considered variables in isolation, system theorists study the relationships between several of them. Their researches have suggested that there is no one best way of designing organisations, and, because of volatility and change, the 'best' way is dependent (or *contingent*) upon prevailing conditions. Thus the contingency approach has developed out of system's thinking. Both recognise that an organisation is a complex structure with many interacting elements and that it must continually adapt to an uncertain and changing environment.

The American researchers, Lawrence and Lorsch, first used the term contingency approach. They examined the operations of a number of firms to assess the effects on the *tasks* and *attitudes* of managers in various functions operating within different structures and environments.

The firms chosen for study ranged from plastics companies, where the environment was uncertain and volatile, through firms in the packaged food industry with a moderate degree of uncertainty, to firms in the container industry, where the environment was considered stable and predictable.

Task Differentiation

The main emphasis of the Lawrence and Lorsch study was on task *differentiation* which covered the differences and attitudes of the managers concerned as well as the division of specialisation or functions. The functional area differences are summarised in Figure 6/5 which should be studied with the explanatory notes.

	Functions		
	Production	**Sales**	**Research**
Function Structure[1]	High	Medium	Low
Managerial Time Orientation[2]	Short Term	Medium Term	Long Term
Managerial Objective Orientation[3]	Techno/Economic	Market	Scientific and Techno/Economic
Interpersonal Orientation[4]	High Task Motivation	Socially Oriented	Low Task Motivation
Sub Unit Environment[5]	High Degree of Certainty	Moderately Uncertain	Considerable Uncertainty

Figure 6/5 Summary of Functional Differences

Note 1. The function structure refers to the relative formality of the unit in terms of hierarchy, rules and procedures. For example, the production functions had clear, formalised procedures, narrow spans of control, numerous levels as compared with the more informally structured and organised research area.

Note 2. This is the managerial expectation about the time required to produce results from their efforts.

Note 3. This relates to the main concern of the functional area. For example, deadlines, cost reduction, efficiency are major objectives of production functions.

Note 4. This relates to the manager's motivation towards establishing personal relationships as compared with task performance.

Note 5. The environment of each function – or sub-unit of the organisation – differs because each one is engaged in different types of activity, interacts with different parts of the environment and has greater or lesser contacts with the environment external to the organisation as a whole.

The study also examined the extent of integration and amount of internal conflict within the organisation. Integration was considered to be the quality of the collaboration that existed between the departments and function and was discovered to be an important factor in controlling the conflicts which inevitably arise between functions with the widely differing characteristics outlined in Figure 6/5.

Task Differentiation Study – Conclusions

In spite of some criticism of their methodology the Lawrence and Lorsch study was an important landmark in the development of a theory of organisation which took account of change, uncertainty and the interaction of key variables. The main conclusions were as follows:

(a) The more volatile and diverse the environment, the more task differentiation, and consequent integration, is required to achieve successful organisation.

(b) More stable environments do not require as much differentiation but still need substantial integration between the functions that exist.

(c) It is more difficult to resolve conflict in organisations with a high degree of differentiation.

(d) Better methods of conflict resolution result in higher performance and lead to types of differentiation and integration that suit the organisation's environment.

(e) In a predictable environment integration is achieved through the management hierarchy, particularly at higher levels, and through rules, procedures, budgets etc. In an uncertain environment, integration is achieved at lower levels mainly through personal inter-relationships with only a moderate use of administrative methods.

Adaptation and Environmental Variability

Another important study using the contingency approach was that conducted in Britain by Burns and Stalker. A number of electronics firms were studied to see how they adapted to changes in their environment, particularly with regard to changes in market and technical conditions. The studies resulted in a classification of organisations into what were termed *mechanistic* and *organic systems*; the properties of which are summarised in Figure 6/6.

Mechanistic Systems	Organic Systems
Stable Environment with High Certainty & Predictability	Uncertain Environment, Low Predictability
High Functional Specialisation	Low Functional Specialisation
Detailed Differentiation of Duties and Responsibilities	Less Structured Management with more Adjustment and Re-Definition of Roles
Hierarchical Control, Authority and Communication with Largely Vertical Interactions	Lateral Communications with a Network of Control and Authority
Authoritarian Style with Clear Superior/Subordinate Relationships and Emphasis on Loyalty and Obedience	More Consultation with Information and Advice Being Communicated Rather than Decisions and Instructions
Low Rate of Innovation	High Rate of Innovation

Figure 6/6 Properties of Mechanistic and Organic Systems

Mechanistic and Organic Organisations in Practice

The two systems were seen as extremes with many intermediate forms possible. Traditional industries, for example, steel, textiles and shipbuilding are mechanistic in nature where management controls and methods are based on well defined rules and procedures which experience little change.

Industries facing rapidly changing environments, for example, computers, pharmaceuticals and so on have to adapt their systems of management in order to survive so that, according to the Burns and Stalker findings, organic systems are more appropriate. This latter point has met with some criticism as it is far from proven that full organic systems are necessary in order to cope with change.

Some large organisations have coped with change quite successfully even though having a substantial degree of structure and formality by ensuring that they are sensitive to changes in the organisation's environment and by a process of step-by-step or incremental adjustment. Indeed the avoidance of unexpected and traumatic large scale abrupt change by making continual incremental adjustments appears to be a feature of many successful companies. A classic British example of this process is Marks and Spencer who avoid the need for unsettling, large scale change by a continual process of incremental adjustments which are in tune with the needs of the market place.

Technology and the Organisation

The studies of manufacturing firms conducted by Joan Woodward observed that many organisational characteristics were directly related to the technology used by the firm. The organisations were categorised on the basis of the technology used as follows:

(a) Small batch or individual item production.

(b) Large batch or mass production including assembly line production.

(c) Continuous process production including refineries, chemical and gas production and so on.

Based on this categorisation Woodward found that there were clear patterns relating to things like the span of control, chain of command and systems of management.

The various features found are summarised in Figure 6/7.

	Categories of Technology		
	Small Batch/ Individual Item	Large Batch/ Mass Production	Continuous Production
Number of Levels in Chain of Command	Few	Medium	Numerous
Span of __ Top Control Management	Small	Medium	Large
Span of __ Middle Control Management	Large	Medium	Small
Span of __ Supervisors Control	Small	Medium	Small
Ratio of Management/Operatives	Low	Medium	High
Type of Management System	Mainly Organic with Fewer Rules and Close Personal Relationships	Mainly Mechanistic with Clear Cut Procedures and more Rules and Impersonal Relationships	Mainly Organic with Fewer Rules and Close Personal Relationships
Communication	Mainly Verbal with Little Paperwork	Mainly Written with Considerable Paperwork	Mainly Verbal with Little Paperwork

Figure 6/7 Organisational characteristics and technology

Woodward's Findings

Woodward found that the more successful firms in each group were those whose various organisational characteristics, as summarised above, tended to bunch around the average for their particular category. This means, for example, that a mass production firm would tend to be more successful if operated in a formal, mechanistic way with a flatter and broader organisation structure than a process production company.

The importance of the Woodward studies was the conclusion that the method of production was an important factor affecting organisation structure and that there was a particular type of structure and management style suitable for each of the types of production. It was found that the ideas of the classical theorists seemed only to be appropriate for firms engaged in large batch and mass production, not for the other categories studied.

The work of Woodward was continued and extended by other studies into structure, technology and the environment; an example being the work done at Aston University by Pugh and others. The Aston group's study examined more variables than Woodward and the findings to some extent contradicted Woodward's, partly due to the inclusion of larger companies in the sample studied.

The Aston group found that size was an important factor in determining structure as well as the technology used. As firms grow they become more formally structured and the study found that larger size tends to lead to:

- more standardisation
- more formalisation of structures, procedures and decision rules
- more specialisation of tasks and functions

but

- less centralisation i.e. the concentration of authority.

Centralisation, and its converse, decentralisation, are important influences on organisations and are dealt with in more detail later in the book.

Systems/Contingency Approach – Conclusion

Although there is a natural yearning for the certainties and simplicities of the classical approach it is now generally accepted that there are no universal solutions to organisational problems. It is recognised that what is right for one organisation is not necessarily right for another and what is right for a given organisation at one time may not suit the organisation at a different stage of development or when the environment changes.

Organisations are always faced by the two opposing forces of uniformity and diversity. By nature, they prefer the predictability and efficiency of uniformity but the need for adaptability and the uncertainty of the environment require diversity.

Key Point Summary

- Motivation is the driving force or commitment people have for doing things.
- Schien's classification of assumptions about motivation was: Rational-Economic man, Social man, Self-Actualising man, Complex man.
- Maslow's hierarchy of needs range from physiological needs to self-actualisation needs and Maslow suggests these are satisfied in sequence.
- McGregor's Theory X person is lazy and needs close control. The Theory Y person will accept and seek out responsibility.
- Herzberg considered that factors called motivators led to satisfaction whereas other factors known as hygiene factors could lead to dissatisfaction.
- There is no complete understanding about what motivates people but the assumptions a manager uses strongly influences the way he carries out his task.
- Modern approaches emphasise the need to take individual circumstances into account when designing organisations.
- The contingency approach to organisations was pioneered by Lawrence and Lorsch.
- Their studies studied the differences between the tasks carried out by managers in different functions.
- The main conclusion from their studies was that the more volatile the environment the more diversity is required but that integration becomes more difficult.
- Burns and Stalker categorised organisations into mechanistic and organic.

- The type of technology used by the firm was found to influence the organisational structure.
- Woodward's studies of technology and organisation concluded that there was a particular type of structure and management style suitable for each type of production and that formality increased with size.

Self Review Questions

1. What view did the early management theorists take of motivation?
2. Define and explain Schein's classification of motivational assumptions.
3. What is Maslow's hierarchy of needs and why is it important in the study of motivation?
4. What are the characteristics of Theory X and Theory Y people?
5. Distinguish between motivators and hygiene factors and give examples.
6. Why is it necessary to study motivation?
7. What is the key thrust of the modern approach to the study of organisations?
8. What is the task differentiation and why was this studied by Lawrence and Lorsch?
9. What are mechanistic and organic systems?
10. Summarise the main findings of Woodward's studies of technology and the organisation.

7 Organisations: Structure, Information and Culture

Objectives

After you have studied this chapter you will:

- understand the relationship between the formal and informal organisation.
- know the advantages and disadvantages of both types of organisation.
- be able to describe the ways that departmentation may be achieved.
- understand functional, geographical, product or service specialisation.
- know what is meant by matrix structures.
- know the characteristics of flat and tall organisation structures.
- understand centralisation and decentralisation.
- know the importance of information systems in organisation.
- understand what is meant by an organisation's culture.

Elements of Organisation

From previous chapters we are aware that organisations are more than just groups of people.

Organisations:

- have purpose i.e. their objectives
- have formal patterns of relationships i.e. their structure
- practise division of labour i.e., who does what
- specify formal sources of authority i.e. who makes decisions.

These are the key elements of organisation and the way that they are dealt with largely determines the nature of the organisation, what departments and functions it contains, the forms of relationships and communication practised, the levels of management, the amount of centralisation/decentralisation, and so on.

That an organisation exists, by definition means that there is some form of structure or formality. However, within the *formal organisation* also exists an *informal organisation*.

Formal and Informal Organisations

The formal organisation is the pattern of relationships and tasks defined by official rules, policies and systems. The formal organisation is designed to achieve the objectives of the organisation in a rational, efficient manner. It is usually depicted on *organisation charts*. These are diagrams which show the official relationships, departments, levels of management and so on which make up the formal organisation.

The way that the organisation works is affected not only by official procedures and relationships but also by the behaviour of the people who work in it. People form small groups and social relationships and develop non-standard, informal ways of getting things done. This is known as the *informal* or *unofficial organisation* and exists, to a greater or lesser extent, within every organisation. The social groups develop behavioural patterns, beliefs and objectives which are different from, and sometimes opposed to, the requirements of the formal organisation.

The informal organisation exists because:

- formal relationships are considered too impersonal.
- it fulfils human needs for friendship and belonging.
- the security of the group provides psychological support for the individual.
- it provides a power base for those dissatisfied with their official influence.
- the formal organisation is not considered efficient or flexible enough.

This latter point is particularly important regarding communication and information flows. As everyone knows, news travels far quicker through the 'grapevine' than through official channels!

The possible advantages and disadvantages of formal and information organisations are summarised in Figure 7/1.

It should be realised that the two types of organisation are not alternatives, they exist side by side in every organisation. Accordingly, it is vital that management try to harness the beneficial aspects of informal organisations and to ensure that the formal organisation, as far as possible, meets the needs of their employees. If not, people will give more attention and loyalty to the informal organisation with a consequent reduction in organisational efficiency.

	Possible Advantages	Possible Disadvantages
Formal Organisation	Unity of objectives and effort	Less innovative and adaptive
	Clear hierarchy of command and control	More 'red tape', formality and inflexibility
	Well defined relationships, duties and responsibilities	Slower, more cumbersome decision making
	Stability and predictability	Inefficient information flows
	Assists control and co-ordination	Lack of individual fulfilment
Informal Organisation	May improve communication	Managerial authority may be undermined
	May use unofficial but efficient methods	Group objectives may run counter to organisational objectives
	May provide more personal satisfaction	Rumours and distortions rather than facts may be communicated
	Activities may be co-ordinated better	More loyalty and effort may be given to group than organisation
	More flexible and adaptive	Bad decisions may result from protecting group interests

Figure 7/1 Formal and Informal Organisations

Specialisation and Departmentation or Divisionalisation

Specialisation is concerned with the division of labour. This means that the various tasks and activities needed to meet the objectives of the organisation should be suitably grouped and divided up. In virtually all organisations the tasks and activities are grouped into *departments*, hence the term departmentation. By specialising, people are able to concentrate on one task or group of related tasks and develop proficiency, knowledge and expertise, thus raising organisational efficiency. As organisations grow in size and complexity there seems an inevitable tendency for there to be more specialisation and the creation of more departments and divisions.

For example, a small business is likely to have one person responsible for all aspects of sales and marketing. By the time the organisation reaches the size of say, ICI there will be numerous departments dealing with specialised aspects e.g. Market Research, Advertising, Brand Management, Retail Sales, Trade Sales, Export Sales etc.

Depending on the nature and objectives of the organisation departmentation can be achieved in various ways. For example, by function, by product or service, by geography or by some mixture of these. The various forms are explained below.

Functional Specialisation

This means that tasks are linked on the basis of common functions; for example, Production, Finance, Personnel. This basis is the most widely used and seems to be logical.

Figure 7/2 shows how a manufacturing company might be departmentalised on a functional basis.

Figure 7/2 Functional organisation structure for a manufacturing company

Advantages of functional specialisation

(a) Professional expertise is enhanced.

(b) Usually effective in practice.

(c) Because it is the traditional form and widely encountered it is readily accepted by employees.

Disadvantages

(a) May encourage narrow departmental interest to the detriment of overall objectives (known as *sub-optimality*).

(b) May be difficulties in adapting to change e.g. geographical dispersal, product diversification.

(c) Narrow functional experience is less suitable as training for management.

Geographical Specialisation

The activities of many organisations are dispersed across the country rather than being concentrated in one place. Examples include; banks, insurance companies, multiple retail outlets. In such circumstances the organisation is often divided up on a regional basis and local management given responsibility for the activities of the branch, area or region as the case may be.

Advantages of geographical specialisation

(a) On the spot decision making using local knowledge.

(b) Speedier reactions and better service creates customer goodwill.

(c) Some operating costs are lower e.g. transport and storage.

(d) The all round experience is good training for managers.

Disadvantages

(a) Loss of control by head office.

(b) Problems of co-ordinating local activities.

(c) Duplication of some jobs (note that local units rarely have responsibility for all activities. Some activities usually remain centralised; one typical example being Finance).

Product or Service Specialisation

Another commonly encountered form of organisational specialisation is by category of product or service. This is frequently encountered in large organisations – in both the public and private sectors – which have a wide range of services or products.

For example a local authority organises its employees into service related areas typically; Education, Social Services, Highways, Rating and Valuation and so on. The National Health Service groups its employees (nursing, para-medical and others) according to the nature of the service i.e. psychiatric, orthopedic, gynaecology, surgery and so on.

In the private sector, a tyre and rubber manufacturer might be organised on a product basis as shown in Figure 7/3.

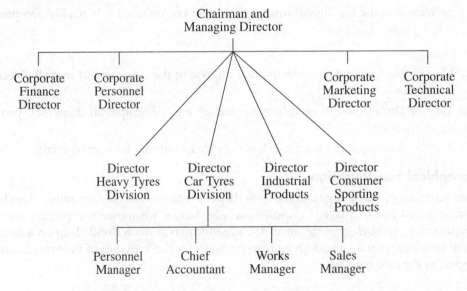

Figure 7/3 Possible product-based organisational structure for tyre & rubber manufacturer

Advantages of product or service specialisation.

(a) Develops expertise in dealing with a particular product or service.

(b) Enables responsibilities to be clearly identified which may increase motivation. For example, a manager is given responsibility for all aspects of Product X, including profitability. In effect it becomes his own business.

(c) Diversification and technological change is easier to handle.

Disadvantages

(a) managers may promote their product or service to the detriment of the organisation as a whole.

(b) Possible co-ordination problems and loss of top-management control.

Flexible Forms of Structure

Organisations choose structures which are thought to be the most efficient for their particular circumstances and operating conditions. This means that they often use a mixture of types in an attempt to combine the best features of functional, product, and geographical specialisation. For example within an organisation grouped into Product Departments, functional areas such as marketing, production, personnel still operate. Mixed forms of structure are commonly encountered reinforcing the contingency view of organisations that the best way depends on individual circumstances and that there are no universal answers.

Burns and Stalker in their study of environment-structure relationships in the electronics industry considered that organic organisations (described in the previous chapter,) were more appropriate in changing conditions. The features of organic organisations – lateral communications, network control structures, advisory/encouraging management styles, flexible work assignments – all have their effects on organisation structures. Current trends in flattening organisation structures, removing middle management levels, giving staff more responsibility and authority (i.e. empowerment) are characteristic of organic organisations.

One unusual form of mixed structure developed to meet particular needs, the *matrix structure*, is described below.

Matrix Structures

Organisation structures are constantly evolving in order to overcome the deficiencies of earlier forms in coping with new activities, relationships and technological change. One particular concept that has developed from the aerospace and other high technology industries is the matrix form. In matrix structures, project teams, each with a designated manager, are combined with a conventional functional structure. The project teams are multi-disciplinary and are formed to achieve specific goals such as; the launch of a new product, the development of a new automatic gearbox, the development of a new system of collecting taxes. The project leaders liaise with the functional heads for services and the functional heads provide technical expertise and facilities and give structure to the organisation. In addition to the functional relationships mentioned, the project manager has a direct or line relationship with his superior, usually the Chief Executive or General Manager.

An illustration of a matrix organisation applied to a manufacturing company is shown in Figure 7/4.

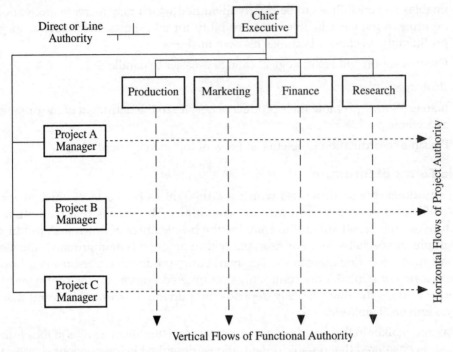

Figure 7/4 Possible matrix organisation in manufacturing

The matrix form attempts to combine the efficiency and stability of the more conventional departmental and functional form with the flexibility and directness of a project based approach. It is a compromise between a traditional functional organisation and a full scale programme based approach such as that used for the American space developments, such as Apollo, Skylab and the Space Shuttle.

The matrix form of organisation can increase motivation and is a help in directing productive effort. However, it does suffer from the disadvantage that conflicts may arise over divisions of responsibility between project groups and functional heads and the consequent way resources are allocated. Also, particularly if newly introduced, functional management may resent the apparent downgrading of their responsibilities.

The various forms of specialisation or departmentation described in the paragraphs above show typical ways in which organisations arrange the tasks to be done. However, it is not sufficient merely to consider the reasoning behind the departments by the numbers of department and the consequent levels of management. A major influence on this is the *span of control*.

Span of Control

It will be recalled that the span of control is the number of subordinates over which a supervisor has direct control.

The classical theorists tended to favour a narrow span of control; Urwick for example recommended a maximum of 6, but practice varies greatly with organisations successfully using spans ranging from one to fifty or more. Smaller forms of control are common in technical, professional and managerial groups where the work is diverse and complex. Larger spans are usually found where the work is routine.

In general, where the span is too wide for the particular conditions the supervisor may spend too much time supervising and co-ordinating and will thus have insufficient time for decision making, training and support. Where the span is too narrow the tendency will be for the manager to become too involved in routine tasks and to interfere in the tasks he has delegated to others causing frustration and the breakdown of trust.

The number of subordinates cannot be determined in advance but will always depend on a variety of factors; the main ones of which are:

- the complexity of the work. The more complex, the narrower the span.
- degree of environmental change. Fast rates of change require narrow spans to increase adaptability.
- ability of subordinates. More able and better trained people require less supervision and support.
- riskiness or danger associated with the work. If mistakes could be costly or there are physical hazards, narrower spans are required.
- the ability of the manager. Good organisers and communicators will be able to deal with larger numbers.

Within a given organisation the spans of control will vary. They are likely to be narrower at higher levels and broader at the lower operational levels. The number of levels of management or authority varies from organisation to organisation and is dependent on a variety of factors. The number of levels determines the *configuration* or *shape* of the organisation.

Configuration and Levels

An organisation may contain many levels of authority or management such as, for example, in the Civil Service, or it may have just one or two as in many small businesses. It is the number of levels between the workers and top management which determines the configuration or shape of the organisation.

In general, organisations can be *flat* or *tall* in relation to their size as shown in Figure 7/5.

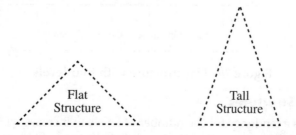

Figure 7/5 Flat and tall organisation structures

Numerous factors influence the number of levels in an organisation, the main ones of which are:

- Size of organisation
- Complexity and nature of operations
- Production methods
- Technology
- Management style and attitude to authority
- Amount of delegation practised
- Spans of control
- Ability of management and personnel

The characteristics of flat and tall structures are summarised below:

Flat Organisation Structures

The key features of flat structures are:

- Relatively small size (but not always)
- Few levels of authority and management
- Short chain of command
- Tendency to suit mass production operations (Woodward studies)
- Broad span of control

As an example Figure 7/6 shows an organisation with 4 levels, typical of many small and medium sized organisations.

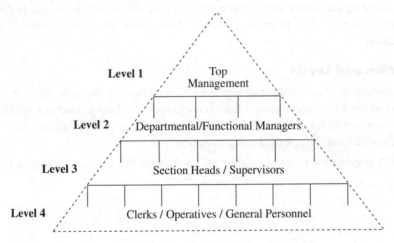

Level 1 — Top Management

Level 2 — Departmental/Functional Managers

Level 3 — Section Heads / Supervisors

Level 4 — Clerks / Operatives / General Personnel

Figure 7/6 Flat structure with four levels

Tall Organisation Structures

Although there is a tendency for the number of levels to increase with the size of organisation this relationship does not continue indefinitely. It would be rare to find more than 8 or 10 levels of authority even in very large organisations.

The key features of tall structures are:

- Characteristic of larger organisations
- Numerous levels of authority and management
- Narrow span of control
- Long chain of command
- More formality, specialisation and standardisation

Figure 7/7 shows a possible structure for a medium/large organisation.

It does not follow that organisations in the same field will have broadly the same structures. The number of management levels reflects many factors including; management style; the organisation's history, the amount of delegation and so on. For example, the Ford Motor Company has 13 levels of management whereas Toyota has 6.

Shorter and flatter organisations increase discretionary power in the lower and middle levels. Organisations where risk is unacceptable, where there is a reluctance to delegate, will keep the spans of control small and the number of levels high.

Studies conducted by Aston University researchers found that size tends to lead to more specialisation and formality with an increase in the number of levels. Taller structures increase vertical communication problems and lengthen decision times so that they may be inherently less flexible. They can, however, support a greater degree of specialisation and seem better suited to the more stable bureaucratic type of organisation, where 'bureaucratic' is used in accordance with Weber's definition and not in a derogatory sense. The Aston group found that as organisations grow they tend to grow taller, and perhaps because of the sheer volume of decisions required, there is less centralisation.

Centralisation, and its converse, *decentralisation* are important influences on the organisational structures and the way the organisation works.

Centralisation and Decentralisation

Drucker states that 'decentralisation is the best principle of organisation *where it fits*' but warns that the requirements for its application are stringent. Decentralisation, in the organisational sense, refers to the *dispersal of authority* to the parts of the organisation and does not describe physical locations. Accordingly, a decentralised organisation is one where authority to commit resources (e.g. personnel, materials, money) and to take real decisions, is spread throughout the various levels of the organisation, as compared with a centralised organisation where authority is exercised only by top management.

As organisations grow and there is more specialisation, the organisation has to decide how much authority, and of what type, it can delegate from the centre. A.P. Sloan in the 1920s, then President of General Motors, was a pioneer of decentralisation in organisations and expressed his philosophy as: 'decentralised operations with centralised policy control'. This remains a good description of how successfully to decentralise.

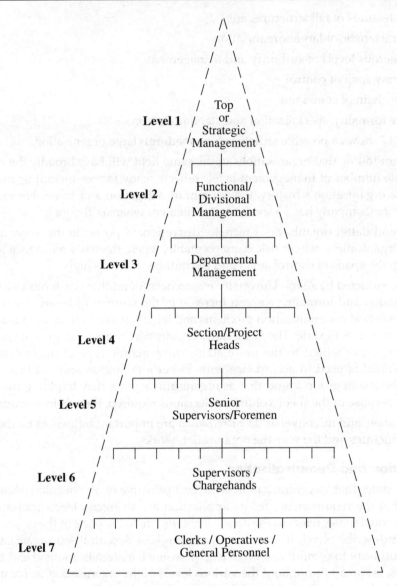

Figure 7/7 Tall structure with seven levels

What Functions can be Decentralised?

Because of their nature certain functions are more easily decentralised than others. Production and Marketing would be in this category whilst Finance and Research are examples of functions which often remain centralised even in a largely decentralised organisation. To avoid fragmentation of the business, Drucker argues that three main areas of decision must always be reserved for top management alone i.e.

- decisions about what technologies, markets and products to go into and what businesses to start or to abandon.
- decisions on corporate finance.
- decisions on corporate personnel policy and on key appointments.

If these types of decision are not centrally controlled the organisation will become fragmented with no real cohesion.

There are no absolute standards to judge the extent to which an organisation is decentralised. An organisation may have numerous operating divisions but with all decisions of any significance taken at the centre whilst another may have few or no identifiable divisions yet has genuine, decentralised decision making. The natural consequence of a policy of decentralisation is the creation of semi-autonomous operating divisions where the local management has considerable, but not absolute, discretion and has responsibility for divisional profitability.

Typically there are two levels of financial responsibility for divisions. They may be established as *profit centres* and thus become responsible for the revenue and expense consequences of their operations. In some cases responsibility is increased and the division is designated as an *investment centre*. This means that the division becomes additionally responsible for the use of capital resources and the return on capital employed as well as revenues and expenses. It is in such circumstances that formal appraisal and monitoring systems become necessary and good informations flows vital.

Factors in Favour of Decentralisation

Properly organised and controlled, decentralisation should:

(a) Improve local decision making. Divisional management are in close touch with day-to-day operations and are in a position to make more informed and speedier decisions.

(b) Improve strategic decision making. Central management are relieved of much lower level and routine decision making and thus able to concentrate on strategic considerations.

(c) Increase flexibility and reduce communication problems. The ability to take decisions near the point of action reduces response time and means that adjustments can be made more swiftly to cope with changes in market or supply conditions. Shorter communication lines mean quicker decisions and fewer chances of errors caused by communication channels.

(d) Increase motivation of divisional management. This is a key feature of decentralisation and arguably is the most important factor contributing to increased efficiency. Research shows that people value greater independence and respond in a positive manner to increased responsibility particularly when this is linked to the reward system of the organisation.

(e) Better Training. The spread of genuine decision making and the increased responsibility this entails, provides better training for junior management. In many organisations there are movements within divisional management and between divisional and central management thus enhancing career opportunities for able and ambitious managers. The existence of these opportunities helps to attract people of the right calibre and increases morale and motivation.

Problems with Decentralisation

Inevitably there are potential problems with decentralisation and these include:

(a) Possible sub-optimal decision making. This is potentially the greatest problem and occurs when local management take decisions which benefit their department or division but where the local gains are more than offset by increased costs or losses of benefit in other parts of the organisation. Where there is any conflict between local and organisational objectives those of the organisation should be paramount. This is not easy to achieve and well designed reporting and information systems are essential.

(b) More problems of co-ordination. With a decentralised organisation, top management must ensure that the parts of the organisation work together. They must ensure that local, parochial attitudes do not develop to the detriment of the organisation as a whole. Without overall co-ordination it becomes difficult for the various functions to integrate their activities. For example, production, selling, distribution and stocking activities must be meticulously co-ordinated to avoid losses in efficiency, increased costs and customer dissatisfaction.

(c) Problems of control, monitoring and communication. One of the advantages of decentralisation is that certain aspects of communication are improved. For example, those relating to operational decisions which, being taken locally, do not have to travel up and down several levels of the organisation. However, top management must have sufficient information to maintain overall control. There must be the correct type of information so that top management can monitor the performance of junior management with regard to the tasks delegated to them.

(d) The supply of the right type of manager. Decentralisation places extra demands upon junior management so that there is a continuing need to recruit, train and develop well motivated and intelligent personnel. Although most people react positively to increased responsibility, some do not and top management need to monitor personal performance closely and must ensure that the organisation's personnel policies and practices attract and retain the right people. Whilst decentralisation puts extra responsibility on to junior managers it also requires top management to reconsider and redefine their own tasks and responsibilities.

As well as commercial companies, organisations in the Public Sector are also encountering the need to be more flexible and efficient:

In 1991 the Audit Commission, which reports on the effectiveness of public spending, said that it had found wide variations in organisation between the 43 police forces in England and Wales.

Some had 10% of staff working on administrative jobs at headquarters; others had 20%. The commission said that moving police officers out of the central offices would lead to more flexible groups of officer's fully accountable for the quality of day-to-day policing in their areas.

If decentralised forces were to be created the police's divisional officers, effectively the middle management level, could become redundant. The commission reported that 'those forces which have reviewed their divisional structures have tended to reduce or remove them'.

Centralisation Combined with Decentralisation

Recent research by Peters and Waterman suggest that more successful companies practice both centralisation and decentralisation. Centrally, clear performance guidelines are established within core values relating to the quality of product and service and then decentralisation by the operating units is encouraged.

For example, within organisations such as Courtaulds, Lucas and BTR the operating units – which may be subsidiary companies or designated business units – are encouraged to be more entrepreneurial and to act as largely independent entities in order to achieve the designated targets in their own individual ways. With this style of operation, the organisation as a whole becomes more flexible and responsible whilst adhering to centrally imposed values and targets.

The need for flexibility is affecting even the giants of industry.

IBM was once the world's most profitable company and operates on a world-wide basis. IBM's earnings peaked in 1985 but increasing competition, mainly from more flexible small companies, caused earnings to decline in the late 1980s and early 1990s. IBM have identified that there are management and structural problems as well as the more obvious problems of maintaining technical leadership in the fast moving electronics field. As a consequence, operating companies throughout the world are being given much more freedom to take decisions and to react quickly to local competition. IBM is changing from a highly centralised organisation to a more decentralised one. It is becoming leaner and more flexible.

Increasing competition and the need to be able to react quickly are causing all types of organisation to re-examine their structures and to reduce layers of management thus flattening the organisation. For example:

In 1993 Herr Piech, Chairman of Volkswagen, Europe's largest car maker said that there were a mass of people in VW's Group Administration who had to ask themselves what they did to earn their keep and announced that it was VW's intention to reduce the number of management levels from nine to three.

Overall, whilst there are undeniably more advantages than disadvantages of decentralisation, it is well to recall Drucker's remark quoted earlier that decentralisation is excellent, *'when it fits'*.

MIS and Organisations

The key emphasis of this book is that the MIS must be appropriate to the organisation and to the persons receiving the information; indeed it must be tailored to suit organisational and personal needs otherwise it will be of little value. Organisations face different types of environment with varying rates of change. If an organisation operates in a placid, relatively unchanging environment it will evolve a structured and mechanistic control system with a need for more formal information in prescribed forms. In a turbulent and volatile environment, information inputs and outputs cannot be rigidly defined and an adaptive and responsible information system is necessary.

Studies by Earl and Hopwood suggested that the more successful organisations are those that retain a significant level of informality in their organisational structure and the way they handle information.

The technology of organisations also has an influence on structures and thus on information requirements and flows. As an example, mass production systems permit a broader span of control for lower level management at the expense of a lot of paperwork.

In process production, close supervision can be achieved with less paperwork but, because process industries tend to have 'tall' management structures, the information system needs to have strong vertical links.

The MIS should suit each individual part of the organisation and must be designed to complement the control and operating characteristics of the different sections, departments and functions. Contrast for example the precise control systems and definitive information requirements in Production Management to the uncertainty and poorly defined control systems in the Research area.

The extent of centralisation, decentralisation and the spread of decision making throughout the organisation also has implications for MIS design. The centralised, mechanistic type of organisation will tend to have little need for lateral communication flows i.e. flows of information across to the same layers in the organisation, but will need constant flows vertically up and down the organisation structure to cater for the necessary instructions and decisions. Where there is full decentralisation, vertical flows are greatly reduced and the lateral flows will increase and will change in character. They will contain information and advice rather than instructions and decisions.

The use of information technology and modern communication systems may itself be a factor in the way organisations are structured. For example, Piercy in examining the use of information technology in retailing suggests that:

> 'The networking effect of making information instantly available at the centre may lead to the removal of a whole tier of middle management as well as reducing the management role in the store itself'.

Management Today

The same technology may be seen in Banks where the extensive use of information technology is disrupting traditional management hierarchies.

The growing use of the Internet the worldwide information network may radically change many of today's shopping habits and the organisation of the firms which supply the goods and services. For example the bookseller with the world's largest list of books, over one million titles, is an Internet provider based in Arizona with no conventional retail outlets at all. In the UK in 1996, Tesco started a home shopping trial on the Internet to attract shoppers too busy to visit their local supermarket. The service offers 20,000 product lines, a similar number to a full-sized supermarket, at normal prices plus a £5 charge for delivery next day. Andersen Consulting have forecast that home shopping could soon account for 20% of the UK grocery market. If this does happen some experts think that the major supermarket giants may be undercut by smaller operators who would not have the overhead costs associated with conventional supermarkets and who would operate entirely by using the Internet, telephone or fax.

Culture of the Organisation

The culture of an organisation is an all-pervasive influence on how it is structured, how work is done, what its aims are and how management and staff interact within the organisation and with those outside. The culture of an organisation results from shared beliefs and values and has been described by Morgan, a sociologist as 'shared meaning, shared understanding and shared sense-making'.

The primary culture of an organisation usually reflects the vision or desires of the founders, modified by subsequent senior management and by interactions with various internal and external factors. Figure 7.8 summarises some of the major inter-relationships between culture and other factors.

Figure 7/8 Main inter-relationships between culture and other facets of an organisation

Alternative Types of Culture

Professor Charles Hardy has found from his researches that there are substantial differences in the cultures found in organisations. Whilst he accepts that culture cannot be precisely defined and that in most organisations the culture is a mixture of various elements he considers that four main types of culture can be identified thus:

Type	Characteristics
Power Culture	Central control and power. Entrepreneurial typically with clear figurehead and leader.
Role Culture	Culture reinforces the structure. Roles more important than people who fill them. Suits bureaucratic organisations.
Task Culture	Focus is on the job expertise and personal contribution is highly valued. High levels of collaboration within groups.
Person Culture	Suited to individuals working loosely together and sharing common facilities. Formal power unimportant as individuals are experts in their own right.

The culture of an organisation is not static. Various groups (e.g. employees, customers, suppliers, stakeholders) are affected by it and over time, help to influence it.

The manifestations of an organisation's culture came from a variety of sources including; corporate aims and policies, organisation structures, rules and procedures management and peer-group attitudes, technology and so on. These are the specific, readily identifiable elements of the fabric of an organisation but culture is more nebulous, although very important, and can be thought of as the shared beliefs, values and understandings that weld the other factors together to make a unique organisation.

Key Point Summary

- Within every formal organisation exists an informal one.
- Departmentation is the result of grouping people by specialisation.
- Different forms of specialisation exist including; functional, geographical, product or service.
- Mixed forms of specialisation frequently occur.
- Flat structures have a short chain of command with a broad span of control and tend to occur where decentralisation is practised.
- Taller structures tend to occur with increase in size and produce more specialised and formal organisations.
- Decentralisation occurs when authority is dispersed from the centre.
- Decentralised organisation can be more responsible and flexible but overall control and co-ordination are more difficult.
- The MIS of an organisation must be tailor made to suit. There are no standard patterns.

Self Review Questions

1. What are the possible advantages and disadvantages of formal and informal organisations?
2. What is specialisation and how can it be achieved?
3. What is a matrix organisation and what are its advantages and disadvantages?
4. What are the factors which affect the number of levels in an organisation?
5. What are the features of flat organisations?
6. What are the features of tall organisations?
7. What is decentralisation and what are its possible benefits and problems?
8. What are the features of organisations which affect lateral and vertical information flows?

8 Management: Introduction and Functions

Objectives

After you have studied this chapter you will:

- have had an introduction to the chapters on management.
- understand the problems of managing change.
- be able to describe Theory Z.
- know what roles a manager must perform.
- be able to define the basic three levels of management.

- know, in outline, what are the functions of management including: Planning, Organising, Motivating and Control.

What is Management?

Fayol's classic definition of management was derived from his own experience and is repeated below.

> 'To manage is to forecast and plan, to organise, to command, to co-ordinate and to control.'

More modern definitions are largely variants of Fayol's but with more emphasis on the need to guide, lead and motivate people rather than merely command. Management is a down to earth process which has practical consequences. As Drucker says:

> 'Management is a practice not a science. It is not knowledge but performance.'

Management have to make decisions about *work*, *people*, *structures* and *systems* and some typical examples are shown.

- *Work of the organisation*

  What should it be? How should it be divided and organised? How will tasks be co-ordinated?

- *People in the organisation*

  Who should they be? How should they be treated and motivated? How will they be managed and led? Who does what?

- *Structure of the organisation*

  What will be the groups/departments? What will be their relationships? How will authority and responsibility be arranged? Where will decisions be taken? (Centralisation/decentralisation.)

- *Systems of the organisation*

  What systems will there be? How will the operating systems (i.e. sales, production, finance etc) work? What type of information/communication system will there be?

Change Management

The single most pressing problem that faces any organisation is how to cope with change. Change occurs in many ways including; competitive pressures (e.g. a competitor introduces a new model or reduces prices), legislation (e.g. the change from the Poll Tax to the Council Tax), the operating environment (e.g. the de-regulation of the UK milk market in 1994 and the subsequent creation of the farmers' cooperative, Milk Marque,) changing client/consumer preferences (e.g. the desire for more leisure or environmentally friendly products,) the introduction of new technology (e.g. computer network, robotics) and many more.

Not all pressures for change come from outside the organisation. Successful managers seek to anticipate market or environmental movements by initiating change within the organisation and thus adopt a pro-active rather than a reactive approach. One means of making radical changes in organisations is by adopting what is called Business Process

Re-engineering (BPR). BPR moves away from the conventional emphasis on tasks and structures in order to focus on business processes. In effect BPR is a systematic method of lateral thinking which forces people to think beyond normal boundaries and structures. BPR is dealt with in detail in the next chapter.

Organisations do not automatically adjust to change. Adaptation only occurs as a result of management actions. These may cause changes in the way the organisation takes decisions, in the processes used, in the services or products, or in the structure of the organisation itself. Only one thing is certain; the organisation that clings to rigid, traditional methods in the midst of rapid change will be an unsuccessful organisation.

Ways to Manage Change

Many valuable pointers to the way more successful organisations manage change and innovation have come from studies by Moss Kanter, Peters and Waterman and others. Moss Kanter found that organisations who adopt an integrated approach to innovation did it more successfully than those who adopted a more piecemeal approach, which she termed 'segmentalist'. To overcome resistance to change and inertia she suggested the following actions:

- Top management must support innovation in a personal way and must think integratively.
- The organisation must be made 'flatter' i.e. unnecessary layers of hierarchy should be removed and staff 'empowered' by authority being pushed downwards.
- Communication should be improved especially across the organisation and staff mobility encouraged.
- Achievements should be highlighted and a culture of pride cultivated.
- Company plans should be made known earlier and more widely to enable staff to make suggestions and contribute before decisions are made.

Peters and Waterman also investigated how companies handled change. They defined success in handling change in terms of a mixture of above average growth and financial return, and a reputation for continuous innovation. Those that achieved success they deemed excellent companies and found that they had certain attributes in common. These can be summarised thus:

- They have simplified structures with autonomous divisions without large headquarters' staff.
- Entrepreneurship and initiative is encouraged with acceptance that there will be occasional failures.
- Customer service is paramount and they genuinely listen and respond to customers.
- They get things done; once a problem is identified and analysed, solutions are sought.
- The organisation's basic values are emphasised and employees are held in high esteem but expectations are high.
- Control is a loose/tight mixture. Core values such as quality and service are insisted upon but decision making is pushed downwards and not continually monitored as long as objectives are achieved and core values maintained.

It will be seen that the attributes above are the hallmarks of the modern approach to organisations and management. The distinction between the traditional and more modern approaches is summarised in the following two quotations.

> Big is better ... make sure everything is carefully and formally coordinated ... the manager's job is decision making ...analyse everything ... produce fat planning volumes ... get rid of the disturbers of the peace ... control everything ... keep things tidy ... specify the organisation structure in great detail ... write long job descriptions.
>
> *Peters and Waterman*

> Companies are discarding their organisational charts and simplifying their chains of command. This gives chief executives more flexibility, keener and quicker assessment of performance, clearer and faster lines of action, and a quick grasp of the information needed to run their companies ... they are frantically trying to push (decisions:) down to those who are closest to the marketplace, giving more autonomy to plant managers, sales people, and engineers ... creating environments in which compensation depends on performance and freedom to improve performance provides the psychic reward.
>
> *Business Week*

Pointers to the way that organisations may adapt to change are provided by the ideas behind Theory Z organisations.

Theory Z

Theory Z is a term coined by William Ouchi to describe an ideal cultural system based mainly on the successful methods and approach used by large Japanese companies. The culture of an organisation includes the philosophies, tradition, experience and corporate values of the organisation.

The Z culture is one characterised by:

(a) a commitment to people

(b) trust and effective personal relationships

(c) long-term employment

(d) a desire to humanise working conditions

(e) consensus decision making

Theory Z claims that high levels of performance and job satisfaction go together. Although hierarchies and formal structures do exist in Type Z organisations, self direction and mutual trust to a large extent replace traditional hierarchical direction and co-ordination. Type Z organisations are more informal and egalitarian and are characterised by many semi-autonomous work groups. Ouchi reports that in Japan each employee, from top to bottom is simultaneously a member of as many as 10 or 12 work groups, each with a different task. This flexibility should be contrasted with the rigid compartmentalisation which is a feature of many UK organisations.

Theory Z argues that although individual managers might have to accept responsibility for decisions there should be a consensus in decision-making, reached by agreement with subordinates and peer colleagues. This participative approach encourages information flows and *goal congruence* i.e. the alignment of personal and corporate objectives.

The reasoning behind Theory Z is the belief that differences between Japanese and Western management practices in part account for the better record of Japanese companies in matters such as; productivity, quality and motivation. If this is true, it means that Japan's industrial dominance is not just because they use more robots but also because they practise more effective management.

What is a Manager?

Management is a process which takes place at all levels in an organisation. It is not carried out *only* by people with 'manager' in their job title. Section leaders, supervisors, chief clerks, foremen etc all carry out managerial functions although obviously not all of the same type or of equal importance. It is the task which a person performs which is of importance not the job title. The examination of what managers actually do in practice has led to a more detailed analysis of managerial roles. For example, Mintzberg has developed a list of key roles which his researches showed appeared consistently in managerial jobs.

His key roles were:

(a) Entrepreneur (planner and risk taker)

(b) Resource Allocator (organiser and co-ordinator)

(c) Figurehead/Leader (motivator and co-ordinator)

(d) Liason/Disseminator (co-ordinator and communicator)

(e) Monitor (controller)

(f) Spokesman/Negotiator (Motivator and communicator)

(g) Disturbance-handler (motivator and co-ordinator)

This list, based on actual jobs in real organisations, illustrates the all-pervasive involvement with people and the importance of behavioural factors. A manager is concerned not only with physical processes, organisation structures and tasks, he has to deal with people and must take account of their attitudes, beliefs, values and reactions.

Although the roles above are shown clearly separated from each other this is for instructional purposes only. The reality is the the manager must blend together his roles and activities in order to be effective.

There are no artificial dividing lines between the manager as 'entrepreneur' or 'leader' or 'disturbance-handler' nor are there between the activities of planning, controlling, co-ordinating and so on.

Professor Handy has characterised the managerial role as akin to the role of the medical General Practitioner in that he must:

• Identify the symptoms

• Diagnose the cause of the trouble

• Decide how it might be dealt with

• Start the treatment

Levels of Management

Although the proliferation of job titles can suggest otherwise, it is possible to differentiate three levels of management in most organisations.

Strategic Management

e.g. Chief Executive, Board of Directors

Tactical Management

e.g. all types of middle management, departmental managers, functional managers such as the personnel manager, accountant, sales manager.

Operational Management

e.g. foremen, supervisor, chief clerk, charge hand.

A major factor in deciding the category of management is the planning horizon. This ranges from long term at the highest level to short-term, almost day-to-day, at the lowest level.

Figure 8/1 summarises the typical responsibilities, decision types and information needs of the three levels.

Although in many organisations the three levels of management discussed above are still readily discernible there is evidence of the erosion of the middle management level. This is caused by various factors, including:

- the creation, within large organisations, of semi-autonomous business units with considerable discretion over operations. Examples include; Rank Xerox, IBM, Hanson Industries. This has been well described as 'small within big is beautiful'.

- the developments in information technology and communication networks enabling information to be received by Strategic Management direct from the operational level.

- the growing ability of computer based systems to take decisions which traditionally were taken by middle managers. Examples include; stock replenishment decisions in supermarkets, credit scoring in banks and so on.

Interrelationships of Levels

The activities of the three levels are interrelated and must not be thought of as self-contained and separate bands. Information flows in both directions, discussions, instructions, advice, results and so on continually flow between the levels in order to achieve co-ordinated activities and better decision making. As an example, consider the activities and interrelationships which are necessary in just one area:

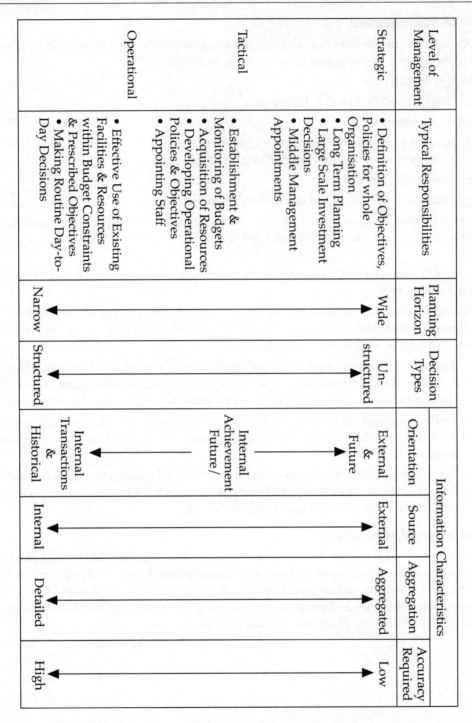

Level of Management	Typical Responsibilities	Planning Horizon	Decision Types	Information Characteristics			
				Orientation	Source	Aggregation	Accuracy Required
Strategic	• Definition of Objectives, Policies for whole Organisation • Long Term Planning • Large Scale Investment Decisions • Middle Management Appointments	Wide	Un-structured	External & Future	External	Aggregated	Low
Tactical	• Establishment & Monitoring of Budgets • Acquisition of Resources • Developing Operational Policies & Objectives • Appointing Staff			Internal Achievement Future / Internal Transactions & Historical			
Operational	• Effective Use of Existing Facilities & Resources within Budget Constraints & Prescribed Objectives • Making Routine Day-to-Day Decisions	Narrow	Structured		Internal	Detailed	High

Figure 8/1 Levels of management and characteristics of information

Materials and inventory control:

- *at the operational level*

  materials/inventory control is dependent on; physical movement and storage, clear parts/material identification, prompt and accurate recording of transactions, clear guidelines on stock levels, order quantities and so on.

- *at the tactical level*

  materials/inventory control is dependent on; accurate summarisation of all operational matters affecting materials and inventory, the setting of key decision values (stock levels, reorder quantities etc.), setting of materials budgets within policy guidelines, order, price, negotiations and so on.

- *at the strategic level*

  materials/inventory is dependent on; correct summarisation of activities at the tactical and operational levels, gathering and analysis of environmental information (price trends, competitors' actions, political factors and so on), setting of long term policies on materials and inventory, long term price agreements and contracts perhaps involving exchange deals or barter.

Functions of Management

A useful way of grouping the functions of management is into the following categories:

- *Planning.* All activities leading to the formulation of objectives or goals and deciding upon the means of meeting them.
- *Motivation and Leadership.* Behavioural processes where a manager influences others to contribute to the achievement of objectives by gaining their commitment.
- *Organising and co-ordinating.* Determining the necessary activities, structures and responsibilities and combining these factors to achieve the required objectives.
- *Control.* A monitoring process where actual results are compared with planned results in order to bring activities in line with plans or to amend the plans.

In addition the all-pervasive function of *decision making* takes place within each of the above categories.

Each of these functions is covered in detail in the chapters which follow.

Key Point Summary

- There are numerous definitions of management but Fayol's original one remains relevant.
- Change occurs in many ways and adapting to change is a primary management responsibility.
- Theory Z organisations are characterised by trust, good personal relationships and consensus decision making.
- Management takes place at all levels.
- Various roles have been identified as appearing in a manager's job including: Entrepreneur, Spokesman, Figurehead, Monitor.
- Decision making, which is choosing between alternatives, is an integral part of all management tasks.

- The main three levels of management are: Strategic, Tactical, Operational.
- There is a constant interchange of information, advice, decisions, results and so on between the levels.
- Management functions can be grouped into: Planning, Motivating, Organising, Control with Decision Making taking place within each function.

Self Review Questions

1. How has Fayol's original definition of management been modified by modern writers?
2. Give examples of change which affects organisations.
3. How do organisations adapt to change?
4. Describe a Theory Z organisation.
5. What are the seven roles identified by Mintzberg?
6. Define the three basic levels of management and give the typical responsibilities of each level.
7. What are the reasons for the decline in importance of middle management?
8. Give the functions of management and explain what each means.

9 Leadership, Organising and Coordinating

Objectives

After you have studied this chapter you will:
- be able to classify the main theories of motivation.
- be able to define leadership and explain its importance.
- understand the trait, style and contingency theories of leadership.
- know the importance of organising work.
- be able to describe job enlargement and job enrichment.
- understand what is meant by participation and delegation.
- know the principles of MBO.
- understand the importance of co-ordination and some of the ways it can be improved.
- understand what is meant by Business Process Re-engineering.

Management and Motivation

The objectives of any organisation will be achieved more efficiently when the people who work in it have drive and commitment, in other words, when they are *motivated*.

Management try to increase motivation by using motivators (e.g. pay, status, recognition etc.), by their style of management, and the way they practise leadership.

There are numerous theories about motivation and the kind of theory a manager believes in, even at a sub-conscious level, influences his approach to management. Some of the earlier motivation theories have already been covered (Maslow's Hierarchy of needs, Herzberg's hygiene factors and motivators and so on) and these theories can be grouped under three headings.

- *Satisfaction Theories:* These theories suggest a satisfied employee will work harder although there is little evidence to support this view.
- *Incentive Theories:* These suggest that a person will work harder to obtain a reward. There is some evidence that positive reinforcement can work if the individual performance can be recognised and rewarded.
- *Intrinsic Theories:* These theories suggest that people will work hard to realise higher-order needs contained in the job itself; self fulfilment, responsibility, participation and so on.

Motivation in Practice

The manager trying to increase motivation is faced with a complex problem with no universal solutions. Managers in practice may adopt the carrot or stick approach. The stick approach could include; reprimands, demotions, or threats of dismissal. On the other hand, the more positive carrot approach may be achieved by either external motivators such as pay or promotion or by offering 'internal' satisfaction for the individual through a sense of achievement or responsibility.

Management use a variety of methods to make jobs more fulfilling and more motivating including; job enrichment, job enlargement and job rotation, delegating authority to subordinates, and encouraging participation in decision making, all of which are dealt with later in this chapter. Before this it is necessary to consider leadership for there seems general agreement that behaviour in organisations is affected by leadership styles and leadership behaviour. Accordingly, the following paragraphs analyse individual leadership characteristics in organisations and the influence of leadership on motivation.

Leadership Defined

In general terms, leadership can be defined as the ability to influence the behaviour of others. The definition can be expanded when considering leadership in organisations to include the fact that the leader exerts influence within a working group in order that the group may achieve group tasks or objectives.

Although there is no doubt that leadership is a vital factor and greatly influences the whole organisation,(consider, for example, Sir John Egan at Jaguar, Alan Sugar at Amstrad and other similar leaders) it is very difficult to lay down general rules for effective leadership to fit all situations. According to Bennis and Nanus, many organisations are over-managed and under-led. The difference is crucial; managers are people who do things right, but leaders are people who do the right things.

Some of the more important leadership studies and theories are briefly described below, the more modern ones of which indicate that leadership is always related to the situation. There is a growing awareness that there is a continuous interaction between the factors present in any given situation, including for example, the personal characteristics of the leader, the tasks, the environment, the technology, the attitudes, motivation and behaviour of the followers and so on.

The approaches to the problem of trying to explain leadership are described under the following three headings:

- trait theories
- style theories
- contingency theories.

Trait Theories

The earliest studies of leadership attempted to discover the distinguishing personal characteristics, or traits, of successful leaders. The assumption was that the individual was more important than the situation and that there were innate qualities of leadership in certain people. The various studies identified numerous characteristics including:

- Intelligence
- Initiative
- Self Assurance
- Imagination
- Courage
- Decisiveness
- Energy.

Unfortunately the different studies produced highly variable results. Professor Handy has pointed out that in over 100 studies of these kind only 5% of the traits discovered were common throughout. Accordingly, trait theory in its original form has been heavily criticised and largely discredited as a basis for a workable theory of leadership, although more modern studies are beginning to highlight once again the importance of the individual amongst many other factors.

Style Theories

These theories concentrate on the behaviour or style of the leader rather than his personal attributes, i.e. they concentrate on the way he manages. The assumption is that employees will work harder for managers who employ given styles than they will for managers who use other styles. The two extremes of style usually compared are the authoritarian or structured style and the democratic or participative style; the main features of which are summarised below.

Authoritarian management style:

- All power resides in the leader.
- Decision making is carried out by the leader alone.
- Only the leader can exercise control, reward, punishment etc.

Democratic management style:

- Group participation and discussion.
- Shared power.
- Group decision making, control etc.
- Delegation.

Clearly the above two positions represent extremes and management style in practice is likely to be somewhere between the two. The fact that there is a continuum between the polar positions is aptly demonstrated by Figure 9/1 which was developed by Tannenbaum and Schmidt who wished to demonstrate that managers have choice in selecting a leadership style. They considered that the choice is influenced by three factors; the manager himself, his subordinates, and the requirements of the situation.

There is some evidence, by no means conclusive, that participative styles are associated with higher-producing work groups. It seems that such styles bring increased subordinate satisfaction and reduce inter-group conflict and tend to satisfy higher order/personal needs such as esteem and self-actualisation. There is also evidence that some people prefer to be directed and that in repetitive work a structured style of leadership leads to higher productivity, at least in the short term. It does seem however that leadership effectiveness is dependent on more than style alone. Hence what are called contingency theories of leadership.

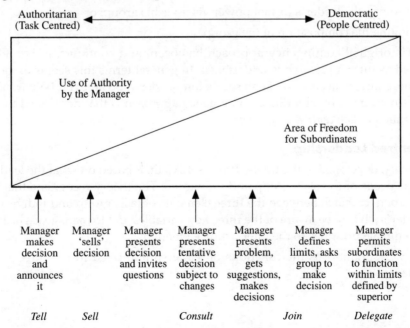

Figure 9/1 Tannesbaum's and Schmidt's continuum of leadership styles

Contingency Theories

The contingency theories, pioneered by Fiedler, consider that leadership effectiveness depends on a range of factors; in particular, the task, the work group and the position of the leader within the work group.

Fiedler's view was that group performance depends on the manager adopting a style appropriate to what he termed the 'relative favourableness' of the situation. He found that a more authoritarian style was most effective when the situation was very favourable or very unfavourable to the leader. When the situation was only moderately favourable then the participative style worked best. Fiedler thought that situations favourable to the leader were characterised as follows:

(a) the leader was liked and trusted by the group

(b) the task was clearly defined;

(c) the power of the leader in respect of the group was high and where he had organisational backing.

Fiedler's findings seem to be supported by practical experience. A strong, well respected leader with a clearly defined task would get best results by being fairly directive. Where the task is ill-defined and he is in a weak position, best results are still likely to be achieved by a more authoritarian style. Alternatively, a respected leader confronted by an ambiguous task (i.e. only a moderately favourable position) would probably obtain best results by drawing out from the group all the contributions they can make.

Fiedler's researches have received some criticism but his approach is useful in that it emphasises that there are occasions where the best results are achieved by a more formal, task-centred approach rather than the apparently more appealing democratic style. He considered that organisations could do much to help the individual leader by either:

(a) defining and structuring the task more clearly; or

(b) improving the leader's formal power vis-a-vis his group; or

(c) changing the composition of the group.

Fiedler's original contingency approach has been, and continues to be, refined and modified as further research is undertaken. In general terms this seems to indicate that even more factors need to be analysed before leadership can even be partially understood. An example of a modified contingency approach is that developed by Professor Adair, called *Action centred leadership*.

Action Centred Leadership

This theory, developed in the UK by Professor Adair, is based on what the leader does to meet the needs of the task, group and individual. The theory recognises that there will not be a perfect match between the three elements of task, group and individual so that the leader's job is to be aware of the three key variables and to manage each situation by giving suitable priorities to the inter-acting elements.

Figure 9/2 summarises the functions of leadership applied to the three inter-acting variables.

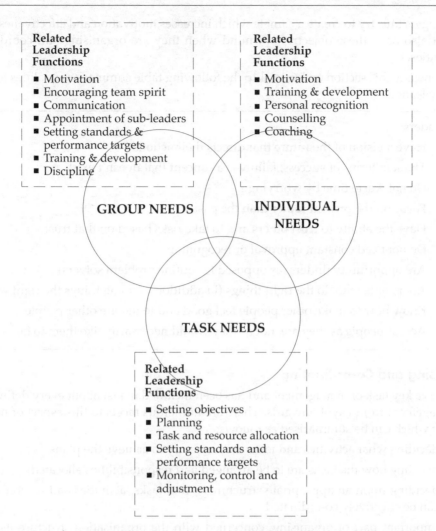

Figure 9/2: Functions of leadership – Adair's action centred leadership

Changing social attitudes to authority and the need for adaptability are causing major changes in management styles. Maccoby's study of leadership styles showed that:

> modern managers exhibit more 'flexibility about people and organisational structure, and a willingness to share power'. Thus, rather than acting as a traditional 'boss' or 'decision maker', leaders are becoming more like a coach, teacher and catalyst.

Characteristics of leadership found to be effective in practice include:

• Leading by enthusiastic personal example.

• Taking a visible, consistent and supportive role.

• Creating a climate positive to the wider objectives of the organisation.

• Keeping in touch by spending time with as many people as possible, known as MBWA (management by wandering around).

Managers thus try to create a climate which increases motivation and effectiveness. They must also have these objectives in mind when they are organising and coordinating activities.

To conclude this section on leadership the following table summarises qualities found in many leaders.

Leaders:

- Have a vision of the future that directs their actions
- Think in terms of success; failure is a concept that doesn't exist
- Do not waste time by worrying
- Focus on the present rather than the past
- Have the ability to trust others and to take risks based on that trust
- Do not need constant approval or recognition
- Are opportunity finders (as opposed to routine problem solvers)
- Are people who do the right things (in addition to doing things the right way)
- Know how to make other people feel good and to inspire other people
- Accept people as they are, not as they would necessarily like them to be.

Organising and Co-ordinating

This is a key task of management and has been included in just about every definition of management from Fayol onwards. There are numerous facets to this aspect of management which can be summarised as follows:

(a) deciding what activities and tasks are necessary to achieve the plans;

(b) deciding how the tasks are to be arranged and responsibilities allocated;

(c) deciding upon an appropriate structure so that tasks, activities and responsibilities can be effectively co-ordinated.

An important part of organising, concerned with the organisation structure itself, has already been dealt with in earlier chapters. It will be recalled that these chapters dealt with the influences of factors such as technology and the environment, the degree of functionalism, the extent of centralisation and decentralisation, the contributions of managerial theorists over the years and so on. Although the design of the total organisation is outside the scope of most managers, every manager has some responsibility for the design of jobs under his control. The scope of the jobs, the amount of responsibility accorded to individuals, the type of control and supervision exercised, the amount of participation and other similar problems must be faced by every manager. Accordingly, the following paragraphs deal with these issues.

Design of the Job

Designing or redesigning jobs is not easy. It causes change in the tasks to be done, in job relationships, in supervisor/supervised relationships, in the pattern of working groups, in training and skill requirements and so on. When work is designed effectively the individual can benefit from more challenging and satisfying tasks and the organisation may benefit from improved productivity. Poor design and organisation may result in stress and tension, low motivation and reduced productivity.

The Department of Employment has suggested that the following factors are important if a job is to satisfy human needs:

(a) Every job should have some goal to aim for and the job-holder's role should be made clear.

(b) There should be a degree of autonomy over the way tasks are to be achieved and people should be responsible for their own work and the resources used.

(c) There should be an element of variety in the job with a minimum of repetition and where possible the job should enable the completion of a complete item or cycle.

(d) There should be some arrangements for providing job-holders with feedback on their performance.

(e) The job should be arranged to provide some social contact.

(f) There should be opportunities to learn and to extend the job-holder's knowledge and skills.

There are several ways of designing jobs to increase employee satisfaction and the following are covered in this book.

- Job enlargement
- Job enrichment
- Autonomous work groups
- Participation
- Delegation

These individual methods of designing jobs are described first followed by an outline of a more radical approach to organising work known as *Business Process Re-Engineering*.

Job Enlargement

This can be termed 'more of the same' or the horizontal enlargement of jobs. It is done by adding tasks of the same type and level but without adding more responsibility or needing more skill. Rotating jobs within the same grade, which is commonly practised, is a form of job enlargement. This approach does increase variety and there is some evidence that the process may increase morale and productivity. However, there are limits to the extent that job enlargement will increase motivation. As Child points out:

> ... adding one Mickey Mouse job to another does not make any more than two Mickey Mouse jobs.

Job Enrichment

This is the process of increasing the scope, challenge and breadth of a task. It is a vertical extension of job responsibilities so that the job-holder has a more rounded job. It is a reaction to the industrial engineering approach to work with its emphasis on the micro-division of labour. The process is a conscious effort to implement some assumptions about the motivation to work by including in a job factors which Hertzberg has termed motivators. The approach gives an individual more scope, more autonomy, more responsibility, more variety, and seeks to satisfy an individuals higher order needs.

Numerous organisations such as Shell, Philips, IBM, Volvo etc. have reported success with job enrichment schemes.

Care is needed with job enrichment and some schemes have ended after a period because their usefulness came to an end. Not everyone is capable of doing a bigger job so that selection, placement and training become much more important. Job enrichment is not a once-off process, it needs constant self-renewal. Properly done it does appear to offer genuine advantages to both the individual and the organisation.

Autonomous Work Groups

These are self-organised work groups which are held responsible for the rate of quality of their output. These groups have been used successfully in Scandanavia, especially at Volvo, where quality improved, overheads were reduced and job satisfaction increased. Within the group the employees are multi-skilled and accept full responsibility for the deployment of group members and for the designated task in terms of quality and output. Although there have been dramatic success stories with this type of work organisation, there appears to be some doubt as to how long the effects will last.

Participation in decision making by employees is a form of both job enlargement and job enrichment.

Participation

This is a word with a wide range of meanings; from mere consultation at one extreme to full worker control at the other. The most relevant meaning from our point of view however is that participation means the sharing of decision making between managers and managed. Although there is an intuitive feeling in us all that participation is always good, it may not always produce beneficial results in practice unless certain criteria are met. These can be summarised as follows:

(a) The manager must genuinely want participation and not indulge in it because he feels he ought to.

(b) The invitation to employees to participate must be genuine. If the decision is already taken or if the group decision is not accepted, then there is not genuine participation.

(c) The decision must be worth the time and effort of all concerned. Trivial matters, matters outside the individual's or group's concern, situations where there is no effective control over the factors concerned and so on will cause participation to become meaningless.

Where these conditions are met, participation will tend to result in increased commitment from the individual although studies of participation in practice have been inconclusive. Job enrichment and autonomous work groups are examples of participation at the job level and clearly are limited in their scope. The existence of job enrichment does not, for example, mean that there is participation in strategic decision making which is likely to affect the individual far more than decision making at the task level.

An important consequence of participation is the need for more information at lower levels. Effective decision making requires good information so that pushing decision making down the hierarchy requires radical changes in the organisation's MIS.

Delegation

This is the process where a manager transfers part of his own authority to a subordinate so that the subordinate can carry out some task. The responsibility for the task remains with the manager and is not delegated. True delegation is delegation with trust and the minimum of necessary controls. The art of effective delegation is about getting the trust/control ratio right and there are two main guidelines:

(a) The area of trust for each individual must be clearly defined and the individual must be allowed full control within the defined limits.

(b) There should be control of results not means. The monitoring of results after the event is not a violation of trust but control of the ways of achieving the result will generally be seen as a violation of trust.

Reasons for Delegation

In effect a manager who delegates is sharing his workload with a subordinate in whom he has confidence. The main reasons why delegation is practised are:

(a) A manager is relieved of some less important or less immediate tasks and thus has time for higher-level work.

(b) Delegation can be more efficient because decisions are taken lower down the hierarchy and communication delays are reduced or eliminated.

(c) Delegation is good training for junior personnel. They learn to make decisions and to live with the consequences. It is more challenging for them.

(d) Delegation makes the organisation more flexible and adaptable.

(e) Delegation satisfies 'higher-order' needs and is a necessary part of job enrichment programmes and is consciously practised by many organisations as part of staff development programmes.

Delegation Guidelines

There is always risk involved with delegation because the manager may not be sure that the subordinate can be trusted to carry out the delegated task, yet knows he still carries ultimate responsibility for its successful completion. Such risks can never be eliminated entirely but the following guidelines will help to reduce them as much as possible.

> To ensure effective delegation the manager should:
>
> (a) set clear objectives and indicate the standards of performance expected;
>
> (b) clearly define the level and limits of authority delegated and ensure that sufficient resources are allocated;
>
> (c) give what briefing, advice, training and guidance is necessary;
>
> (d) establish a control system to monitor results;
>
> (e) ensure that the task is completed and review the performance with the subordinate.

Some managers find it difficult to delegate and when they do, they continually interfere during the execution of the task. Others do not delegate because they think they may lose touch with day-to-day operations or because they feel threatened by the thought that a subordinate is doing part of their job.

It is generally recognised that in any organisation above the very smallest management must delegate some authority. However by delegating authority to subordinates the manager takes on two extra tasks:

1. The need to monitor the results of decisions and the performance of subordinates.

2. The need to coordinate the efforts of different subordinates.

Management by Objectives (MBO)

MBO is a structured form of delegation which seeks to harmonise the goals of the individual with those of the organisation. MBO concentrates on results achieved (in relation to objectives) rather than on the processes of achieving results. A key element of the system is that there must be participation by the managers concerned in the goal setting process. This helps to achieve a sense of common purpose and direction throughout the organisation.

A system of MBO develops logically from the overall planning system of the organisation whereby corporate and department objectives are broken down into individual manager-objectives. At its best MBO is an all-embracing approach to management both from the point of the organisation's need to achieve objectives and the needs of the individual.

The distinctive features of MBO are given below:

(a) clear definition of individual responsibilities;

(b) clear definition of key tasks and targets expressed in terms of results;

(c) participative goal setting;

(d) development of agreed measurements for both qualitative and quantitative factors;

(e) joint review and appraisal with recognition of achievement in current post;

(f) joint review of a manager's potential ability in his next job.

Although much broader in scope, there are clear similarities between the above features of MBO and the guidelines for effective delegation given earlier.

The MBO process is summarised in Figure 9/3.

The advantages and disadvantages of MBO are:

Advantages of MBO

- A scheme for converting strategic plans into management action plans.

- Helps planning, control, co-ordination and communication.

- Each manager knows what is required of him and the agreement of targets ensures commitment to them.

- Serves as a basis for the analysis of managerial training needs

Disadvantages of MBO

- It can be a time consuming process with the possible danger of creating inflexibility.
- It requires a major change in the attitudes of senior management and the style of leadership which is not easy to achieve.
- It can overstress the need for individual achievement at the expense of teamwork.

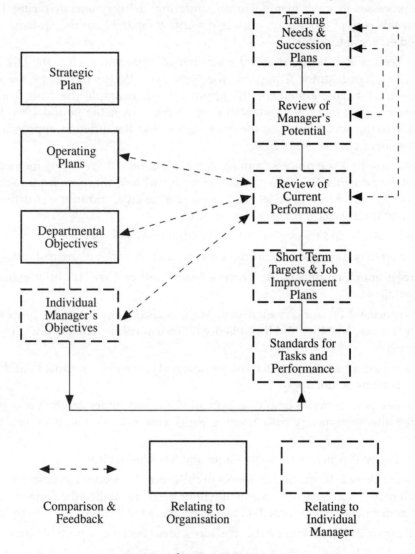

Figure 9/3 The MBO process

Business Process Re-engineering (BPR)

BPR is claimed to be a radical approach to the way organisations view work to be done. BPR was initiated by Hammer and Champy in 1993 and defined by them thus:

'Re-engineering ... is the fundamental rethinking and radical redesign of business processes to achieve dramatic improvements in critical contemporary measures of performance, such as cost, quality, service and speed'.

109

BPR is a systems oriented approach to organising work and concentrates on *business processes* not on traditional tasks and structures.

Hammer and Champy describe processes as:

> A collection of activities that takes one or more kinds of input and creates an output, that is of value to the customer.

Typical processes include; manufacturing, ordering, delivery and invoicing. It will be seen that this way of looking at work is directly, comparable to the systems approach described earlier in Chapter 3.

BPR has been, and is being, used by a number of organisations e.g. the UK Treasury, Lloyds Bank, Ford Motor Company, the New York Police Department and many successes have been claimed for the approach. For example the New York Police Department claims that the substantial drop in crime over the period 1994–1996 was partly due to the streamlining of the organisation and the different approach to work which resulted from the use of BPR.

BPR seeks to rethink the process from scratch without regard to existing methods, structures and departments. It is claimed that the re-engineering approach leads to numerous changes in the way work is done, how employees behave, and in the structures of the organisation itself. Typical of these changes are:

- individual jobs and tasks get combined with related jobs and tasks
- jobs tend to become more multi-dimensional and comprise a range of tasks
- there is more emphasis on process teams rather than traditional functional departments
- empowerment of workers increases. More decisions are made by process teams, there is more flexibility and less reliance on formal rules, there are fewer checks and controls
- work is performed where it is most sensible and efficient i.e. normal boundaries and demarcations do not apply
- there needs to be more emphasis on education and understanding *why* the job is done rather than merely basic training which concentrates mainly on *how* the job is done
- organisational structures become flatter and less hierarchical
- there are likely to be major differences in culture and attitudes e.g. customers become much more important, advancement will be based on ability, the focus for payment and performance will be based on results measured in terms of value to the customer
- challenging traditional methods, structures, ideas becomes a normal part of work.

Naturally enough some of the more extravagant claims made for BPR have been challenged by other writers. Coulson-Thomas, for example, thinks that much of what is termed BPR is only process simplification within existing frameworks and is a cover for cost reduction and down-sizing (i.e. reduction in staffing levels).

The staff that remain after BPR are pressurised and have to work much harder. Other writers, such as Talwar, think that much of BPR goes beyond the scope of work design and is more applicable to strategic management and organisational change.

Co-ordination

Co-ordinating is a primary management function and can be defined as:

the process of integrating the work of individuals, sections and departments towards the effective achievement of the organisation's goals.

A co-ordinated organisation meshes together as a team, with obvious benefits. However a lack of integration brings problems of which the following are examples:

- Complaints by clients, customers about poor service, late deliveries and of receiving conflicting messages from different parts of the organisation.
- Conflicts and 'buck passing' between individuals and departments.
- The presence of excessive rules, committees and 'red tape' in an attempt to enforce integration.
- Repeated short term 'panic' decision making to cope with today's crisis.

Reasons for Poor Co-ordination

Any one, or combination of the following reasons could contribute to poor co-ordination in an organisation and to loss of morale.

Possible reasons for poor coordination

- Poor communications between departments and between individuals.
- Poor organisation structure and inappropriate departmental groupings.
- Inadequate planning and objective setting. Does each department know, in detail, what it has to do?
- Differences in leadership style.
- Inter-departmental and inter-personal dislikes and rivalries.
- Difficulties of combining different disciplines. Can the accountants work with the marketing people?

Improving Co-ordination

As with many management problems there is not a single, universally applicable, solution.

Management have to examine the particular circumstances and difficulties and try to deal with them in a progressive fashion. Some of the approaches found useful in practice are as follows:

Administrative procedures

Standardising rules, procedures and specifications. These will have been derived from clearly defined operational plans and policies. A well developed MIS is essential to disseminate the required information.

Committees and Meetings

Formal and informal committees and meetings provide a simple but effective structure by which co-ordination may be improved. Membership should be drawn from the pool of interested people/departments. The greatest care must be taken to ensure that committees have specific tasks to perform and do not become just talking shops. Committees should not consist of the unwilling, drawn from the unfit, doing the unnecessary.

Establishing co-ordinating roles and departments

These would act as intermediaries between existing departments or functions. For example, between Social Services and the local Health Authority, between Research and Marketing and so on.

Project teams

These are used to combine and integrate different functions and departments to achieve a project objective. In effect they are a stage in the development of a full matrix structure.

Making structural changes

Depending on circumstances co-ordination may be improved by combining specialisations in different ways, or by creating more coherent service or product groups or some other structural change.

Apart from these formal changes management should try to cultivate an attitude for co-operation between departments and should actively foster teamwork.

Key Point Summary

- A manager's beliefs about motivation affects his style of management and how he leads.
- The theories on motivation include those based on satisfaction, incentives and intrinsic or personal fulfilment.
- Leadership is the ability to influence others.
- The more modern views on leadership consider that successful leadership must always relate to the specific factors in the situation.
- Trait theories attempted to identify the personal characteristics of successful leaders.
- Style theories concentrated on the way a manager manages, the two extremes being Authoritarian and Democratic.
- Contingency theorists consider that leadership effectiveness is dependent on such factors as the task, the work group and the position of the leader.
- Organising includes: deciding what tasks are necessary, how tasks are to be arranged and designing an appropriate structure for the organisation.
- There are numerous factors influencing job design including; provision of goals, some autonomy and feedback, variety, social contact and the opportunity to learn.
- Job enlargement is essentially more of the same.
- Job enrichment involves more scope, more autonomy and seeks to satisfy higher order needs.
- The conditions for genuine participation must be met otherwise there will be pseudo-participation.
- Delegation is where a manager transfers part of his authority (but not responsibility) to a subordinate.
- When delegating the manager should set clear objectives, provide what training etc is needed, monitor results and review performance.
- Management by Objectives (MBO) is a formal, structured form of delegation where the emphasis is on results achieved, not on the ways that the results were obtained.

- Business Process Re-engineering is a radical way of looking at work and concentrates on business processes not conventional tasks and structures.
- Co-ordination is the process of integrating work to achieve the organisations objectives.

Self Review Questions

1. Why is it necessary to study motivation?
2. What are the three main theories of leadership?
3. What is the problem discovered by investigations of the traits of successful leaders?
4. What are the characteristics of an authoritarian and a democratic style?
5. What are the key features of the contingency approach?
6. What elements are included in the organising function?
7. What factors do the Department of Employment suggest are needed in the design of jobs?
8. What is Job Enlargement?
9. What is Job Enrichment and what are its advantages and disadvantages?
10. What is an autonomous work group?
11. What guidelines should be followed to ensure successful participation?
12. What is delegation?
13. Why do managers delegate?
14. How should you delegate?
15. What is MBO?
16 What is Business Process Re-engineering?
17 What is co-ordination?
18. How can co-ordination be improved?

Assessment and revision section

Assignments

1. Investigate several organisations (or different parts of a large organisation) and try to find out what spans of control different managers have to deal with. If they vary greatly, find out the reasons. Can you find any general guidelines which determine the span of control?

2. Try to find the Organisation Charts of different organisations. If you find that an organisation does not have a chart try to develop one for that organisation.

    Why do the charts differ between the organisations? How many management levels are there?

3. By observation or interviews or discussions try to find out what factors motivate a person of your choice. Do the things that motivate them also motivate you? Does anything you discover relate to the theories of motivation covered in the book?

4. Imagine you are starting a 20 person Design Consultancy employing 12 professional designers, 4 computer specialists and 4 clerical staff.

    Explain, with reasons, how you would deal with the following:

    (a) Hierarchy of Authority;

    (b) Degree of Centralisation;

    (c) Specialisation.

5. Major changes are taking place within the UK Civil Service. An important part of these changes is the 'Next Step' programme. Find out what this is. What changes in management and organisation will be necessary for this to succeed? What are the problems?

6. Try to find in the literature or by investigation examples of structural changes made by organisation to cope with change or the introduction of new technology or in an attempt to become more efficient.

7. Effective Communication and presentational skills are important from both a personal and organisation viewpoint.

    Prepare a set of guidelines which could be used in an organisation to make both its internal and external communications more effective.

8. Find out some examples of large groups which practise divisionalisation. Why do they do this? What centralised control is there? Can you find out what information flows between the divisions and headquarters?

Mini-Case 1 – Organisation Structures

BKM plc is a group consisting of numerous manufacturing plants; some in the North West, some in the Midlands and some on the outskirts of London. The Group's activities include automotive products and components and assemblies for the aerospace and defence industries. Some factories sell direct to outside customers, others both sell direct and manufacture parts which are assembled in other factories in the Group.

The Group is administered by a holding company with a substantial head office staff dealing with the following functions:

- Purchasing for the Group.
- Personnel; including recruitment, selection and training. The department also administers salaries and runs a detailed staff appraisal scheme.
- Industrial engineering; including designing production layouts, management services etc.
- Data Processing with Group wide responsibility for systems analysis, design and implementation.
- Central Accounting with small accounting departments at each factory reporting to head office.

Task 1   Describe the Group's organisation structure.

Task 2   Give the advantages of such a structure.

Task 3   Give the disadvantages.

Mini-Case 2 – Improving Service Performance

Westonshire is a largely rural D.C. with three large towns within its boundaries. Like most councils it is under pressure to reduce expenditure. There is also political pressure to use outside contractors wherever possible but the Council would like to keep as many services as possible under its own control. A preliminary investigation has shown that the performance of the Council's own domestic refuse collection and disposal service compares unfavourably with that of a neighbouring Council who use private contractors.

Task 1   Explain how the Council may improve the performance of its own service.

Task 2   Investigate what has been the experience of Council's who have sub-contracted out this service.

Task 3   Explain what are the organisational consequences of sub-contracting out such services.

Mini-Case 3 – Leadership and Group Working

As part of the Davill Group's Management Development programme John, a young graduate was put in charge of a small warehouse which had been established some years ago to act as a central supply source for the Group.

The programme called for John to have three-monthly review meetings with the Group Personnel Officer. At his first meeting John was very enthusiastic and confident and described in detail the numerous developments and improvements he had already initiated and his ideas for the future. When asked about problems John mentioned the 'stick-in-the-mud' attitude of the staff and the lack of co-operation he had received.

Enquiries among the staff by the Personnel Officer discovered that there was dissatisfaction about John's leadership. The staff felt that he was in too much of a hurry and they were a little apprehensive about what they considered to be risky and ill-thought out decisions that John had taken. They thought that he had little interest in them and they were not sure whether their work was up to his requirements. One thought that a Group decision had already been taken to close the warehouse and John had been sent to do a hatchet job. The Personnel Officer knew that this fear was quite unfounded.

Task 1   What managerial problems are revealed by the above case?

Task 2   What should the Personnel Officer do?

Task 3   What should John do to improve the present position?

Task 4   How do you think the situation should have been handled from the beginning?

Mini-Case 4 – Flattening the Organisation

WH Jones plc has a nationwide chain of retail outlets specialising in the sale of magazines, books, stationery and related products. Competition is increasing and various ways of reducing costs are being examined. One possibility is to eliminate one of the in-store management levels saving three or four staff at each store.

Task 1   Describe the main effects of eliminating the management level.

Task 2   Give the advantages and disadvantages of the proposal.

Task 3   Give examples of the changes in management and staff practices and attitudes that will be necessary to make a success of the elimination.

Examination Questions (with Answers)

A1.   Critically evaluate the contribution of the classical/traditional school of management theorists to our understanding of organisation.

CIMA

A2.   Outline the principal advantages and disadvantages of decentralised forms of organisation.

CIMA

A3.   Describe the main principles of the Human Relations School, as developed from the Hawthorne Studies carried out in the Western Electric Company between 1924 and 1936. In what way did the post-war work of the Tavistock Institute (especially E.L. Trist and K. Bamforth) in describing 'social-technical systems' develop this earlier pioneering work?

ACCA

A4.   Motivation of subordinates is an important aspect of a manager's job.

(a) What do you think motivates a person to work well?

(b) What steps can a manager take to motivate his subordinates?

ICSA

A5.   Compare and contrast functional authority with line and staff authority. Why is an understanding of the scope of functional authority essential to the organisation and management of the accounting activity within an enterprise?

ACCA

A6.   You are required to

(a) describe five characteristics of a flexible organisation;

(b) explain five pressures which a flexible organisation may exert on individuals.

CIMA

A7. Why does conflict develop between different departments in an organisation and how might it be prevented?

CIMA

A8. Classical writers on organisation structure focused on the search for a common set of principles applicable to all circumstances.

(a) State and briefly explain any *four* such principles

(b) Discuss why the Classical Approach based on principles has been criticised by later writers and whether it has anything of lasting worth to contribute to our understanding of organisational design.

IAM

A9. 'Successful management depends upon the effective delegation of authority'.

Analyse the main principles by which authority may be delegated.

Comment on the advantages to both manager and subordinate of effective delegation.

ACCA

A10. A manager has recently been promoted from head of a department in one of the subsidiaries of a large company, to the same function at head office. In the few months since his arrival there has been a decline in morale and productivity in that function. Using concepts from the behavioural sciences, suggest some of the possible reasons for such a decline.

CIMA

A11. Who are the major stakeholders in an organisation and what will they each be looking for from the management of the organisation?

ACCA

A12. (a) Explain what is meant by a functionally-based business organisation, and described *two other* ways of organising the structure of a business.

(b) Discuss the advantages and disadvantages of *one* way of organising the structure of a business.

CIMA

Examination Questions (without Answers)

B1. Discuss whether 'scientific management' could be applied in today's conditions.

B2. What are the advantages and disadvantages of Weber's bureaucratic form of organisation?

B3. (a) What are the advantages and disadvantages of large international companies from the management point of view?

(b) How can the disadvantages be reduced?

CIMA

B4. The view of an organisation as a socio-technical system suggests that there is a substantially different role for management from that which emerges from traditional theory.
Discuss this suggestion.

CIPFA

B5. (a) What are the main features of a bureaucratic organisation?
(b) How effectively do bureaucratic organisations respond to changing circumstances in the environment?

ICSA

B6. M Ltd employs between 200 and 300 people. It was formerly part of a large group of companies with a centralised personnel function.
The responsibilities of this function were
(a) recruitment services, including preparing personal specifications, and inter-viewing;
(b) appraisal procedures, including the design of forms and maintenance of records;
(c) determining salary scales, including job evaluation;
(d) employment services, including maintaining personnel records and dealing with legal issues.

M Ltd has now become independent, through a management buy-out. The new managing director is considering whether to establish a central personnel department to take responsibility for the above matters or whether to devolve the responsibilities to the managers of the operating departments.

You are required to explain the implications of decentralisation versus centralisation for each of the functions (a) to (d) above.

CIMA

B7. You are required to
(a) distinguish between 'formal' and 'informal' groups;
(b) list, with examples, five conditions which will encourage highly cohesive groups.

CIMA

B8. Identify the factors which bring about change in organisations.

CIMA

B9. Describe ways in which specialisation in an organisation may be achieved. What are the advantages of these various ways?

CIMA

B10. Because of the unexpected resignation due to illness of the previous manager, George Smith has taken charge of a department of his father's business. The department employs 50 people, and is divided into six sections headed by junior managers. Although the department is efficient and running well, there are half a dozen employees whose time-keeping is irregular, and who periodically leave early or take time off. What steps should George take to eliminate this problem?

CIMA

B11. What factors would influence your decision to delegate work to a subordinate? What are the major barriers to delegation?

CIB

B12. Describe what you understand by a system of management by objectives. What do you think are the advantages and disadvantages of such a system?

CIB

B13. Your chief executive office (CEO) has been considering reorganising the company. Currently, the business is involved in the provision of a range of different products. Recently, there have been problems because employees appear unsure about who is responsible for some of the activities. The CEO has been told that a matrix structure would probably work well.

Write short briefing notes explaining a matrix structure (include a diagram), possible problems and why it may be suitable for the organisation.

ACCA

Additional Reading

1. Handy, *Understanding Organisations*, Penguin
2. Mintzberg, *Power in and around Organisations*, Prentice-Hall
3. Simon, *Administrative Behaviour*, Harper and Row
4. Cole, *Management – Theory and Practice*, Letts Educational (formerly published by DP Publications)
5. Drucker, *The Practice of Management*, Heinemann
6. Harvey-Jones, *Making it happen: Reflections on Leadership*, Fontana
7. Child, *Organisation*, Harper and Row
8. Peters and Waterman, *In Search of Excellence*, Harper Collins
9. Likert, *New patterns of management*, McGraw-Hill
10. Robbins, *Organisational Behaviour*, Prentice-Hall

10 Planning

Objectives

After you have studied this chapter you will:

- understand the relationship between planning, decision making and control.
- be able to define key terms used in planning.
- know how planning is carried out at the three management levels.
- understand the elements of corporate or strategic planning.
- know the major types and sources of planning information.
- understand how models and simulation may assist planning.

Planning, Decision Making and Control

Planning, decision making and control are intimately related managerial functions. Although these activities are often separated for instructional purposes, as they are in this book, in practice they are effectively inseparable and this point should be kept in mind whilst studying the chapters which follow.

> A complete cycle containing these functions would include the following phases:
> (a) Objective setting
> (b) Planning
> (c) Decision making and action
> (d) Accomplishment
> (e) Feedback
> (f) Control

What is Planning?

Planning is the managerial process of deciding in advance *what* is to be done and *how* it is to be done. Planning is not an end in itself, its primary purpose is to provide the guidelines necessary for decision making and resulting action, throughout the organisation. Planning is done on both a formal and informal basis and the planning process uses information from internal and external sources. The process gathers, translates, understands and communicates information that will help to improve the quality of current decisions which are based on future expectations.

Planning, like decision making and control, is heavily dependent on information flows so repays close study by information specialists.

In summary, planning means decisions by management about:

> - *what* is to be done in the future
> - *how* to do it
> - *when* to do it
> - *who* is to do it

Because planning deals with the future, uncertainty is always present. This means that flexibility must be incorporated into plans. Even where there is considerable uncertainty, plans give direction and purpose to an organisation.

Without plans, the organisation is rudderless. The essence of planning is well captured by the Vice Chancellor of Aston University in the foreword to the University's Academic Plan.

> 'Whether as individuals or as members of departments and professions; whether at the level of the Faculties or of the entire University, we all make plans for the future. To be realistic, they must take account of our personal strengths and weaknesses, and of externally-imposed constraints on our actions. If they are well formulated, they will anticipate threats and opportunities that might arise, and be capable of dealing with them as contingencies.
>
> Of course, they will not be able to foresee *all* threats and opportunities, but that only strengthens the argument for planning thoughtfully, and retaining as much flexibility as possible. Counsels of inaction deriving from the fact that the future can never be perfectly known must be rejected if progress is to be made.'

Planning terms

In the literature on planning a bewildering variety of terms are used, not always consistently. For clarity the terms used in this book are defined below:

- *Mission:* description of the purpose of the organisation as a whole.
- *Objectives:* statement of aims or goals to be achieved.
- *Plans:* statements of specific actions and activities to achieve objectives (Plans are sometimes described as strategies.)
- *Policies:* limits to acceptable behaviour expressed in terms of priorities, ethical and moral values, standards, social responsibilities and so on.

Thus objectives are *ends*, plans are *means* and policies are *statements of conduct*. Policies are not actions in themselves but they cause management to take actions in certain ways. For example it is the policy of Marks and Spencer only to sell goods under their own brand name of St Michaels.

Some organisations think it worthwhile to produce a *mission statement*. This is a general overall statement about the purpose, values and principles of the organisation which should, ideally, serve as the framework to the objectives, plans and policies pursued. Whilst some organisations consider such statements as merely public relations exercises and too general to relate to specific strategies, others take mission seriously. Examples of mission statements for the WH Smith Group and Oxfam are given below.

Group Vision

We will have a range of products and a quality of service which meets our customers' needs more effectively than any of our competitors.

We will develop a climate which emphasises directness, openness to new ideas, personal accountability and the recognition of individual and team achievement. We want all who work for the Group to contribute as much as they can to its success.

We will achieve a consistent and competitive growth in profits and earnings for our shareholders, our staff and the community. *W.H. Smith Group*

We are committed … to a process of development by peaceful means which aims to help people, especially the poor and under-privileged regardless of the politics or style of regime under which they live. *Oxfam*

Figure 10/1 shows the relationship of the planning elements described above.

Because of their importance in providing direction to the whole organisation objectives and policies are further described below.

RELATIONSHIP OF PLANNING ELEMENTS

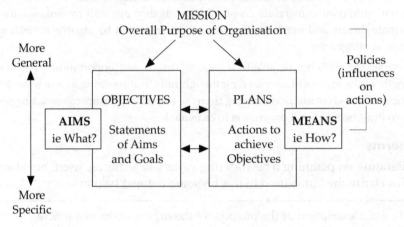

Figure 10/1

Objectives

The objectives of the organisation are usually of two levels of detail. At the highest level there are those that state the purpose or overall objective of the organisation. Naturally these are in broad general terms intended to be relatively permanent. In addition somewhat more detailed objectives would be set stating the organisation's long term aims. These should be specific enough so that it is possible to assess, say over a 5 year period, whether or not they have been achieved. If the objectives are highly specific and quantifiable they are likely to be tactical or operational level objectives rather than true strategic ones.

The nature of overall or strategic objectives is influenced by many factors including; the attitudes of the owners, political pressures which reflect different views of society, the history of the organisation, the type of business or service and so on. Traditionally in profit seeking organisations there was a heavy emphasis on financial objectives such as; return on capital employed, earnings per share and profit levels. This was a relatively narrow view which has been termed the *shareholder theory of the firm*.

A more modern tendency is what is called the *stakeholder theory*. When this view is adopted objectives are set not only for the good of the organisation but also for the other groups which are beneficiaries of the organisation, known as the stakeholders. These may include; employees, customers, suppliers and the public at large.

As an example of organisation which takes the stakeholder view consider the objectives of Sainsburys plc.

Sainsbury's plc objectives

- To discharge the responsibility as leaders in our trade by acting with complete integrity, by carrying out our work to the highest standards and by contributing to the public good and to the quality of life in the community.

- To provide unrivalled value to our customers in the quality of goods we sell, in the competitiveness of our prices and in the range of choice we offer.

- In our stores, to achieve the highest standards of cleanliness and hygiene, efficiency of operation, convenience and customer service, and thereby create as attractive and friendly a shopping environment as possible.

- To offer our staff outstanding opportunities in terms of personal career development and in remuneration relative to other companies in the same market, practising always a concern for the welfare of every individual.

- To generate sufficient profit to finance continual improvement and growth of the business whilst providing our shareholders with an excellent return on their investment.

Note the balancing of the needs of the various stakeholders; the customers, staff and shareholders, with the needs of the community as a whole. Note also the part of the first objective relating to the public good and quality of life in the community. This is the area of *social responsibility* which is taken seriously by many leading organisations which initiate or contribute to activities in the Arts, Education, Welfare and so on. For example:

- *In education:* support for universities e.g. Nottingham (Boots), Liverpool (Littlewoods), funding of Chairs e.g. by Lloyds, Arthur Andersen and others.

- *Community projects:* Sainsbury's, Tesco and other firms support numerous local and national projects. Boots are sponsoring a scheme to beautify towns and cities.

- *Arts:* donations to the National Gallery, Royal Philharmonic by the Getty Foundation, Bankers Trust Company and others. Financing of a major extension at the National Gallery by Sainsburys, sponsorship of the Royal Shakespeare Company by Allied-Lyons.

- *Business assistance:* funding of the London Business Agency to help small business jointly by Marks and Spencers, Barclays Bank, BP, United Biscuits and others.

Activities such as those above are predominantly charitable in nature and should be distinguished from promotional activities such as sports sponsorship which are usually funded from the advertising and public relations budgets of the large organisations concerned.

Because of the increasing world-wide attention to environmental matters a number of organisations have, in addition to more normal objectives, also established specific environmental objectives. For example:

Environmental Objectives – ICI plc.

- Compliance with regulatory legislation and standards wherever ICI operates is the minimum basis of the Group's four environmental objectives.

- To require all its new plants to be built to standards that will meet the regulations it can reasonably anticipate in the most environmentally demanding country in which it operates that process. This will normally require the use of the best environmental practice within the industry.

- To reduce wastes by 50 per cent by 1995, using 1990 as the baseline year. It will pay special attention to those which are hazardous. In addition, ICI will try to eliminate all off-site disposal of environmentally harmful wastes.
- To establish a revitalised and more ambitious energy and resource conservation programme, with special emphasis on reducing environmental effects so as to make further substantial progress by 1995.
- To establish a clear policy and practice on waste recycling.

The importance of environmental issues was underscored by the first ever listing in 1993 of corporate environmental performance by 'Fortune', the international business magazine.

Policies

Policies are a guide to managers causing them to take actions in certain ways. They express the organisation's official attitude to various forms of behaviour. When the organisation's objectives have been established, policies provide guidance on the way they will be achieved.

Policies are formal expressions of the organisation's culture and belief systems. Some are so fundamental that they form the rationale for the whole organisation. For example, the Fairtrade Foundation has a policy of ensuring that Third World growers of coffee receive a higher price than the normal world market price for their coffee beans. At present Café Direct is their only product and is being sold in an increasing number of supermarkets. There are plans to apply these same policies to the cocoa and chocolate trade.

Examples of policies published by other organisations include:

- Marks and Spencer has policies of selling goods only under their own brand name and of concentrating their buying in the UK.
- The Body Shop has strong environmental policies which include the avoidance of animal testing, using recyclable containers and natural ingredients.

Levels of Planning

All levels of management make plans but naturally the type of planning done at each level varies in scope and time scale. Planning has a natural hierarchy and must commence at the strategic or top level of the organisation. Planning at tactical and operational levels takes place within the guidelines of strategic plans which is obviously essential otherwise the organisation will not have a sense of direction or overall purpose.

Figure 10/2 shows an outline of the three levels of planning with indicative time horizons.

Planning Problems

Planning is a vital process in all organisations yet it is often shirked and management sometimes seek ways to avoid planning if at all possible. There are numerous reasons for this of which the following are the most important.

(a) Planning is an intensive, time consuming task and there often seems to be more immediate jobs to be done.

(b) Planning is hard mental work so it may be neglected.

(c) Planning makes evident the uncertainty of future events so that paradoxically, the future may seem more uncertain after planning than before.

(d) Planning reduces the apparent freedom of action. When plans are made managers are committed to a narrower range of actions than when no formal plans are made.

(e) Plans are often made and then ignored. This tends to happen with imposed plans which do not represent real agreement.

(f) Lack of knowledge about the purpose and objectives of the organisation and of other departments. Good planning encourages co-ordination.

(g) Lack of confidence by managers about their ability to meet targets.

(h) Lack of appropriate information.

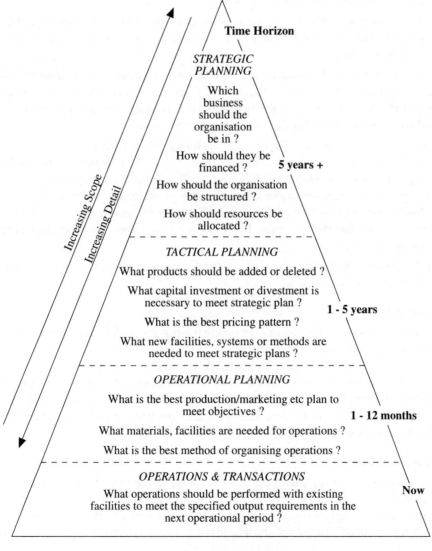

Time Horizon

Increasing Scope

Increasing Detail

STRATEGIC PLANNING

Which business should the organisation be in ?

How should they be financed ?   **5 years +**

How should the organisation be structured ?

How should resources be allocated ?

TACTICAL PLANNING

What products should be added or deleted ?

What capital investment or divestment is necessary to meet strategic plan ?   **1 - 5 years**

What is the best pricing pattern ?

What new facilities, systems or methods are needed to meet strategic plans ?

OPERATIONAL PLANNING

What is the best production/marketing etc plan to meet objectives ?   **1 - 12 months**

What materials, facilities are needed for operations ?

What is the best method of organising operations ?

OPERATIONS & TRANSACTIONS

What operations should be performed with existing facilities to meet the specified output requirements in the next operational period ?   **Now**

Figure 10/2 Levels of planning

Strategic or Corporate Planning

As previously pointed out, planning within an organisation must start from the top or strategic level. Strategic planning, or as it is sometimes known, corporate planning, seeks to obtain a consensus among the top people of an organisation about the overall direction of the organisation over the medium to long term. It is more than 'business planning' (which are plans for parts of the business), it is more than 'budgets' (which are tactical plans expressed in money terms), it is more than finance, marketing or manpower planning.

Corporate planning is about issues which affect the whole organisation at the highest level; it is a top-down process whereby the organisation as a whole is given planning guidelines which spell out the direction which the organisation will take and how the parts of the organisation fit into the plan.

In summary, corporate planning can be defined as the systematic planning of the direction and total resources of an organisation so as to achieve specified objectives over the medium to long term.

Excessive detail should be avoided because this has a tendency to reduce flexibility and the scope for opportunism and initiative; vital factors in dealing with future problems and opportunities. Argenti recommends that the corporate plan should provide 'a coarse grained strategic structure for the long term future'.

In the early days of corporate planning it was thought that corporate planning should be a very detailed, numeric exercise carried out by specialist planners using sophisticated planning techniques. Nowadays it has been realised that true corporate planning must be done by top management themselves, that the plan should address only the topmost issues facing the organisation and that few advanced techniques are relevant. Although the overall process has become more informal and less numerate, a methodical approach is still necessary.

Figure 10/3 summarises the corporate planning process and the following paragraphs expand some of the key stages.

The Planning Team

The task facing the planning team is to tackle the top issues facing the organisation. This is not something that can be delegated away or given to a specialist corporate planning department. Accordingly the planning team must consist of the Chief Executive, however designated, and other members of top management. The planning team would normally be served by a planning assistant (or several) whose task is to write reports, make calculations, undertake investigations and generally provide what assistance the top management require.

The Assessment Stage

The primary task is for the planning team to establish the overall purpose of the organisation, i.e. the corporate objective. To do this some assessment of the numerous factors that influence the organisation is required. These range from the expectations of what can be termed 'stakeholders' i.e. shareholders, employees, customers, ratepayers etc, to the planning team's judgement of the future. Assessment may be on an informal basis or it may take the form of special investigations and reports by the planning assistant.

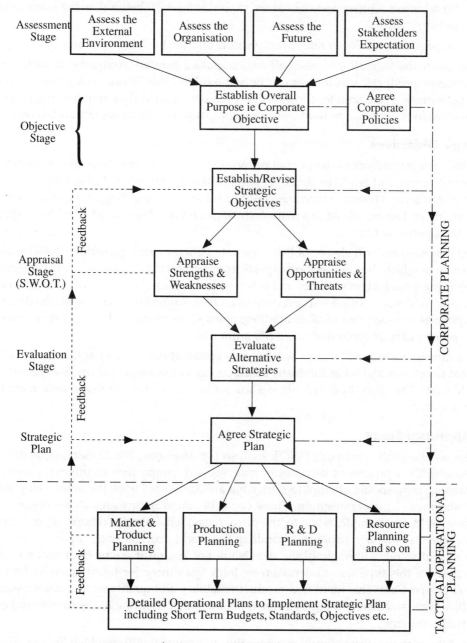

Figure 10/3 Overview of corporate planning

The Objective Stage

This is in two stages; firstly the statement of the overall objective or purpose of the organisation followed by the establishment of the strategic objectives or aims of the organisation over the medium to long term.

The statement of purpose for the organisation is intended to be relatively permanent and would be framed in broad, general terms, for example:

'to achieve a return on shareholders' capital at least 2% better than the average in the industry', or

'to provide a service to ratepayers, visitors and the business community'.

Although the overall purpose of, say, a public limited company manufacturing consumer products, would seem to be self-evident, this is not so for many types of organisations. For example, consider the problems involved in arriving at a corporate objective for a charity, a mutual insurance company, a building society and so on.

Strategic Objectives

Within the framework of the overall purpose, the strategic objectives are also written in general terms and relate to different parts of the organisation. For example, within a Local Authority, strategic objectives could be set for Housing, Education, Social Services, Planning and so on, whilst in a manufacturing company they could relate to marketing, finance, personnel etc.

Top management will also establish corporate policies which provide guidelines on the manner in which the organisation expects its objectives to be achieved. Policy statements reflect the organisation's culture and belief system and can be powerful influences on the ways activities are carried out and decisions taken. Consider, for example, the difference in policies between two local authorities; one a Conservative controlled rural area and the other a Labour controlled inner-city authority.

It is during this stage that gaps will become apparent between what the planning team want to achieve and what forecasts, based on current strategies, show is expected to be achieved. The 'gap analysis' often shows the size of the strategic task facing the organisation.

The Appraisal Stage

This is colloquially known as SWOT analysis (i.e. Strengths, Weaknesses, Opportunities, Threats). By a process of discussion, analysis and comparison of internal factors, the planning team should attempt to rank what are considered to be the main strengths and weaknesses of the organisation. These could be found in any area of the organisation. They could, for example, relate to; the price, range, reliability (or otherwise) of the products; the training, age structure, morale of the workforce; size, age, capability of equipment and so on. Although all the details are not known it seems clear that a detailed analysis of this type was undertaken by John Egan (now Sir John) when he first took over Jaguar Cars. This identified product reliability and quality as the major weakness which was remedied in a highly professional manner, resulting in the turn-round of the whole company.

Next the planning team should consider the environment within which the organisation operates to try to identify the trends and factors which will have material effect on the organisation in the medium to long term. This process will involve considerable discussion with outside experts and analysts, perhaps special investigations, examination of national and international statistics. Depending on the size and scope of the organisation the appraisal could include local, national or international factors. Threats and opportunities maybe identified in various aspects of the environment, for example:

(a) Political factors such as privatisation, changes of government at home and abroad, legislation, wars.

(b) Market factors such as new and current competitors, market share, changes in distribution (e.g. city centre to out of town shopping).

(c) Economic and social factors such as unemployment, inflation, social mobility.

(d) Technology factors such as automation and robotics, new materials, process.

It has to be recognised that all these appraisals mean trying to peer into a misty and uncertain future. When change is in a continuous pattern it is possible to project existing trends and thus make reasonable assumptions as to the actions and reactions required. The problem is that much change is discontinuous and unexpected. With truth it has been said that the only thing we know for certain about the future is that the unexpected will happen. This unpredictability means that judgement and intuition always play a part in long-term forecastings. Statistical forecasting, of whatever level of sophistication, is based on the implicit assumption that existing trends, patterns and cycles will continue in the future. Of course they may, but on the other hand they may not.

Evaluating Alternatives

By this stage the planning team will be aware of:

(a) the scale of the strategic task ahead;

(b) the major forecasted trends and factors which are expected to influence the organisation either as threats or opportunities;

(c) the aspects of the organisation which are strong and those which are weak.

The team are now able to consider alternative corporate strategies which will form the basis of the agreed corporate plan. The strategies should be sufficiently clear so that they can be evaluated as to whether they have been achieved or not, but not so specific that they constrain the organisation. Specific targets can only be set at tactical and operational levels for shorter periods of, say, up to one year.

The information system of the organisation can be of considerable assistance to the planning team when considering alternative strategies. The team will continually require answers to a series of questions beginning, 'What would happen if...?' Possible answers to these, and similar questions, are provided by the process termed *modelling* which is dealt with in the later part of this chapter.

The Strategic Plan

By this time there will be a consensus on the strategies for the organisation so that the remaining stages add increasing amounts of practical detail. The task is to prepare action plans for the various departments and functions of the organisation. These plans will contain targets and will be in sufficient detail so that tactical level management know the task they have to perform. The plan should show not only the new tasks, but how existing operations will dovetail into the new targets over, say, the next five years. The strategic plan will be used by tactical management to prepare operational plans, budgets, set short term targets and so on.

An example is shown below of a 5 year Strategic Plan for Wolverhampton Metropolitan Council.

The Corporate Strategy embodies the principles upon which the Council works and provides the context for service strategies and organisational change. Over the next five years, Wolverhampton Council will:

- efficiently implement the Council Tax and any other national changes in the financial structure of local government.

- thoroughly reassess its own functions services and assets base in the light of changing needs, financial constraints and the priorities of its elected Councillors.

- continue to meet the requirement for clearer definition of purchasing and contracting roles, a controlled 'internal market' for professional services and the devolution of decision-making authority within a strong corporate framework.

- demonstrate that services to be provided in-house are at least as effective and efficient as those provided by private sector competitors.

- strengthen the working relationship with and influence the activities of public agencies delivering services and setting policies for Wolverhampton.

- strengthen the processes of formal and informal consultation with the business community, residents and tenants, voluntary and community groups.

- develop a positive and consistent presentation of Wolverhampton Council and its work through a new strategy for public relations and communications.

Monitoring and Control

There is little point in any planning exercise if progress is not monitored after the plans have been implemented. This is to see whether activities need to be adjusted to bring them into line with the original strategies or to see whether, because of unforeseen circumstances, it is time to review the strategies themselves.

Monitoring and control at all levels works by the feedback of information. This is a major function of the information system of the organisation and is dealt with in detail later in the book.

Formal and Informal Planning

In the 1960s and 70s the fashion was for highly formal planning systems and for formal information systems to support them. Informal planning and information systems were thought of as imprecise and somehow amateurish. Experience and major unforeseen disturbances such as the oil price explosion of the mid 1970s, the stock market crash of 1987, the collapse of the property market in 1990 and others showed that highly structured systems are slow to respond to change, perpetuate static organisational assumptions and offer little or no protection from unpredictability. Indeed a survey by Grinyer and Norburn found no correlation between formal planning procedures and financial performance; instead informality and diversity of information, especially from external sources, seemed to be the critical factor.

Informal systems are more flexible and adaptable. They deal with information which is more current and significant and, because of the social contact involved, they can convey nuances which formal systems cannot handle. They do, however, suffer from bias, noise and do not always provide a complete picture. What is required is a blend of formal and informal so that the completeness, accuracy and detail of the formal systems complement the flexibility the adaptability of the informal. To achieve the right mixture is difficult for both managers and information specialists but to be aware that there is no single, all-embracing, simple solution, is an important first step.

Various reviews of formal planning procedures suggest that they encourage inflexibility whereas the real requirements, especially at the strategic level, are responsiveness and adaptability. The greatest care must be taken to ensure that the environment is continually scanned and monitored so that the organisation can adapt in progressive, controlled fashion. This is always more efficient than enforced traumatic changes made after a period of stagnation.

Type and Sources of Planning Information

By now it should be apparent that planning requires a great deal of information. The types of information and their sources will naturally vary from organisation to organisation but there is one general principle. For long term planning, environmental information is of critical importance. At lower levels, and in the short term, internal information is important but for planning the long term direction of the organisation and ensuring survival and success, external information is all important.

The following tables give examples of the *types* of information that might be required for strategic planning and typical *sources* of such information.

Types of *external* information

- *Markets and competition*

  Is the market segment increasing or decreasing? Where should our products/services be positioned? What are our competitors doing? etc.

- *Demographic trends*

  How is the population structure changing? Can we deal with an ageing population? Is the age profile of our customers changing? etc.

  Economic conditions. What are the forecasts for growth, inflation, GDP etc? What will be effect of the European Community Single market? etc.

- *Industrial structure*

  Is there a process of rationalisation/concentration taking place? What will be the consequences of privatisation? How many new firms are entering the industry? etc.

- *Social factors*

  What will be the effect of the changing family patterns, the role of women in society? What changes are expected in attitudes towards consumption and savings? etc.

- *Political factors*

  What will be the effect of political decisions? Is there likely to be political instability (especially important in overseas markets)? etc.

- *Technological Change*

  Can the organisation adapt to/take advantage of new technology? How will it affect the organisation? etc.

Types of *internal* information

- *Marketing and sales information* on performance, revenues, market shares, distribution channels etc.
- *Production and operational information* on assets, capacities, lead times, quality standards etc.
- *Financial information* on profits, costs, margins, cash flows, investments etc.
- *Personnel information* on labour skills and availability, training, labour relations etc.
- *Research and development information* on new products and developments, patents, knowledge base etc.

Typical *sources* of information

- *External*

  Formal: Published reports, government statistics, scientific and technical abstracts, company reports, commercial data banks, Trade Associations, special investigations.

  Informal: Discussions, social contact of all types, media coverage, conferences, business and holiday trips at home and abroad, correspondence.

- *Internal*

  Formal: All outputs of the organisation's MIS including control and monitoring reports, forecasting and enquiry systems, modelling and simulation, investigative reports, budgets, job descriptions, organisation charts, correspondence, video displays.

  Informal: Discussions, meetings, social contact, telephone conversations, personal record keeping, correspondence.

Note: The above are not exhaustive lists but are indicative of typical sources.

In spite of the wealth of external information available and its obvious importance in planning there is evidence that organisations fail to explore the sources in a thorough comprehensive manner.

A survey conducted by UWIST, Cardiff of 27 South Wales engineering firms with turnovers ranging from £1m–50m employing 9000 people in total, found that 50% based market forecasts solely on the opinions of the existing sales force. Only 4 out of 27 took advantage of information services available externally.

Models

The MIS of an organisation provides considerable general assistance for planning and decision making as outlined previously. One particular development, the use of models, is proving to be of especial importance because their use extends intuition and experience by analysing the effects of uncertainty and by exploring the likely consequences of different planning assumptions.

A model is any simplified abstract of reality. It may be a physical object such as an architectural scale model or it may be what is termed a 'symbolic model'. These are representations of reality in numeric, algebraic, symbolic or graphical form.

Business models are symbolic models which represent the operations of the organisation by sets of logically linked arithmetic and algebraic statements. Such models enable operations to be explored at low cost and with nil risk. Models are invariably computer-based and use the processing power of the computer to enhance a manager's analytical ability.

Figure 10/4 provides a broad classification of models used for management purposes.

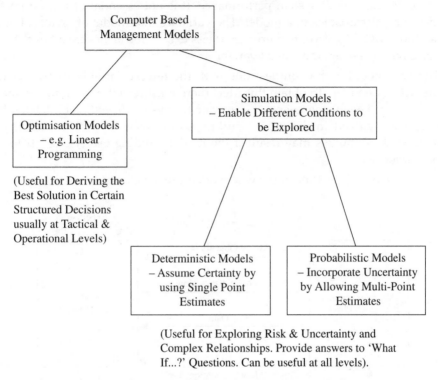

Figure 10/4 Classification of management models

Models maybe used at various levels; at the economy level, at the level of the organisation or to deal with a narrow aspect of operations. Some examples follow:

- The Treasury Model is a complex, large scale model used to predict the progress of the UK economy as a whole so as to guide fiscal and monetary policy.

- In the US, a model was developed at Harvard which analysed the domestic market for detergents and included factors such as relative prices, state of the economy, introduction of new products and firms, marketing patterns and so on.

- Many organisations use models to investigate the interaction of their investment decisions, earnings and cash flow.

- Typical lower level models include, determining staff and service points where queues exist, predicting stock levels where there are variations in supply and/or demand and so on.

Model Development

To develop a model, which is realistic and has adequate predictive qualities, is a collaborative effort between management and information specialists.

The key points are:

- The model should have a purpose and be objective orientated.

- Model building is an iterative, creative process with the aim of identifying those variable and relationships which must be included in the model so that it is capable of predicting overall system performance. It is not essential or indeed possible, to including all variables in a model. The variables in a model of greatest importance are those which govern, to a greater or less extent, the achievement of the specified objectives. These are the critical variables.

- The best model is the simplest one with the fewest variables that has adequate predictive qualities. To obtain this ideal there must be a thorough understanding of the system. The management who operate the system have this understanding and must be involved in the model building, otherwise over elaborate and overly mathematical models may result if the model building exercise is left to systems professionals.

Figure 10/5 shows an outline of the way models are developed and used.

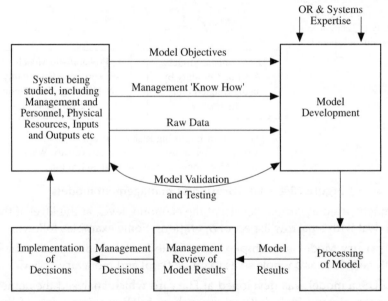

Figure 10/5 Model development and use

A Simple Planning Model

A typical planning model consists of a number of linked arithmetic, algebraic or financial statements which reduces different answers with different input values. A highly simplified example of a deterministic simulation model is as follows:

$$\text{Sales} = \text{input variable}$$
$$\text{Cost of sales} = 0.45 \times \text{sales}$$
$$\text{Gross margin} = \text{Sales} - \text{cost of sales}$$
$$\text{Operating expenses} = \pounds200{,}000 + 12.5\% \text{ sales}$$
$$\text{Profit before tax} = \text{gross margin} - \text{operating expenses}$$
$$\text{Taxes} = 52\% \times \text{profit before taxes}$$
$$\text{Net profit} = \text{profit (before taxes)} - \text{taxes}$$

Given any value of input variable, say £1m, a profit plan may be prepared thus:

Profit plans for year ended 19..

		£
Sales	=	1,000,000
less: cost of sales	=	450,000
Gross margin	=	550,000
less: operating expenses	=	325,000
Profit before tax	=	225,000
less: Tax	=	117,000
Net profit	=	108,000

The above example, although unrealistically simple, illustrates the general form of a planning model including:

(a) A format for presenting the results from processing the model.

(b) A set of input data.

(c) A set of processing statements (formulae, logic statements, equations, flowcharts etc) to operate on the input data.

More Comprehensive Models

To be realistic models must be much more comprehensive and contain many more elements than shown above. For example, ways of increasing the realism of the above model would be to include the factors underlying the Sales instead of entering the final figure. These factors could include:

• National estimate of GNP.

• Disposable income of consumers.

• Industry sector sales trends.

• Level of advertising last year.

• Level of advertising current year.

• Level of competitive advertising last year.

• Estimate of level of competitive advertising current year.

• Last years sales.

• Last years price levels.

• Changes anticipated in price levels, etc.

To develop the model into a probabilistic simulation model it would be necessary to include probability frequencies for the important variables. For example, probabilities for various possible sales levels could be calculated from historic data and management judgement and a similar process undertaken for the cost of sales using past cost records and judgement. Then, when the model was entered, random sets of these factors would be chosen in accordance with the chance they have of turning up in the future. In this way a profile of likely results would be more informative than the single value output obtainable from a basic deterministic model. The incorporation of probabilistic elements into the process is sometimes termed 'Monte Carlo' simulation. An example is given below.

A Probablistic Simulation

A common application of simulation is to examine the behaviour of queues in circumstances where the use of queueing formulae is not possible. The following example is typical.

A filling station is being planned and it is required to know how many attendants will be needed to maximise earnings. From traffic studies it has been forecast that customers will arrive in accordance with the following table:

Probability of 0 customers arriving in any minute 0.72.

Probability of 1 customers arriving in any minute 0.24.

Probability of 2 customers arriving in any minute 0.03.

Probability of 3 customers arriving in any minute 0.01.

From past experience it has been estimated that service times vary according to the following table.

Service Time (in minutes)	Probability
1	0.16
2	0.13
3	0.12
4	0.10
5	0.09
6	0.08
7	0.07
8	0.06
9	0.05
10	0.05
11	0.05
12	0.04

If there are more than two customers waiting, in addition to those being serviced, new arrivals drive on and the sale is lost.

A Petrol pump attendant is paid £20 per 8 hour day, and the average contribution per customer is estimated to be £2.

How many attendants are needed?

Solution

It will be seen that there are two factors whose values change; the rate of arrivals and the rate of service. These are the probablistic elements and their individual values would be repeatedly selected during the simulation using either, a random number generator if a computer is used, or a printed random number table if the simulation is done manually.

The first step is to derive the model (i.e. the logic) of the problem.

This can be expressed as a linked series of statements, a computer program or as a flow-chart. In this simple example, a flowchart is used. See Figure 10/6.

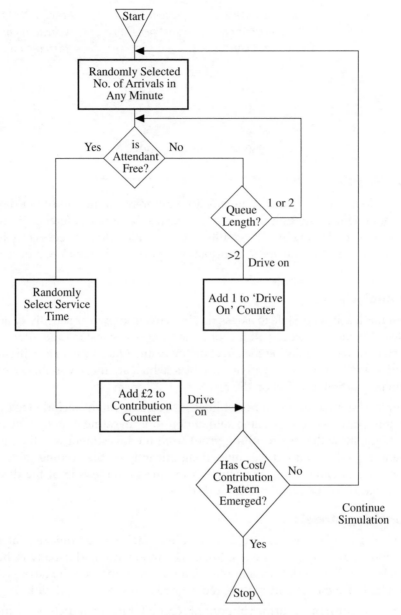

Figure 10/6 Model of filling station simulation

When the logic has been established the simulation is carried out for a number of iterations each representing 1 minute's operations; first with 1 attendant, then 2 attendants then 3 and so on. During the cycles the counters would be clocked up and, at the end of the simulation, a summary of results would be prepared.

The above simulation has been worked through for several day's operation with 1, 2, 3 and 4 attendants and the results obtained are tabulated below.

No. of Attendants	Average Contribution per Day	Attendant(s) Cost per Day	Average No. of Vehicles/Day driving on
	£	£	
1	156	20	81
2	260	40	29
3	288	60	16
4	300	80	2

Results of simulation

From the table it will be seen that there is little difference in net profit per day between 2,3 and 4 attendants, although there is of course a substantial difference in the average number of vehicles driving on. The results of a simulation do not necessarily indicate an optimal solution but provide more information upon which a reasoned decision can be taken.

Sensitivity Analysis

With most models it is possible to assess risk by what is known as sensitivity analysis. At its simplest this means holding all the variables, bar one, constant and altering that one variable step by step and noting the effect on the result. One object of sensitivity analysis is to identify the 'critical' or 'sensitive' variables, which are those variables which have a more than proportionate effect on the result.

For example, a simulation of an investment programme might include factors such as; cost per unit, price per unit, volume sold, amount of investment and so on. Sensitivity analysis might show that the resulting profit from the investment was little affected by the cost and price per unit but was altered significantly by the volume sold. Sensitivity analysis can be extended from this simple example to the testing of the design of the system, the nature of the relationships and so on.

Reasons for Using Models

- **The model is cheaper**. Manipulation of the model may be quicker, safer and less hazardous than trying out the real thing. The model can and usually is, built before the real event. The model is manipulated and if the proposed scheme or system looks to be a bad idea the scheme may be redesigned or not proceeded with.

- **Study and redesign**. A further important reason for using models is the insight they give management into the working of the real system and the assistance they can give in trying our various designs, arrangements and plans. The proper use of models enables time scales to be compressed so that the results of several years operations can be studied in a few hours.

- **Specialised assistance**. Considerable expertise is available to management from such groups as OR specialists, systems analysts and accountants. However, these groups are better able to provide this assistance when specific problems have been identified and require solutions. The process of model building with its combination of management and specialist expertise and the necessity to define objectives carefully is a fruitful area of co-operation between line management and technical specialists. It is a process from which both groups will gain, providing the manager with an awareness of the possibilities of modern mathematical, financial and computer techniques and giving the technical specialists an insight into the practical problems that exist which often limit or modify the use of specialised techniques.

Simulation and modelling is such an important facet of the work of the computer that most manufacturers have developed simulation languages to assist the process. Typical examples are GPSS, CSL, SIMULA etc.

Key Point Summary

- Planning is deciding in advance what is to be done and how it is to be done.
- Common terms used in planning include; objective, goal, strategy, plans, policy.
- Planning is long term at strategic levels and virtually immediate at operational levels.
- Corporate or strategic planning is about issues which affect the whole organisation.
- Corporate planning is the *key* task of strategic management.
- Strategic objectives are set within the overall purpose of the organisation.
- The appraisal stage is know as SWOT analysis.
- During the evaluating of alternatives the organisation's MIS can be of great value.
- The output of the corporate planning process is the strategic plan.
- It is important to use a blend of informal and formal planning.
- There are numerous sources of planning information, external and internal, formal and informal.
- Models are representations of reality and simulation models are useful for exploring the consequences of different actions.
- The best models are simple, objective-orientated and are those in which management has been involved.
- The object of sensitivity analysis is to identify the sensitive or critical variables.
- Models are used because they are cheaper and less risky and they provide insights into problems.

Self Review Questions

1. Define planning.
2. Define the following terms: objectives, strategy, plans, policy.
3. What is the relationship between aims and means in planning?
4. What are examples of the areas covered by the three levels of planning?
5. Define corporate strategy.
6. Who should carry out corporate planning?
7. What takes place during the objective stage of corporate planning?
8. What is 'gap analysis'?
9. What is SWOT analysis?
10. What is the strategic plan?
11. What is the relationship between formal and informal planning?

12. What are the main sources of planning information?

13. What is a model and what type of model is most appropriate for management purposes?

14. How are models developed?

15. Outline the basics of a planning model.

16. What is sensitivity analysis and how is it carried out?

11 Decision Making

Objectives

After you have studied this chapter you will:

- be able to define decision making.
- know Simon's four phases of decision making.
- understand the distinction between programmed and non programmed decisions.
- know how decisions vary with the level of management.
- be able to distinguish between certainty, risk and uncertainty.
- know what conditions are necessary for rational decision making.
- understand expected value and decision trees.
- know what is meant by satisficing behaviour.
- be able to explain why reviewing the decision process is necessary.
- know the main ways the organisation's MIS can assist decision making.

What is Decision Making?

Decision making is an integral part of management and occurs in every function and at all levels. Naturally the type of decisions taken vary enormously but all decision makers have to go through a similar process. All of them must decide by some means to choose the outcome or outcomes which are considered necessary or desirable to them and to do so after some form of appraisal of the situation.

H.A. Simon, a leading authority on management decision making, considers that decision making comprises four principal phases: finding occasions for making decisions, finding possible courses of action (i.e. alternatives), choosing among courses of action, and evaluating past choices.

Figure 11/1 shows a summary of these phases using Simon's terminology.

It is important to realise that although there is a general flow from intelligence to design to choice to review, at any time there could be a return to an earlier phase. For example, a decision maker in the choice phase who finds no suitable alternative among those currently available, would return to the design phase to develop more alternatives. Decision making is an iterative process and although it is useful to separate out the various phases in order to discuss them, very few decisions are taken in this neat, logical sequence. There is feedback, inter-relationships between decisions; there is flair, intuition, judgement and creativity.

Phase 1 INTELLIGENCE	– Searching the environment for conditions calling for decisions.
Phase 2 DESIGN	– Inventing, developing and analysing possible courses of action. This involves processes to understand the problem, to generate solutions and the testing of solutions for feasibility.
Phase 3 CHOICE	– Selecting an alternative or course of action from those available. A choice is made and implemented.
Phase 4 REVIEW	– Assessing past choices.

Figure 11/1 Simon's Phases of Decision Making

Decision making is based on information. Information is the trigger to knowing there is a problem, information is needed to define and structure the problem, information is needed to explore and choose between the alternative solutions and information is needed to review the effects of the implemented choice.

Programmed and Non-programmed Decisions

Simon classified decisions into two categories according to the extent that the process of decision making can be pre-planned. The categories are *programmed* and *non-programmed*, as follows:

- *Programmed decisions:*

  Characteristics: repetitive, routine, known decision rules or procedures, often automated, usually involve 'things' rather than people, can be delegated to low levels in the organisation.

  Examples: inventory control decisions, machine loading decisions, scheduling.

- *Non-programmed decisions:*

  Characteristics: novel, non-routine, decision rules not known, high degree of uncertainty, cannot be delegated to low levels, may involve 'things' but always involve people.

  Examples: acquisitions, mergers, launching new products, personnel appointments.

Note: Alternative terms for these two categories are *structured* and *unstructured*.

The two categories should be thought of as the extreme ends of a range of decision types with many decisions containing elements of both categories. The terms programmed and non-programmed are not related to computer processing. They refer to the nature of the decision process and to the extent that the process can be pre-planned.

There is some relationship between the level of management and the decision type; broadly more programmed decisions at lower levels and more unstructured decisions at higher levels, but this is not an absolute rule. Some high level decisions contain structured elements, an example being a costly plant replacement decision which is likely to be taken at the highest level and for which decision rules are available using replacement analysis and investment appraisal techniques.

Levels of Decision Making

Decision making takes place at each level of management in organisation although there are markedly different characteristics at each level. Each level has substantially different information requirements and figure 11/2 summarises the main characteristics and information requirements of the various levels.

The tactical level of management occupies an intermediate position between the two extremes with some of the characteristics of both. Much of the development of formal aids to decision making, such as, for example, optimising models, has been directed at the operational and tactical levels of management. At the strategic level, decision making is much more dependent on human factors and judgement. Such decision making is based on guided trial and error and because of uncertainty and ambiguities, all possibilities cannot be explored. This type of decision making is known as *heuristic* and is based on rules of thumb rather than explicit decision rules.

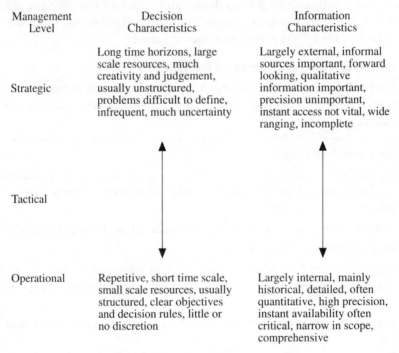

Management Level	Decision Characteristics	Information Characteristics
Strategic	Long time horizons, large scale resources, much creativity and judgement, usually unstructured, problems difficult to define, infrequent, much uncertainty	Largely external, informal sources important, forward looking, qualitative information important, precision unimportant, instant access not vital, wide ranging, incomplete
Tactical		
Operational	Repetitive, short time scale, small scale resources, usually structured, clear objectives and decision rules, little or no discretion	Largely internal, mainly historical, detailed, often quantitative, high precision, instant availability often critical, narrow in scope, comprehensive

Figure 11/2 Levels of decision making

Figure 11/3 gives examples of decision making at the three levels with typical information requirements.

Management Level	Decision Examples	Information Requirements
Strategic	Mergers and acquisitions, new product planning, capital investments, financial structuring	Market and economic forecasts, political and social trends, legislative, environmental and technological constraints and opportunities
Tactical	Pricing, capacity planning, budget preparation, purchasing contracts	Cost and sales analyses, performance measures, summaries of operations/production, budget/actual comparisons etc
Operational	Production scheduling, maintenance, re-ordering, credit approval	Sales orders, production requirements, performance measures, customer credit status, deliveries, despatches etc

Figure 11/3 Decision and Information Examples

The preceding paragraphs and diagrams are not absolutes and indicate tendencies only. In practice, decisions should be taken at the level where they are most effective.

Peter Drucker says decisions should be made at the *lowest possible level* which accords with their nature, and as close to the scene of action as possible.

They should always be taken at the level which ensures none of the activities and objectives affected are forgotten.

There is increasing evidence that many decisions are being taken at lower levels in the hierarchy. Authority to take decisions is being delegated down the line especially in modern service industries. Examples include; telephone banking and insurance, and British Telecom. This process is called *empowerment* and means that the organisation is able to answer queries and take a variety of decisions more quickly thus providing a better and more flexible service. Empowerment is also one of the reasons why some middle management jobs are disappearing.

Certainty, Risk and Uncertainty

Decisions can also be categorised in terms of knowledge about the outcomes of the various alternatives, as follows:

Outcome State	Explanation
Certainty	There is only one outcome for each alternative and there is complete and accurate knowledge of the outcome.
Risk	There are multiple possible outcomes for each alternative and a value and probability of occurrence can be attached to each outcome.
Uncertainty	The number of outcomes, their values and probabilities is not known.

Where there is certainty or risk, various *optimising techniques* (i.e. techniques which select the best possible outcome) can provide useful guidance to the decision maker. Examples are given later in the chapter.

Taken literally, where there is uncertainty, decision making is not possible. This is because decision making, by definition, means choosing between alternatives and if you do not know what the alternatives are you cannot chose between them. Of course, what happens in practice is that, by using judgement and any available information, estimates are made of the values and likelihoods of possible outcomes. In effect transforming uncertainty into risk. If this was not done decision making could not take place in the real world where uncertainty, to a greater or lesser extent, is always present.

Prescriptive and Descriptive Decision Models

A prescriptive or normative model of decision making is one which automatically selects the best option. Such models have usually been developed by operational researchers, economists and management scientists. Examples include: linear programming, cost/volume/profit analysis, statistical decision theory, investment appraisal techniques and so on. These models are well defined and structured and treat decision making as an entirely rational process. They are optimising techniques which assume that conditions of certainty or risk exist.

On the other hand, descriptive models have been developed by behavioural scientists and seek to explain actual behaviour in decision making. Actual decision making is less structured and is not completely rational. In practice, decision makers simplify the factors involved and, because of practical difficulties, are prepared to accept a satisfactory solution rather than attempt to find the theoretical optimum.

These two categories are expanded below.

'Rational' Decision Making

This model of decision making, developed from classical economic theory, is summarised in Figure 11/4.

This model assumes perfect knowledge of all factors surrounding the decision and adopts a rational mechanistic approach to decision making. It will be realised that all the criteria of the model – single, known objective, perfect information and so on – are rarely met in practice, yet many decision making techniques make these assumptions and are widely used.

For example, most decision making techniques drawn from accounting use the above approach.

The use of the pure rational decision making is more suited to operating and tactical levels of management where the factors are more clear cut and there is less uncertainty. The decisions are more structured and the formal MIS of the organisation is thus able to provide considerable assistance. However, care is always necessary to ensure that the particular 'rational' decision making technique being used actually does suit the individual circumstances. Various studies have shown that things are not always as clear cut as they seem; for example.

'Users tend to explain their actions in terms of rational behaviour, whereas their actual performance may be governed by intuition rather than by rational analysis. Studies of managers at work have shown that there is a discrepancy between how managers claim to take decisions and their actual observed decision-making behaviour'.

Argyris and Schon

In many cases the results produced from a rational decision making technique are not used uncritically. They are treated as one of many types of information and management may well adjust to the apparent 'optimal' decision because of other factors. These could include; conflicting objectives, uncertainty, social, psychological and political considerations.

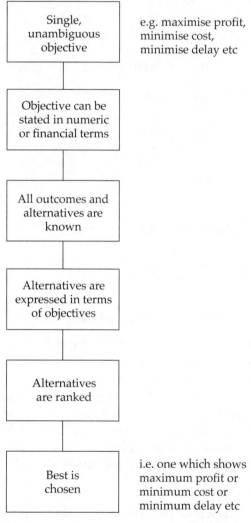

Figure 11/4 Characteristics of rational decision making

Rational Decision Making Objectives

The starting point of the rational decision making process is a statement of the single objective. This may be to; maximise profit, or maximise return on capital employed, or minimise cost per unit, or maximise utility (used in the economic sense of satisfying wants or desires), or, where risk exists, maximise expected value.

Expected value is a widely used decision making criterion and can be defined as the total of the probability or likelihood of each outcome times the value of each outcome.

As an example, assume that this is required to choose between three alternatives A, B and C each of which has three possible outcomes. The objective is to maximise profit and all outcomes and probabilities are known, as follows:

	Alternative A		Alternative B		Alternative C	
	Prob'y	*Profit*	*Prob'y*	*Profit*	*Prob'y*	*Profit*
Optimistic Outcome	0.2	5000	0.3	4000	0.1	3000
Most Likely Outcome	0.6	7500	0.5	7000	0.7	6500
Pessimistic Outcome	0.2	9000	0.2	9500	0.2	10000

Solution

Expected values:

Alternative A

$(0.2 \times 5000) + (0.6 \times 7500) + (0.2 \times 9000) = 7300$

Alternative B

$(0.3 \times 4000) + (0.5 \times 7000) + (0.2 \times 9500) = 6600$

Alternative C

$(0.1 \times 3000) + (0.7 \times 6500) + (0.2 \times 10000) = 6850$

Thus, in terms of the objective, Alternative A is preferred.

Expected value is commonly used and has the advantages of arithmetically taking account of all the variabilities and being easy to understand. It suffers from the fact that by representing the various outcomes by a single summary figure, it ignores other characteristics of the distribution, such as the range and skewness. Furthermore, expected value can strictly only be interpreted as the value that would be obtained if a large number of similar decisions were taken with the same range of outcomes and associated probabilities. Hardly a typical decision making situation!

Decision Trees

Often decisions are not taken in isolation but as part of a sequence. In such circumstances the analysis can usefully be presented in the form of a decision tree. Decision trees are a pictorial way of showing a sequence of inter-related decisions and outcomes. They invariably include probabilities and are evaluated using expected values. By convention, decision points are represented by square nodes and outcomes (which vary according to circumstances) by circles. Figure 11/5 shows the general form of a decision tree.

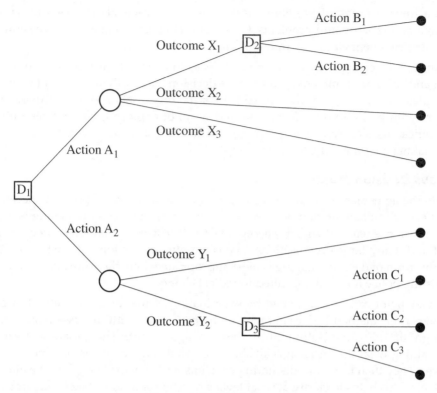

Figure 11/5 Decision tree

Notes on Figure 11/5

(a) The decision nodes are points where a choice exists between alternatives and a managerial decision is made based on estimates and calculations of the returns expected.

(b) The outcome nodes are points where the events depend on probabilities. For example, assume that Action A1 was – Build branch factory – then outcomes X1, X2, and X3 could represent various possible sales; high, medium and low, each with an estimated probability.

Decision trees are evaluated from right to left, working back from the later decisions to the first.

Satisficing or Bounded Rationality

This view of decision making is a descriptive, behavioural model which takes account of imperfections of knowledge and behaviour.

The term 'satisficing' was coined by Simon to describe the behaviour of decision makers operating in a complex and partially unknown environment. Decision makers are not fully aware of all the alternatives available nor is there always a single, clear cut objective. They make only a limited search to discover a few satisfactory alternatives and finally make a decision which satisfies their aspirations, hence the term satisficing. There is not complete rationality but bounded rationality which means that decision making is rational but within the imperfections of information and the decision maker's ability to perceive alternatives and outcomes. The choice of an alternative which is good enough, from a limited range of possible alternatives, is a practical approach to day-to-day managerial pressures and problems. Observation and personal experience show clearly that satisficing behaviour is commonplace.

An important consequence of this type of decision behaviour is that subjectivity, judgement and rules of thumb are used to make decisions rather than the use of explicit decision rules. This means that the formal MIS of the organisation should provide decision makers with background information and ways of exploring alternatives rather than mechanical decision rules and procedures. The ways in which the MIS can assist decision making are outlined later in the chapter.

Consensus Decision Making

Where the agreement of individuals and groups in positions of power is necessary for the effective implementation of a decision then consensus decision making is practised, i.e. a decision is reached which is acceptable to all. This is a common strategy in government and many large organisations. The conventional wisdom, at least in the West, is that this form of decision making is most appropriate where there are only small changes to existing policy and it is not suited to radical changes.

This viewpoint can be questioned by examination of the Japanese method of decision making. Their method is decision making by consensus with discussion and argument throughout the organisation until there is agreement. The Japanese focus is on determining what the decision is all about i.e. what is the question first, not what is the answer. They then bring out dissenting opinions which helps to explore the alternatives available. This helps to clarify at what level a decision should be taken and, importantly, it eliminates the 'selling' of a decision in order to get effective action and support. This method has been used for the most radical decision making and although it has been criticised in the West as being long-winded, once a decision has been reached, implementation and action follow with great speed and effectiveness.

By its nature consensus decision making involves more people so that there is more chance of the real problem being identified. This is a vital, if not the most vital, part of the process. The recognition of what is the real problem requires much questioning and thought. For example, a firm is experiencing a drop in sales. What is the problem? Is it the price of the product, the quality, appearance, style, capability? Is it poor sales and marketing? Is it the lack of advertising or of the right type of advertising? Is it the lack of an appropriate incentive scheme for the sales force? Is it the appearance on the market of a superior competing product? Have the consumers' tastes changed? etc.

Only when the real problem has been identified can alternatives be developed to deal with it and a decision made.

Reviewing the Decision Making Process

It is often invidious to review the actual decision made because totally unforeseen circumstances may turn a correct decision, honestly made in the light of the then prevailing knowledge, into an incorrect one. What is possible, and indeed essential, is to review the quality of the decision making process itself to ensure that decisions are made in a systematic fashion after a thorough review of all relevant factors.

The quality of a decision process is dependent on a decision maker who:

(a) Considers the full range of objectives to be fulfilled and makes explicit any compromises necessary between competing objectives.

(b) Explores a wide range of alternative courses of action using formal and informal sources of information including discussions with peers and subordinates.

(c) Carefully evaluates the costs and risks of negative consequences as well as the positive consequences of each course of action using, where necessary, aids to analysis such as simulation.

(d) Seeks out new information, from various sources, to assist his evaluation of alternatives.

(e) Assimilates and takes account of information and expert opinion even when this runs counter to his own preferences.

(f) Re-examines the positive and negative consequences of all known alternatives, include those originally regarded as unacceptable, before making a final decision.

(g) Makes detailed plans for implementing the chosen course of action including discussion with those affected, training, contingency plans to cope with problems which might arise and so on.

(h) Reviews the effectiveness of past decisions in order to learn.

Decision Making and Information Systems

In broad terms the organisation's MIS can perform one of two functions with respect to decision making:

either (a) it supplies information, explores alternatives, and provides support *where the manager takes the decision*

or (b) *the MIS takes the decision itself*. This is only appropriate with routine operational decisions where the rules are known.

At operational levels many, but not all, decisions are structured with known decision rules and clearly defined objectives. It is these types of decisions which are now routinely being taken by computerised MIS as part of the day-to-day transaction processing of the organisation. Semi-structured and unstructured decisions do exist at operational levels but are increasingly common as one moves up the management hierarchy. These decisions have to be taken by managers but they need information to assist them to define the problem, evaluate the likely results of different alternatives, test effects and so on.

Figure 11/6 provides a broad overview of decision making at the three levels and the assistance that MIS can provide.

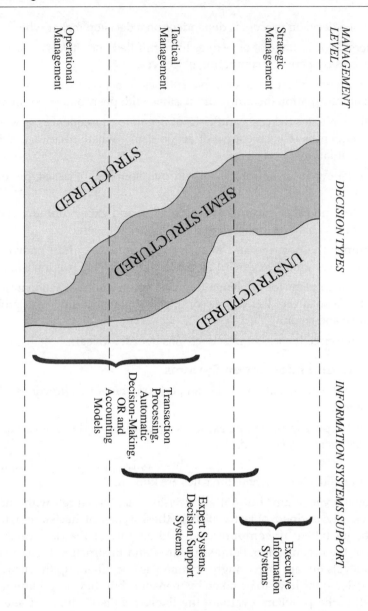

Figure 11/6 Decision-making and MIS support

The various aspects of MIS support; transaction processing, automatic decision making – expert systems and decision support systems – executive information systems – are described in detail later in the book.

The boundaries between structured and unstructured decisions are constantly changing. As new techniques and systems are developed, there is a tendency for more and more decisions to be dealt with using pre-determined rules and procedures. As an example, inventory control decisions were originally a middle management task involving experience and a degree of judgement. Routinely nowadays decisions on re-order levels, order quantities, when to order and so on are taken using programmed decision rules, often computer based. It is expected that this process will continue.

Key Point Summary

- Simon considers that decision making has four phases – Intelligence, Design, Choice and Review.
- Decisions can be categorised into programmed or structured, and non-programmed or unstructured.
- The characteristics and information requirements of the levels of decision making vary greatly.
- All decision making has problems of risk, unquantifiable factors and how to recognise the real problem.
- Prescriptive decision models tell the manager how to make decisions whereas descriptive models explain how decision making takes place.
- Rational decision making assumes perfect knowledge of all factors and is a mechanistic approach.
- Expected value is a well known decision making criterion.
- Decision trees are a useful way of presenting a sequence of decisions.
- Satisficing or bounded rationality acknowledges that imperfections exist and that to seek a satisfactory outcome is a practical approach.
- Consensus decision making, although protracted, saves time in implementation.
- It is important to review the process of decision making to ensure that decisions are made in a systematic fashion.
- The organisation's MIS provides support for semi-structured and unstructured decision making and may take the decisions for structured, well defined problems.

Self Review Questions

1. What is decision making and what are Simon's four phases?
2. Distinguish between programmed and non-programmed decisions.
3. What are the decision and information characteristics at the three management levels?
4. What are some of the practical problems in decision making?
5. What are prescriptive and descriptive decision models.
6. What are the stages of 'rational' decision making.
7. What is expected value?
9. What is consensus decision making?
10. On what factors does the quality of the decision process depend?
11. Explain in outline how the organisation's MIS can assist decision making.

12 Elements of Control

Objectives

After you have studied this chapter you will:

- understand the importance of the control function.
- be able to describe the basic elements of the control cycle.
- know the importance of feedback loops.
- be able to distinguish between single loop feedback and double loop or higher order feedback.
- understand how lower level control loops nest into higher level ones.
- know the function of negative feedback.
- understand positive feedback.
- be able to describe Pareto analysis.
- understand the law of requisite variety.
- be able to explain feedforward and explain its importance.

The Concept of Control in Management

Control is a primary management task and is the process of ensuring the operations proceed according to plan. A comprehensive definition of management control given by Mockler is reproduced below:

> 'Management control can be defined as a systematic effort by business management to compare performance to predetermined standards, plans, or objectives, in order to determine whether performance is in line with these standards and presumably in order to take any remedial action required to see that human and other corporate resources are being used in the most effective and efficient way possible in achieving corporate objectives.'

The type of control activity varies according to the level of management, and the amount of time spent controlling also varies according to level. As an example, control activities will occupy most of the time of a supervisor or foreman at the operational level and most operational control systems involve the use of formal, systematic rules with clear, unambiguous targets expressed in quantitative or financial terms. At higher levels, planning and control are more interlinked, with management being concerned both to monitor progress against the original plans and to review the suitability of the plans themselves for current and anticipated future conditions.

Control is necessary because unpredictable disturbances occur and cause actual results to deviate from the expected or planned results. Control activities seek to keep the system outputs in line with the original plan, what is known as 'steady state', or to enable the system to change safely to meet the new conditions.

Disturbances can range from minor matters such as a short delay in the delivery of raw materials, to disturbances which threaten the organisation itself, for example, the unexpected entry of a large, new competitor into the market.

Control of Systems

To be successful, any organisation, whether a factory, local authority or school, must produce outputs in the form of goods, services, or facilities that meets its objectives. To do this planning must take place and, when the plans have been implemented, control must be exercised to ensure conformity to the plans and that the plans remain relevant. It is meaningless to consider any form of control activity without a clear idea of what is to be achieved i.e. a plan. Correspondingly, a vital element in any planning process is consideration of the controls and control systems necessary to ensure adherence to the plan. In physical systems, control is an integral part of the design and is based on direct and immediate measurement and sensing of voltages, pressures, temperatures, flows, weights and so on. Well known examples being engine governors, heating thermostats and overload switches.

In organisational and management systems the need to monitor activities is not always so apparent and there must be a conscious effort to include appropriate control systems throughout the organisation. A crucial difference between organisational and mechanical systems is that in organisational systems, control is exercised by the use of information. Most managers do not see the actual operations and rely on information about the activities that have taken place in order to be able to exercise control. It is this fact which makes formalised information systems so essential, particularly for operational and tactical level management.

Information Equivalents

Much of the information used in organisations represents the tangible inputs and outputs of the system i.e. it may be termed the information equivalents of the physical items and activities.

It is these information equivalents, usually represented by dockets, vouchers, forms, telephone messages, goods received notes, VDU displays, computer printouts etc. that provide the raw material for the information systems which are used for planning and control. For example, a production system may be represented as shown in Figure 12/11.

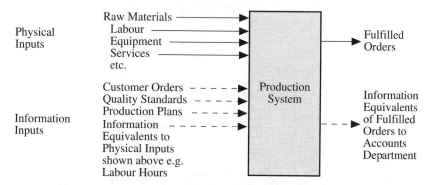

Figure 12/1 Information equivalents

Basic Elements of Control Cycle

Control is the activity which measures deviations from planned performance and provides information upon which corrective action can be taken (if required) either to alter future performance so as to conform to the original plan, or to modify the original plans.

The elements of the control cycle are:

(a) A standard specifying the expected performance. This can be in the form of a budget, a procedure, a stock level, an output rate or some other target.

(b) A measurement of actual performance. This should be made in an accurate, speedy, unbiased manner and using relevant units as measures. For example, time taken, £s spent, units produced, efficiency ratings and so on.

(c) Comparison of (a) and (b). Frequently the comparison is accompanied by an analysis which attempts to isolate the reasons for any variations. A well known example of this is the accounting process of variance analysis.

(d) Feedback of deviations or variations to a control unit. In an organisational context the 'control unit' would be a manager. This type of feedback is 'single loop' feedback which is described more fully below.

(e) Actions by the control unit to alter performance in accordance with the plan.

(f) Feedback to a higher level control unit regarding large variations between performance and plan and upon the results of the lower level control units actions. This is 'double-loop' feedback which is described more fully below.

Feedback Loops

Control is exercised in organisational systems by feedback loops which gather information on past performance from the output side of a system, department or process, which is used to govern future performance by adjusting the input side of the system.

Systems theory gives special names to certain parts of the control and feedback cycle – illustrated in Figure 12/2 and explained below.

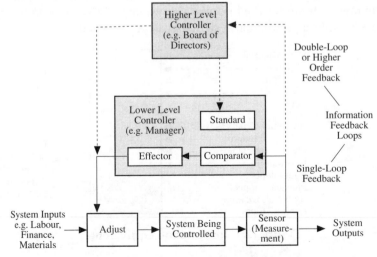

Figure 12/2 Control and feedback cycle

Sensor

These are the measuring and recording devices of the system. In mechanical systems this is some form of automatic metering but in organisational systems the usual sensor is some form of paperwork. Care must be taken to ensure that the sensor is appropriate for the system, is sufficiently accurate and timely and does not introduce bias.

Comparator

This means the way in which the comparison of actual results and the plan is achieved. Typically in information systems this is done by a clerk or by a computer program.

Effector

In an information system the usual effector is a manager or supervisor acting on the report containing the results of the comparisons and issuing the instructions for adjustments to be made.

Single-loop Feedback

Single-loop feedback, usually expressed simply as 'feedback', is the conventional feedback of relatively small variations between actual and plan in order that corrective action can be taken to bring performance in line with the plan. The implication of this is that existing performance standards and plans remain unchanged. This type of feedback is that associated with the normal control systems at operational and tactical levels. Examples include; stock control, production control, budgetary control and standard costing. At lower levels these systems are closed in that they do not interact with their environment, and relatively mechanistic in that the performance standards do not change.

These systems are the first to be computerised and frequently include automatic decision making. Figure 12/3 shows an inventory control system which is a typical operational level control system using single-loop feedback. The diagram shows the distinction between information flows and the movement of physical stock items.

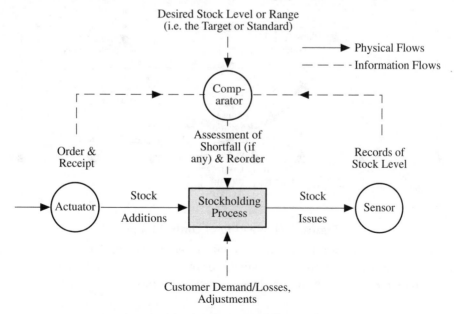

Figure 12/3 Feedback in stock control

Double-loop or Higher Order Feedback

This is a higher order of feedback designed to ensure that plans, budgets, organisational structures and the control systems themselves are revised to meet changes in conditions. Ross Ashby maintains that double-loop feedback is essential if a system is to adapt to a changing environment and, as already pointed out, adaptability is the primary characteristic of organisations that survive. The business environment abounds with uncertainties – competitors' actions, inflation, industrial disputes, changes in tastes and technology, new legislation. The monitoring of trends and performance, so that appropriate adjustments can be made to plans, is likely to be more productive than the rigid adherence to historical plans and budgets which were prepared in earlier and different circumstances.

Although single-loop feedback always appears in lower level control systems, the arguably more important higher level feedback is often omitted or at best is fragmentary. The effect of this is that the organisation as a whole is less adaptable and responds less quickly to changing conditions. A common example of this is a stock control system which continues to use re-order levels and re-order quantities which are inappropriate for current conditions, with the result either that there are excessive stocks, which have to be financed, or stocks run out completely causing a loss of sales. Higher level feedback, which is designed to monitor the performance of the lower level control systems, should avoid this problem.

Note: Although for simplicity only one higher level feedback loop has been shown in Figure 12/2, in reality there are numerous levels of feedback as each control system nests within a higher level system. Links must be designed into these nests of systems so that a higher level system can resolve the conflicts and exceptions of its lower level systems and feed down information on changes in plans and standards to the lower levels. Figure 12/4 illustrates the nesting of control loops commencing with the control of material within an activity as an example.

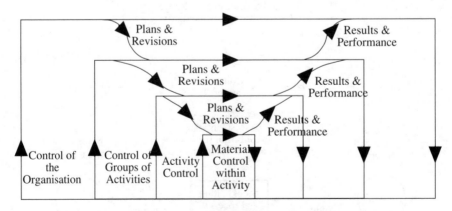

Figure 12/4 Nesting of control loops

The timing of information flows and of control decisions differs from level to level. In general at the lowest level there is the need for more or less immediate information and decision making whereas at higher levels, weekly, monthly and longer review periods are more effective. As an example, reviewing quality on an automatic production line needs to be done minute by minute whereas reviewing the performance of the factory as a whole is likely to be done on a monthly or quarterly basis.

Negative Feedback

Feedback which seeks to dampen and reduce fluctuations around a norm or standard is termed negative feedback. The corrective action would be in the opposite direction to the error. For example, production quantities above the plan would cause action to be taken to reduce production levels by altering some of the inputs – the amount of materials, labour and other resources. Many types of operational and tactical level control systems use negative feedback in order to ensure that operations and activities conform to plans. Examples include; inventory control, budgetary control, standard costing and production control.

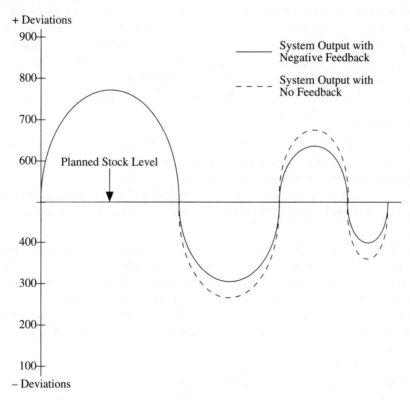

Figure 12/5 Negative feedback in oscillating system

Because the action of negative feedback tends to smooth out fluctuations such systems are inherently more stable and are more likely to conform to norms and standards. For example, Figure 12/5 illustrates the effect of negative feedback in an oscillating system, (i.e. where the system fluctuates between positive and negative deviations from standard).

A fully self-regulating system which was held exactly between desired limits would be termed a *homeostatic system*. Such regularity is possible with some mechanical or biological systems but, although organisational control systems using negative feedback are homeostatic in character, they are far from being perfect homeostats. Disturbances, human unpredictability, noise along information channels, and other factors make organisational control less than an exact science, particularly at higher levels.

Closed Loop Systems

The system of feedback loops described so far, where control is an integral part of the system and where feedback, based on output measurement, is fed back to make appropriate alterations to the input, is a closed loop system.

Many mechanical systems e.g. governors on engines, thermostats in heating systems, are totally closed loop systems. Business systems containing feedback control loops integrated with the system, are essentially closed loop systems although influences other than output monitoring can affect decisions. A typical closed loop business example is a stock control system with a planned level of stock. The actual stock levels are measured and compared with the plan and adjustments made to the stock replenishment order quantities to bring stock levels in line with the plan. Most operational and tactical level control systems use closed loops. By its nature this type of control is best suited to more stable conditions where existing plans and targets continue to be appropriate, and where there are clear-cut quantifiable standards against which to compare output results.

Open Loop Systems

In contrast, open loop systems are where no feedback loop exists and control is external to the system and not an integral part of it. Control action is not automatic and may be made without monitoring the output of the system. An example is an immersion heater without an automatic thermostat. Control is therefore not an integral part of the system and the heater must be externally controlled by switching it on and off at appropriate times.

At operational levels in organisations it would be rare, and somewhat dangerous, to have a system which did not have some form of automatic control built in, but some of the effects of open loop systems may occur if, for example, there was a breakdown in communication in a production control system whereby the measurements of output were not communicated in time to make the necessary adjustments to production inputs. Thus the feedback control loop would not exist for a time and the effect of an open loop system would be achieved. Also a department without a budgetary control system lacks the essential elements of a feedback control loop and control (e.g. by reduction of staff or expenditure limitations) may have to be exercised from outside the department.

At higher levels, especially where the environment is unpredictable or turbulent, management intervention becomes essential and thus open loop systems become necessary.

The key point is the appropriateness, or otherwise, of the plans and targets presently incorporated in the control system. If it is thought that these will be of continued relevance in the future and current variations are relatively small, then the more automatic closed loop system would be preferred. Alternatively, where more adaptation is required, scope for management intervention must be incorporated into the control system and an open loop used.

Positive Feedback

Positive feedback causes the system to amplify an adjustment or action. Positive feedback acts in the same direction as the measured deviation, that is it reinforces the way the system is moving, if this is thought beneficial. As an example, if variances from standard were favourable, positive feedback would encourage this tendency. Positive feedback would not be incorporated in an automatic, closed loop system and requires managerial intervention via an open loop system. Unplanned positive feedback, perhaps caused by excessive delays in producing information, can cause system instability and loss of control.

Planned positive feedback is a feature of systems experiencing growth or decline which thus require plans to be changed to deal with the new circumstances. As an example, a firm might launch three new products and make plans for equal advertising expenditure and production levels. If soon after launch, one of the products was found to be much more popular than the others, positive feedback would be needed to enhance production of the popular ones. In contrast a negative feedback system – if mechanically operated – would attempt to bring all the products back in line with the original, and now inappropriate, plans.

Timing of Control Action

Control action is likely to be most effective when the time lag between the output and corrective action – via the information loop – is as short as possible. Not only will the control action be able to commence earlier but it will be more appropriate. Too great a time lag may cause the resulting control action to be the opposite of what it should be.

Figure 12/6 shows the effect of time lag in control actions, which transforms what should be negative feedback (i.e. damping oscillations) to positive feedback (i.e. amplifying oscillations).

Two factors which influence the speed of control are the organisational structure and the reporting period. If an item of information has to pass through several levels of the organisation's hierarchy before effective action can be taken then there will inevitably be delays.

Peter Drucker has said that decisions should always be made at the lowest possible level, consistent with the nature of the decision and as close to the scene of action as possible. Effective control and organisational protocol may thus be in conflict.

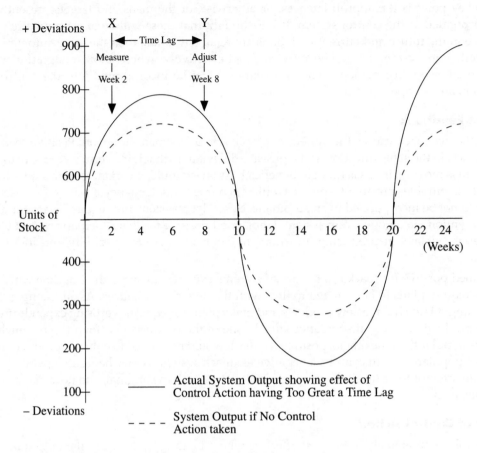

Point X. Measurement — Above Standard and Rising.

Point Y. Adjustment — As Consequence of Measurement at Point X.
Adjust in Downward Direction

(Note that system at Point Y is already moving downward. Adjustment, because of Time Lag, Exaggerates Oscillation)

Figure 12/6 Timing of control actions

There is a tendency for some types of control information, for example budgetary control and standard costing reports, to be produced in accordance with conventional accounting periods – monthly or four weekly – for all levels in the organisation. Because of the procedures involved, such reports are frequently not available until halfway through the next period and consequently much of the information is out-of-date and is misleading as a guide to action.

There is no complete answer to this problem but there should be recognition that the most effective control period is not necessarily the same as an accounting or calendar period such as a week, or month or year. At lower levels in the organisation rapid feedback of a relatively restricted range of matters is likely to be more effective, whilst at higher levels there is less immediacy. Organisations where decentralisation is practised have shorter communication lines and control information. Hence control action, is more immediate and is likely to be more effective.

Research into formal managerial control systems, especially budgetary control, indicates that they are by no means as effective as top management and information specialists would like to believe. Many managers considered the control systems to be ineffective and virtually ignored the reports and statements produced by the systems. The studies showed that there were five main reasons for management's failure to use the information provided:

- Subjects covered were outside the manager's control.
- The information arrived too late for effective action to be taken.
- Insufficient detail was provided.
- The information supplied was thought by the manager to be inaccurate.
- The information was provided in a form which could not be understood.

The first two factors were by far the most important so repay close attention by information specialists.

Delays in the Control Cycle

There are various types of delay in the plan-decision-control cycle, all of which may cause problems. Four types of delay were identified by Forrester in 'Industrial Dynamics', shown in Figure 12/7.

In small organisations or in fully decentralised larger organisations, decision and implementation delays can be minimised. However even in such organisations information delays can create problems and cause inappropriate decisions and control actions to be taken. Contrast the likely delays in the planning/control cycle for a one-man business and a typical large organisation such as a local authority or car manufacturer.

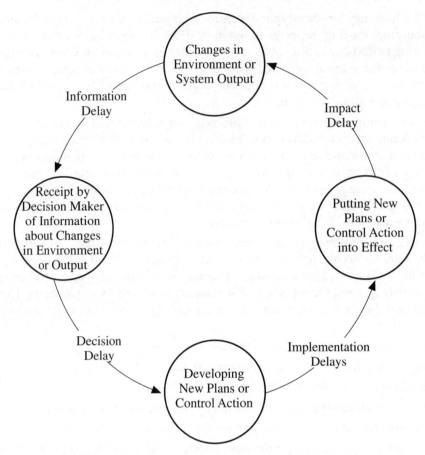

Figure 12/7 Major delays in planning/control cycle

Control Systems and Reward Structures

The targets and levels of performance which are developed at the planning stage are used subsequently during the control process to monitor performance and to provide guidance as to the corrections required, if any. Performance targets should be set so that goal congruence is encouraged i.e. the employee is given the maximum incentive to work towards the firm's goals. Control is effective when it induces behaviour which is in accord with achievement of the firm's objectives as specified in the plans. Where the organisation's reward-penalty system is consistent with the control systems there is evidence from Stedry, Arrow and others, that goal striving behaviour is encouraged.

The reward-penalty system of an organisation is the whole range of benefits and advantages which can be offered to, or withheld from, an employee. Typically these could include: promotions, wage and salary increments, bonuses, share options, profit sharing, company cars and other 'perks', holidays and so on.

If the control system is seen to be unconnected to the reward-penalty system of the organisation it will be perceived to be of little importance by the managers concerned and consequently it will tend to be ignored and so, by inference, will the organisation's objectives.

The incentive element discussed above is but one of the behavioural aspects of control systems, albeit an important one.

Concentration of Control Effort

The full control cycle – continual monitoring of results, comparisons with plans, analysis of variations and reporting – is an expensive and time consuming process. Accordingly it is important that the effort is concentrated where it can be most effective such as areas of high expenditure, vital operations and processes, departments whose objectives are vital elements in the fulfilment of overall objectives and other similar areas.

A good example of this is the use of Pareto analysis (sometimes called ABC analysis or the 80/20 rule) in stock control. It is commonly found that 20% of the items account for 80% of the total inventory value and accordingly the major control effort would be concentrated on these items and correspondingly less time spent on detailed analysis and control of items which have insignificant values. The application of this simple concept is, of course, much wider than just inventory control and its use makes it more likely that control activities will be cost effective.

Law of Requisite Variety

Complex systems such as commercial and industrial firms, public authorities and other types of organisations contain a large number of elements and pursue a range of objectives. The law of requisite variety, discussed by Beer, Ashby and others, states that for full control the control system *should contain variety at least equal to the system it is wished to control*. The effect of this is that relatively simple control systems, for example budgetary control, cannot be expected to control the multi-faceted activities of a complex organisation. At best such control systems may only control a relatively narrow aspect of the organisation's activities.

A major source of the disturbances and variations in organisations is the influence of external variables upon the achievement of the firm's objectives. Many of these external factors are non-controllable so would not be included in a conventional control system which concentrates on controllable internal factors. However where external factors interact with internal variables it is necessary to include them in the overall control system in order that the interactions can be monitored. Examples of external factors which, although uncontrollable by the organisation, are likely to make changes necessary within the organisation, are a sudden increase in advertising expenditure by a competitor or the introduction of a discount campaign by a competitor.

The effect of this law is that closed feedback systems will only be suitable for simple, structured applications because only in these circumstances will it be possible for there to be enough pre-determined control actions to match all possible control conditions. In more complex and uncertain circumstances effective control will only be achieved by open loop feedback systems where managerial intervention is needed to generate enough control variety to meet the unexpected conditions which will inevitably arise.

Feedback and Control Example

To bring together the concepts covered so far, a diagram (much simplified) of a typical production system is shown in Figure 12/8.

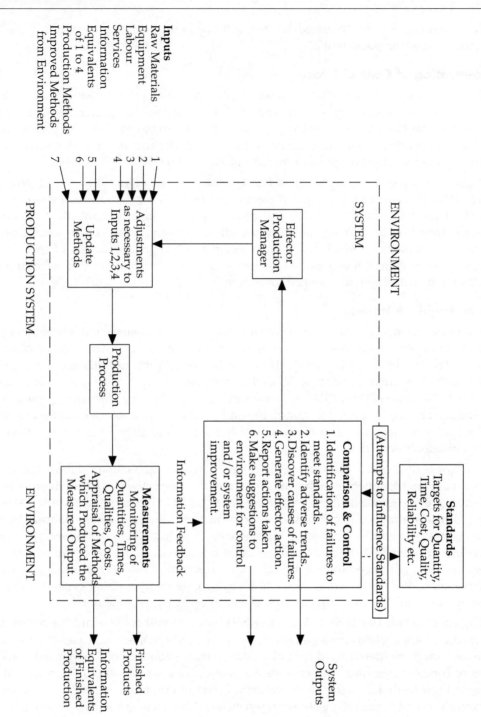

Figure 12/8 Feedback and control in a production system

Feedforward

Close examination of any real system such as a private or public sector organisation will show that there are two types of control loop; feedback loops which monitor past results to detect and correct disturbances to the plan and feedforward loops which react to immediate or forthcoming dangers by making adjustments to the system in advance in order to cope with the problem in good time. In any organisation it is unlikely that pure feedforward or pure feedback control would operate in isolation. Feedback control on its own may be too slow and feedforward control too risky,so that some balance between the two is desirable.

> Feedback monitors the past. Feedforward looks ahead.

Figure 12/9 shows an outline of the two types of control.

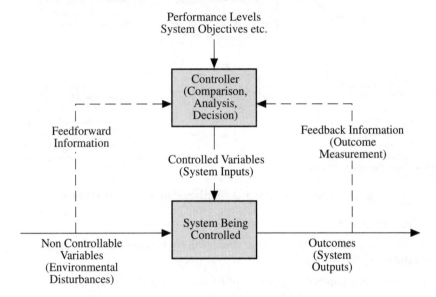

Figure 12/9 Feedforward and feedback loops

Feedforward uses flair and insight and relies heavily on information about the environment to anticipate critical changes in the non-controllable variables before they have an effect on the system. Feedforward is open-loop and does not feed back through the process as does closed-loop feedback control. The ability to sense impending problems and to take prior corrective action, which is the essence of feedforward control, are also the hallmarks of successful managers and businessmen.

Examples of Feedforward

Practical examples of feedforward include; news of political instability in a country which was a major supplier of an important rare metal would cause astute buyers to buy before prices went up and their own stocks were depleted (in contrast a pure feedback system would not react until stocks had actually fallen), or a company hearing of a possible industrial dispute would make alternative production arrangements, such as sub-contracting or engaging non-union labour, in advance of the withdrawal of labour.

Figure 12/10 provides an example of feedforward and feedback in a marketing system.

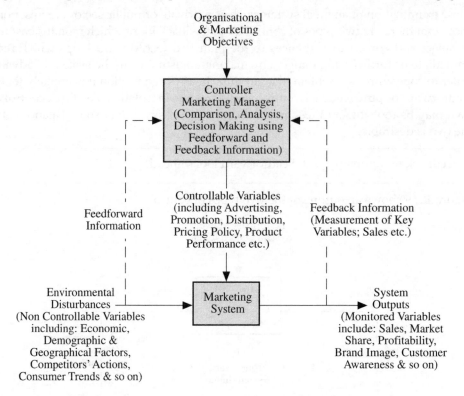

Figure 12/10 Feedforward feedback in a market system

Key Point Summary

- Control is a monitoring process undertaken to ensure that operations proceed according to plan or that the plans are reviewed.

- In organisations control is carried out using information.

- The basic elements of control are: a plan, measurement, comparison, feedback of variations and actions, if necessary.

- Single-loop feedback is feedback of relatively small variations from plan.

- Double-loop or higher order feedback is designed to ensure that the plans, structures and control systems are revised if necessary.

- Negative feedback dampens fluctuations around a norm.

- Closed-loop systems are those where control is an integral part of the system.

- Open-loop systems are where no feedback loop exists and control is external to the system.

- Positive feedback causes the system to amplify (not dampen) a deviation.

- Delays in the control cycle cause difficulties.

- Control effort should be directed where it can be most effective (80/20 rule).

- The law of requisite variety states that the control system should contain as much variety as the system to be controlled.

- Feedforward loops react to environmental disturbances in order to make adjustments to the system.

Self Review Questions

1. Define control.
2. Why is information so important in management control?
3. What are the basic elements of control?
4. What is a feedback loop and what are its components?
5. Describe single and double-loop feedback.
6. What is negative feedback?
7. What are the differences between closed and open loop systems?
8. What is positive feedback and why can it be dangerous?
9. Why is the timing of control actions important?
10. What delays are possible in the control cycle?
11. Why should the control system be consistent with the reward?
12. What is Pareto analysis?
13. Why is the law of requisite variety important in control systems?
14. What is feedforward and why is it important?

13 Control in Organisations

Objectives

After you have studied this chapter you will:

- understand the problems of achieving control in organisations.
- be able to distinguish between operational and managerial control.
- know how the organisation's MIS can assist operational control.
- understand that management control must include behavioural factors.
- know how requisite variety is applied in practice.
- be able to describe the scope of management control.
- understand why many operational control systems produce adverse reactions.
- know some of the ways that behavioural problems can be avoided.
- recognise the changing style of control required to deal with modern conditions.
- understand Total Quality Control and Total Quality Management.

Control in Organisations

Having covered the general principles of control it is now necessary to examine the particular characteristics of control systems at various levels in the organisation. There are two broad categories of control:

(a) **Operational control.**

As the name suggests, this takes place at the operational level of the organisation and is a structured, repetitive form of control with pre-determined rules and procedures.

(b) **Management control systems.**

These are procedures and systems which induce people to behave in ways that will ensure that top management policy decisions are put into practice throughout the organisation down to and including the level of operations. The management control process spans all three management levels merging into operational control at the lower end, through the tactical level and up to the strategic planning level. It follows from this that there is more than one level of management involved, ranging from people above supervisors up to top management.

The broad characteristics of these two categories of control are shown in Figure 13/1 from which it will be seen that management control occupies a broad, intermediate position acting as a bridge between strategic planning and day-to-day operations.

Operational and management control are developed in the paragraphs which follow.

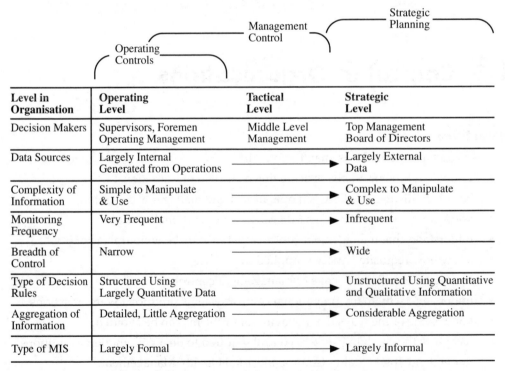

Level in Organisation	Operating Level	Tactical Level	Strategic Level
Decision Makers	Supervisors, Foremen Operating Management	Middle Level Management	Top Management Board of Directors
Data Sources	Largely Internal Generated from Operations	⟶	Largely External Data
Complexity of Information	Simple to Manipulate & Use	⟶	Complex to Manipulate & Use
Monitoring Frequency	Very Frequent	⟶	Infrequent
Breadth of Control	Narrow	⟶	Wide
Type of Decision Rules	Structured Using Largely Quantitative Data	⟶	Unstructured Using Quantitative and Qualitative Information
Aggregation of Information	Detailed, Little Aggregation	⟶	Considerable Aggregation
Type of MIS	Largely Formal	⟶	Largely Informal

Figure 13/1 Characteristics of operating and management control

Operating Control Systems

These systems occur at lower levels of the organisation and are based on unambiguous, clear data of a quantitative or financial nature. The decision rules are predetermined and these systems lend themselves to computerisation. A typical example being a computerised inventory control system where reorder levels, reorder quantities and other control levels are calculated automatically according to precise rules. By their nature, operating controls are repetitive and short term and often use quite complicated formal models but ones which tend to be mathematically or logically certain. Managerial interventions in such control systems are, and should be, few in number. If continued intervention is necessary to deal with non-standard conditions, it is likely that the process is not repetitive or predictable enough to operate as a closed loop automatic system.

The setting up of operating control systems requires considerable technical skill and advice from functional specialists, such as statisticians, operations research analysts, accountants, industrial psychologists, is invariably required.

H.A. Simon has neatly summarised the characteristics of operating controls and his summary is given in Figure 13/2.

Control-related traits

1. Control system is a rational system
2. A set of logical rules is relied upon
3. It focuses on a single task or transaction
4. Basic disciplines employed are economics and physical sciences
5. Scope is precise and narrow
6. Guided by pre-established procedures and decision rules
7. It often uses mathematical models
8. Decisions are not judgement-based, though decision rules are
9. Control is repetitive
10. Control is stable, predictable and prescribed
11. Short-run current perspective is predominant

Data-related traits

1. Data used for control are real time and current (or on line)
2. Data are exact and accurate
3. Units of measurement are monetary and non-monetary
4. Data are collected and reported daily, hourly etc
5. Data are internally generated
6. Data are detailed and less aggregated
7. Cost data are engineered
8. Other measurements are mechanical or technical
9. Reports are in the nature of 'attention directing' and 'score card'

Figure 13/2 Characteristics of Operating Controls

Examples of Operational Control Systems

Any sizeable organisation contains many operational control systems which are based on functional division and sub-division of tasks. Some typical examples within major functional areas are as follows:

*   Production operating control systems include; stores control, work scheduling, job/process control, procurement control and so on.
*   Sales and Marketing operating control systems include; invoicing, delivery, warehousing, packaging, order processing, inventory control and so on.

- Personnel operating control systems include; safety, security, pay-roll, timekeeping, staffing and so on.
- Accounting operating controls include; pay-roll, ledger keeping, credit control, standard costing and so on.

All these and other similar systems generate vast volumes of routine data and a developed, formal MIS is needed to ensure that there is effective information processing and that continuous monitoring of results occurs. The MIS at this level needs to deal with:

- *transaction processing.* This includes the keeping of files, recording day-to-day movements (i.e. weights, volumes, cash flows, labour and materials usage), producing transaction summaries and balances.
- *production of control reports.* Typically these reports show actual results and trends compared with standards or targets. They are often produced on a regular basis but the use of new technology (computer networks, video displays etc) means that now they are often available on demand.
- *handling enquiries.* Efficient operations require information to be quickly (or instantly) available about status, availabilities, balances, times, stocks, deliveries and numerous other factors.

Management Control Systems

Management control attempts to influence or control behaviour to ensure that strategic policy is implemented and strategic objectives are achieved.

Management control systems are complicated and attempt to control numerous factors as compared with the single or limited number of factors with which operational control systems deal.

The word 'control' in management control has a broader meaning than merely monitoring results in order to bring them into line with the original plan. In many cases the aim of the management control system is to help managers to review the plans and to assess the operation of, and targets contained within, the lower level operational control systems. The double loop or higher level feedback described earlier is a necessary part of the input to the managerial control system.

A further extension of the management control process is that it is concerned with behavioural factors as well as quantitative performance levels. Managers need to show leadership, encourage cooperation, develop motivation, be aware of personal aspirations, resolve conflicts and consider numerous other behavioural factors in order to develop goal congruent behaviour i.e. where the employees objectives coincide with organisational objectives.

At this level, control systems must consider a wide range of factors, both long term and short term, otherwise they will not be truly effective. For example if only a single simplified target, such as return on investment, was to be monitored then it is feasible for a manager to achieve this in the short term by storing up troubles for the future. He might for instance, reduce maintenance, stop training, fail to re-equip, curtail product development and research and so on. This point is developed in the next paragraph.

Multiple Control Factors

In order to control the complexities of management behaviour, the information system should provide both quantitative and qualitative information, gleaned from external and internal sources, about numerous facets of the manager's responsibilities. The traditional control system is financially orientated and whilst the profit factor is important, especially in the long term, there is general recognition that it is only one facet of the management task. Profit is relatively objective and is easily measurable whereas some of the other factors are less so. Numerous organisations have attempted to deal with this problem and one of the pioneers was the General Electric Company of America.

General Electric identified eight key result areas which are summarised below.

- Productivity
- Personnel development
- Profitability
- Market position
- Product leadership
- Employee attitudes
- Public responsibility
- Balance between short- and long-term goals

Within each key area various performance targets were established and a manager would be expected to achieve a satisfactory performance level across all eight facets. A high score of profitability would not compensate for poor performance elsewhere.

Non-quantifiable Control Factors

Even in areas which are conventionally thought difficult to assess, General Electric laid down criteria. Take, for example, the area 'Personnel development'. Personnel development is concerned with the systematic training of managers to fill present and future manpower needs to allow for both individual development and organisational growth. The quality of the programme offered by the General Electric department was appraised by informal interviews covering the staff's views on; selection, periodic performance reviews, training available and so on. Also a manning audit was taken annually to assess how well the department could fill its own promotional needs by examining the preparation and training of each manager and the amount of internal and external training undertaken. Finally a ratio was devised of the number of people actually promoted to the number deemed promotable in the department.

Personnel development and other parts of a manager's task are long term in nature and if no attempt is made to measure performance in such areas, a manager might be tempted to ignore them and merely concentrate on a short term factor such as profitability.

It will be seen that the General Electric system was a conscious attempt to introduce 'Requisite Variety' into the control system.

Even at operational levels there is awareness that a single control factor cannot satisfactorily monitor the richness and diversity of any operation. J.G. Miller carried out an international survey to find out what performance measure were used to control and monitor production in Europe, the United States and Japan. The key results are summarised below.

Performance measures listed in order of importance

	Europe	United States	Japan
1	Outgoing quality	Incoming quality	Manufacturing leadtimes
2	Unit manufacturing costs	Inventory accuracy	Direct labour productivity
3	Unit material cost	Direct labour productivity	WIP turnover
4	Overhead costs	Manufacturing leadtimes	Incoming quality
5	On-time deliveries	Vendor leadtime	Vendor leadtime
6	Incoming quality	Set-up times	Indirect productivity
7	Direct labour productivity	WIP turnover	Material yield

Multiple control factors in the public sector

Public sector organisations are equally complex and face a similar range of control problems to those in a typical private sector company. As an example, when in 1988 the government accepted a report from the Civil Service Efficiency Unit that free-standing Agencies should be set up to carry out specific activities, they were faced with the problems of controlling the Agencies. The main objective of the programme, called the Next Steps initiative, was to bring about better performance in the provision of Central Government services. It was realised that to manage better and to improve reporting there was a need for more comprehensive and timely information on all aspects of performance, not just financial performance.

To date over 150 Agencies have been established employing over 450,000 people. There is an enormous range of functions and size. For example, the Social Service Benefits Agency employs approximately 65,000 people whereas the Historic Royal Palaces Agency employs approximately 330. It was decided that performance would be monitored and controlled across four broad headings.

- Financial performance
- Volume of output
- Quality
- Efficiency

Within these broad headings targets are set specifically related to the activities, services or products of the particular Agency and control exercised by comparing actual performance with the targets.

Examples of targets set by the Agencies under the four headings are shown below.

Area	Target	Agency
FINANCIAL PERFORMANCE	Full cost recovery plus unit cost targets	Civil Service College, Central Office of Information and others
	Commercial revenue to offset costs	Met Office
OUTPUT	Number of tests performed	Vehicle Inspectorate
	Number of course days provided; number of students taught	Civil Service College
	Arrange 1.3 million placings (16 per cent long-term claimants; 2.4 per cent people with disabilities; 34 per cent inner city unemployed)	Employment Service
QUALITY OF SERVICE		
(a) Timeliness	Same-day clearance for Social Fund crisis loans	Benefit Agency
	Time to handle applications	Passport Office, Vehicle Certification Agency and others
	Time to issue patent search reports	Patent Office
(b) Quality of product	Proportion of course evaluation indicators in top categories	Civil Service College
	95 per cent of work completed to time and to standards	Military Survey
	Number of print orders delivered without fault	HMSO
(c) Availability	All documents to be available within five days of receipt	Companies House
	23,000 additional basic scale maps available	Ordnance Survey
EFFICIENCY		
(a) Efficiency/economy	Percentage reduction in price paid for stationery and paper	HMSO
	20 per cent reduction in the cost of common services over five years	Patent Office
(b) Unit cost	£20.89 for a car test	Driving Standards Agency
	£472 per productive professional day	Occupational Health Service

Uncertainty and Adaptability

The manager has to deal with multiple goals, a changing environment, personal inter-relationships, conflicts and unpredictable responses to his decisions and control actions. As a consequence management control systems cannot be closed-loop, structured systems typical of those at the operational level. They must allow for creativity and judgement and use both informal and formal information sources. The formal MIS of the organisation are a vital support for the manager but they are not sufficient in themselves.

As an example, computer-based simulation models enable managers to assess risk, explore inter-relationships, test the likely effects of decisions and control actions and so on whilst at the same time allowing managers to apply their own judgement to the problem. Mechanistic optimising formulae and rules which produce a single 'best' answer are likely to be of limited value in volatile conditions.

Although clear cut guidelines and types of control system can be specified for operational control (for example an inventory control system) there is no one best approach or system that can be specified for management control. The complexity and amount of change means that the control system must be designed to suit the circumstances; which is known as a 'contingency approach'.

Scope of Management Control

Management control is concerned with present performance and future objectives and can be sub-divided into different functional areas such as:

(a) Financial Management Control

(b) Production Management Control

(c) Research and Development Management control

(d) Marketing Management Control

(e) Personnel Management Control

Within each of these areas there are numerous activities which need to be monitored and controlled. As examples, typical responsibilities and activities within the Financial and Personnel areas are given below.

Financial Management Control includes:
- All types of budget activity – formulation, monitoring, evaluation of financial and operating budgets.
- Working capital management – cash flow, debtors and stocks.
- Capital expenditure decisions for replacement and enhancement.
- Performance evaluation for profit and investment centres.
- Assessment of accounting operational controls.

Personnel Management Control includes:
- Recruitment, interviewing and hiring.
- Training both internally and externally.
- Welfare activities.
- Remuneration and compensation schemes.
- Industrial relations activities.
- Health and Safety.
- Assessment of personnel operational controls.

The breadth and scope of the above activities should be contrasted with the narrower, defined nature of the operational controls given earlier in the chapter.

General Behavioural Aspects of Control

The attitudes of the people being controlled are of critical importance to the success of any control system. Higher levels of management may obtain feedback information and attempt to alter operations to conform to the plan, but it is the individual staff member who actually exercises control by accepting or rejecting standards, by exercising or not exercising care and other similar behaviour. It is therefore crucial that control systems are designed with due regard to this human factor.

There is a tendency, especially at operational control levels, for the control systems to be too mechanistic with a concentration on rational economic factors with social and psychological considerations being partially or totally ignored. A control system developed to cater solely for the physical aspects of the task will only be a partial system which may well cause strong adverse effects.

Research has repeatedly shown that people react negatively to threatening control systems, systems which are over rational and systems which treat people virtually as machines. Studies and research from the days of the Hawthorne experiment have demonstrated that, given suitable conditions and treatment, people have a great capacity to learn, they are loyal with an ability to work efficiently without supervision. Too often the control system is arranged to suppress these traits rather than complement them.

> Peter Drucker summed up the problem well when he said:
>
> 'So much of what we call management consists of making it difficult for people to work'.

Behavioural Aspects of Operational Control

Many operational level tasks are organised in accordance with the old scientific management concepts developed by Taylor. These include:

(a) High specialisation.

(b) Reduction of skill content.

(c) Repetition of a narrow task.

(d) Limited span of control.

(e) Close, coercive supervision.

This type of organisation with its associated 'rational' control system fulfils only lower order needs, i.e. physiological needs. Higher order needs such as recognition, achievement and fair evaluation remain largely unsatisfied. In such circumstances it is hardly surprising that the task and the control of the task, is performed unsatisfactorily. The emotional involvement of the supervisors and operatives must be considered both in the design of the task and the control system. Industrial psychologists have found that workers' satisfaction can be increased when the operational control system:

(a) provides opportunities for workers to set their own targets;

(b) shows the worker's success in the task performance; and

(c) provides regular feedback to the workers relating to their performance against target.

Adverse Reactions to Operating Controls

Controls which are perceived as threatening can result in various adverse effects such as aggression and rejection which cause lower productivity. Contrary to the view of many operational level supervisors, threat is not leadership. Leadership which encourages trust and co-operation and which uses less formal monitoring methods has been shown to achieve better results than more pressure-orientated, threatening management.

The repetitive nature of some operational tasks and the repetitive nature of the resulting controls create fatigue, frustration and monotony which may lead to lower output and more rapid labour turnover. Job enrichment and group work and more employee-centred, self regulated control are some of the ways that have been tried to alleviate these problems.

In general, operational control systems should be designed so that there is a balance between quantitative and behavioural factors. People are involved and their attitudes, needs and aspirations must be taken into account.

Behavioural Aspects of Managerial Control

To a much greater extent than at the operational level, management controls are human controls. Control originates from the individual so the successful operation of a management control system depends on the social and psychological characteristics of the people involved. Accordingly, the reports and outputs of the formal information system provide only a partial view of the control process. For example, a formal budget report would contain nothing about the bargaining, interactions, conflicts and the people involved with the production and use of the budget.

A manager's control behaviour is influenced by numerous factors and interactions which are summarised in Figure 13/3.

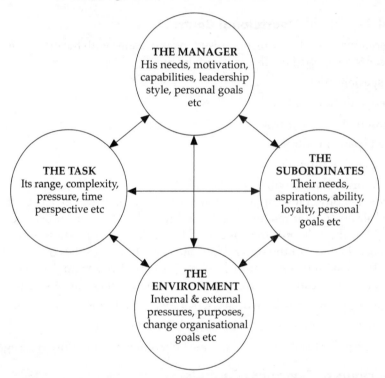

Figure 13/3 Influences on the manager's control behaviour

Dysfunctional Effects of Control

Managers operate controls and use control information in different ways so it is likely that the routine production of standardised reports across the whole of the organisation will not be ideal. The style, content and format of reports must suit the manager, who is the report user, and not the report producer. When managers use control information in a short-term, rigid fashion there is evidence that tension increases, supervisor-supervised relations worsen and dysfunctional behaviour occurs, i.e. behaviour which reduces overall efficiency. On the other hand, where control information is used more flexibly with a longer term perspective there are few, if any, unfavourable behavioural indications.

Badly designed control systems or those which are operated without regard to behavioural factors can produce various adverse effects which are summarised below:

(a) Dysfunctional behaviour may occur where the control system wrongly motivates managers to produce short term results at the expense of long term growth.

(b) Confusion of ends and means. This is where the control is taken to be the end in itself and not as a means of achieving organisational objectives. One manager may view a budget as a guideline towards achieving longer term targets and not as a constraint whereas another may consider budget compliance an end in itself.

(c) Creation of informal systems. If a control system is deemed inappropriate, managers create their own informal systems which may be unreliable, cause duplication and make co-ordination more difficult.

(d) Manipulation and falsification. Where there is excessive control pressure, manipulation of results and falsification of targets may occur.

Avoiding Behavioural Problems

The following guidelines will help to reduce behavioural problems and to produce an effective and adaptable management control system.

(a) Encourage participation in setting control objectives and in the design of the control system.

(b) Tailor the reports, level of detail and complexity of system to suit the participants.

(c) Improve and foster human contacts e.g. have meetings to discuss results and performance levels, avoid creating pressure.

(d) Reduce the information load on managers by intelligent filtering, exception reporting and careful design of reports.

(e) Humanise the information system by recognising individual needs and capabilities.

Changing Styles of Control

Traditionally, controls in organisations have been hierarchical moving from lower to middle to higher management in a regulated way. This pattern suits stable conditions where real decision making is concentrated at the top.

However, conditions are changing rapidly and organisations have to adapt. There is the need for more flexibility and local decision making. This has led to the growth of decentralised decision making and the establishment of smaller, autonomous units operating with considerable freedom and flexibility within a larger framework. Many business organisations already have, or are moving towards this style of operation e.g. Proctor and Gamble, IBM, Rank Xerox. The same tendency can also be clearly seen in the Public Sector.

In education the Local Management of Schools is being introduced. This means almost total transfer of responsibility for the running of a school from the Local Authority to the Governors of each school and the Head Teacher. This includes financial management of all expenditure, including salaries.

In a similar manner, hospitals within the National Health Service may opt for Self-governing Trust status. Trust hospitals have virtually complete control over their operations which includes bidding within the competitive market set up in the Health Service. With Trust hospitals, the 'middle management' level, represented by the District Health Authority, is bypassed and the Trust Hospital answers directly to the Department of Health. Most major hospitals have already opted for Trust status including, Guys in London and St James in Liverpool and there are now over 400 NHS Trusts.

As organisations and the style of operations change so must the style and method of control. Old report-based detailed controls passing up and down the hierarchy stifle initiative and inhibit flexibility. The solution to the problem of achieving both control and freedom is to combine tight control of performance with freedom of operation. This is described by Peters and Waterman as 'Simultaneous loose-tight properties'.

This means that individuals and units are held accountable for mutually agreed goals while being free to achieve the results as they see fit. Results and performance are controlled; methods are not. This places more reliance on individuals and encourages initiative. Operating units become self managing organisations which are are innovative and adaptable.

The effectiveness of another feature of traditional control systems, that of post-event monitoring, is increasingly being questioned. Take for example, labour cost control. Typically, labour costs are collected and at the end of a period an assessment is made as to whether the labour is being used effectively and costs controlled. However, there is growing awareness that the factors which influence labour costs are mainly determined at the planning stage i.e., the investment decisions about the equipment and methods to be used. Once these earlier decisions have been made labour costs are effectively prede-termined and so traditional post-event 'control' is largely illusory.

Proper planning is thus the best method of control. This philosophy has been fully accepted by the Japanese particularly in the all important area of product quality. Take an automatic pop-up toaster as an analogy for a production system. If, from time to time, the toaster pops up burnt toast the traditional Western approach, called Quality Control, was to set up an elaborate recording system to record the number of burnt slices and then a rectification system to scrape them. The Japanese approach is to fix the toaster.

Total Quality Control (TQC)

Advanced Manufacturing Technology (AMT) and Just-in-Time (JIT) systems have a total quality control philosophy in which the only acceptable quality level is zero defects. There is strong evidence that high product and/or service quality is directly linked to long-run success. Examples include; Japanese cars and consumer electronics, Mercedes cars, Marks and Spencer etc. In consequence, control systems relating to quality and the creation of a 'quality culture' are of paramount importance to all organisation.

The most important first step is to realise that quality cannot be inspected in; it must be designed in. Quality is not something which is solely the concern of inspectors at the end of the production line.

The following are the key points at which TQC must operate:

- *Product design*
  Probably the key stage. Product design should have price, performance, ease of manufacturing and quality in mind throughout the design stage. An important factor is simplicity; fewer parts preferably of standard design. Product designers should also liaise closely with manufacturing and process engineers. A well designed product not only works well, it is easy to manufacture. During the design stage the technique of *value analysis* is used extensively. This the systematic examination of cost factors in order to devise ways of achieving the specified purpose, most economically, at the required standard of quality and reliability.

- *Production engineering*
  This is the process of designing the methods for making a product to the design specification. This also includes the tools and processes to be used, the tolerances and finishes required, assembly sequences and so on.

- *Manufacturing*
  Manufacturing considerations must be part of product design because it is estimated that only 20% of quality defects can be traced to the production line. The other 80% being attributable to design factors or poor purchasing. In JIT systems the responsibility for defects has moved away from quality control inspectors to the operatives. Operators are expected to maintain their equipment and produce zero defect output. They are, of course, aided in this by CNC machines and automatic equipment which often incorporates computerised gauging and measuring devices. In addition there is extensive use of Statistical Process Control and Control Charts.

  JIT systems emphasise in-process checks rather than waiting until the product is fully completed before it gets a final inspection. This was the traditional method and is still widely used even though it is a less efficient system.

  (Note: Statistical Process Control and Control Charts are covered in detail in *Quantitative Techniques* by T. Lucey, DP Publications.)

- *Goods inwards*
  The quality of output depends on the quality of input materials. This means that quality requirements are also imposed on suppliers to ensure quality and no inspection is performed on incoming supplies.

- *Output inspection*
  Final inspection is being replaced by in-process checking. Final inspection, based on sampling does still take place mainly to satisfy management that quality control in production is being maintained.

When TQC is properly applied and the incidence of defects decrease, total manufacturing costs, including warranty and service costs, decrease.

This is not surprising because if items are made correctly first time money is saved from the avoidance of detection, reworking, scrapping, repairing in the field and so on.

> *Higher quality* means *lower costs.*

Total Quality Management (TQM)

TQM is where there is a defined culture of quality awareness and quality improvement in every process, in every department and at every level in the organisation. Organisations practising TQM have a long-term commitment to quality and consider quality to be a core value of the organisation. They take an *external* view of quality as compared with the traditional Western *internal* view.

The internal view of quality concentrates on ensuring that items produced conform to their specification within accepted tolerances. This view considers that quality costs money and, as production costs must be minimised, quality factors are always limited by their cost. On the other hand the external view, pioneered by the Japanese, places much more emphasis on the original design which the customer ordered. This view considers quality as the heart of the production process where every part will be fit for its purpose and will be right first time. With this philosophy there is emphasis on continual improvement of the product and *preventing errors* rather than relying on post-production inspection to reject faulty items and to correct mistakes. One of the American consultants who greatly influenced the Japanese acceptance of TQM, Joseph Juran, showed that over 80% of failures in production were attributable to management and stressed that management should deal with the *causes* of production problems rather than the short-term concentration on the *symptoms*, which is all too common.

William Edwards Deming, another of the pioneering Americans who advised Japanese industry, advocated a total quality approach as well as changes in other management practices – a number of which have still to be accepted fully in the West. Key points advocated by Deming include:

- The organisation, at all levels, must accept and practise their commitment continuously to improve customer satisfaction.
- Quality improvement must be embedded in the organisation's culture from top to bottom.
- Aim for constant improvement in products and processes.
- Provide adequate training and equipment and encourage pride in their own work and the product.
- Encourage cooperation and teamwork and develop trust throughout the organisation.
- Encourage self-improvement and education at every level.
- Choose suppliers for quality and reliability rather than price.

Deming had an enormous influence on Japanese industry and can be credited with much of its post-war success. Deming Awards for Quality are given each year in Japan and his portrait has pride of place in Toyota's headquarters. He died in December 1993.

Quality Circles are another facet of the total quality approach which originated in Japan and are spreading to the West. Quality circles are small groups which meet regularly to discuss matters such as productivity, safety and quality. The idea is to develop and implement improvements directly at the work-place. The circles select their own leaders and are seen as a practical way of delegating real powers to employees and of achieving grass-roots participation.

The benefits of Quality Circles include:

- improvements in commitment, motivation and confidence.

- increased awareness of shop-floor problems
- improvements in quality, productivity and safety.

A feature of TQM is that closer links are forged between top management and shop-floor operators. Operatives are encouraged to take more decisions and accept more responsibility. As a consequence, middle management and the formal structures that go with layers of management are being reduced or eliminated.

Professor Handy estimates that over one million middle management positions have disappeared in the USA over the last ten years. The same process is also taking place in Europe.

Many forward looking organisations in the West are adopting a total quality approach. These include service and government organisations as well as manufacturers. As an example, consider Brent London Borough Council. Brent are carrying out a radical overhaul of their management practices. The operations of the Council are to be carried out by some 80 'business units' with substantial powers of decision-making devolved to the lowest possible level. Coupled with the authority to make decisions there is also the need to be accountable for the decisions. Integral to this radical overhaul is a Total Quality Programme which is shown in outline in Figure 13.4 on the next page.

In the UK, national encouragement to improve quality systems is provided by the British Standards Institute, especially BS 5750.

British Standard 5750 (BS.EN.ISO 9000)

BS 5750 applies to all types of organisation and a wide variety have obtained accreditation. These include; travel agents, solicitors, transport firms, tyre and exhaust fitters, local government as well as numerous manufacturers.

BS 5750 seeks to encourage organisations to develop quality management systems and its award provides public recognition that organisations have reached certain standards. BS 5750 is not a product or service testing system, nor does it set specific quality standards. It concentrates on checking whether there is a framework of procedures, systems and records throughout the organisation relating to quality.

To become accredited under BS 5750 the organisation has to satisfy external assessors that it has the main elements of a quality system. These include:

- There must be adequate documentation to support the quality systems across the whole organisation including; customer specifications, product routeing, control and test procedures etc.
- There must be a designated senior manager with the responsibility of ensuring BS 5750 requirements are met.
- Records are required to ensure that customer quality requirements are being met.
- There must be written control of the quality systems to be applied by suppliers and procedures for inspecting and testing incoming goods.
- there must be effective internal quality audit systems and appropriate statistical techniques for monitoring quality standards.
- Quality systems must be planned and developed across all functions in the organisation with adequate resources, equipment and training.

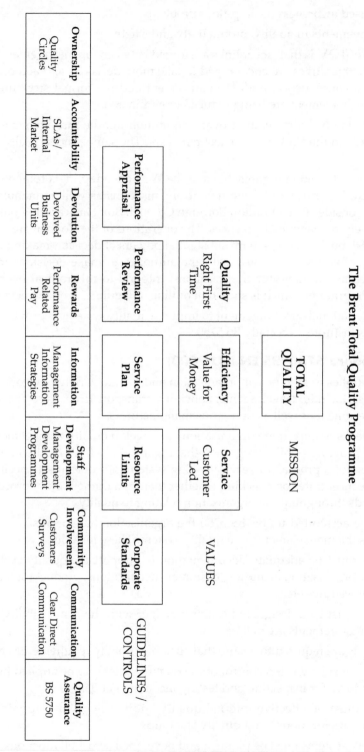

Figure 13/4 (Source: *Certified Accountant,* **March 1993)**

BS 5750 is clearly a major step in promoting the idea that quality is everyone's responsibility and increasingly Government suppliers are required to have accreditation. However it should be pointed out that the Standard, and the voluminous records and manuals associated with it, has received some criticism for being over-bureaucratic and encouraging 'paper-compliance'.

During 1994 BS 5750 and the corresponding European Standard EN.ISO 9000 underwent searching re-appraisals. Following these it was decided that all the European Standards should be brought together into one common standard to be known as BS.EN.ISO 9000 Series which, from 1995, superseded BS 5750.

Planning and Control Example

To bring together the chapters on planning and control an example of the inter-relationships found in one company are shown in Figure 13/5 on the following page.

The example is based on a medium sized company in the North West of England. The firm makes control equipment bought mainly by machine tool manufacturers and firms using assembly line techniques. Although each job is individual there is a high degree of standardisation and the firm have rationalised components and sub assemblies so there is considerable commonality. The diagram shows only the main inter-relationships and information flows and the major inputs and outputs to the environment. The diagram follows a rough time scale. Longer-term at the top moving progressively down to day-to-day operations at the bottom.

Key Point Summary

- Control in practice can be categorised into operating and management control.
- Operating control systems are clear and unambiguous and management intervention should be rare.
- Management control systems are more complicated and attempt to control numerous factors including behavioural ones.
- Research has emphasised the importance of behavioural factors in control and has shown that people act adversely to mechanistic threatening controls.
- To a large extent management controls are human controls.
- Dysfunctional effects can occur when the control system wrongly motivates managers, concentrates on short term factors and where ends are confused with means.
- Modern control systems concentrate on results, not methods.
- Good planning is the best control.
- Total Quality Control aims for zero defects.
- High quality must be designed in.
- Total Quality Management is where there is culture of quality awareness and improvement throughout the organisation.
- BS 5750 (ISO 9000) accredits organisations which fulfil the main elements of a quality system.

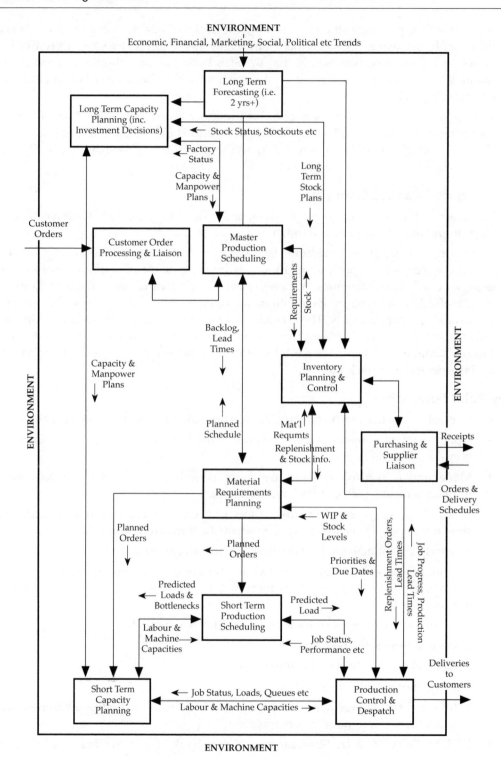

Figure 13/5 Manufacturing Planning & Control Example

Self Review Questions

1. Explain the differences between operational and managerial control.
2. What are the characteristics of operating control systems?
3. What is the meaning of 'control' in 'management control'?
4. What multiple control factors did General Electric identify?
5. Give examples of management control.
6. Why is it important to consider the behavioural aspects of controls?
7. What are the causes of adverse reactions to operating controls?
8. What factors cause dysfunctional effects in managerial controls?
9. How can behavioural problems be avoided in management control?
10. What is 'simultaneous loose-tight control'?
11. What is Total Quality Control?
12. Describe Total Quality Management.
13. What are the main features of BS 5750 (ISO 9000)?

Assessment and revision section

Assignments

1. Find out the policies of two organisations on matters such as race, colour, religion, the environment etc. and contrast them. What evidence can you find that the official policies are implemented in practice?

2. Carry out a SWOT analysis on yourself (try to be honest!). Get a friend to do a SWOT analysis on you independently. Compare the results.

3. Find examples of management by exception being used in practice. How are exceptions recognised? Does the procedure aid management control?

4. In an organisations known to you, find two examples each of strategic, tactical and operational level decisions. What are the key information needs for each decision?

5. Find a practical example of each of the following:

   (a) Negative feedback

   (b) Higher order feedback

   (c) Feedforward

6. An organisation is considering the purchase of a sophisticated, high-volume photocopier. List the factors which would need to be considered before a decision was taken.

7. Find out what organisations in your locality are accredited under BS 5750, (ISO 9000).

8. Empowerment is the process of pushing decision making lower down the hierarchy of the organisation. Try to find an example in practice and details of how this is working, what training was given and whether service has been improved.

Mini-case 1 – Decision Tree

A company is considering whether to launch a new product. The success of the idea depends on the success of a competitor in bringing out a competing product (estimated at 60%) and the relationship of the competitor's price to the firm's price.

Table A shows the conditional profits for each set of prices by the company and its competitor.

Table A (£'000's)
Competitors Price

Company's Price	Low	Medium	High	Profit if no Competitor
Low	30	42	45	50
Medium	21	40	45	70
High	10	30	53	90

The company must set its price first because its product will be on the market earlier so that the competitor will be able to react to the price. Estimates of the probability of a competitor's price are shown in Table B.

Table B (£000's)
Competitor's price expected to be

If company prices	Low	Medium	High
Low	0.8	0.15	0.05
Medium	0.20	0.70	0.10
High	0.05	0.35	0.60

Task 1 Draw a decision tree and analyse the problem.

Task 2 Recommend what the company should do.

Task 3 Consider what other information the company should try to find out.

Mini-case 2 – Setting a Target Selling Price

Japanese manufacturing companies use radically different methods to set selling prices than their Western counterparts who frequently use a form of cost-plus based on existing engineering standards.

The Japanese process is market driven and starts with a specification of what features the new product should have. A target selling price is set based on market research, into which is incorporated the profit margin specified in the strategic plans of the firm. The differences between the two represents the 'allowable cost' for the product which is usually well above the currently achievable cost. As product design proceeds, value engineering and redesign takes place in a continuous cycle until the target cost is reached. The process is shown in Figure MC1 on the next page.

Task 1 Classify the information used into internal and external.

Task 2 Explain the key differences between the Japanese approach depicted and that traditionally used in the West.

Task 3 Describe the main decision points in the Japanese system.

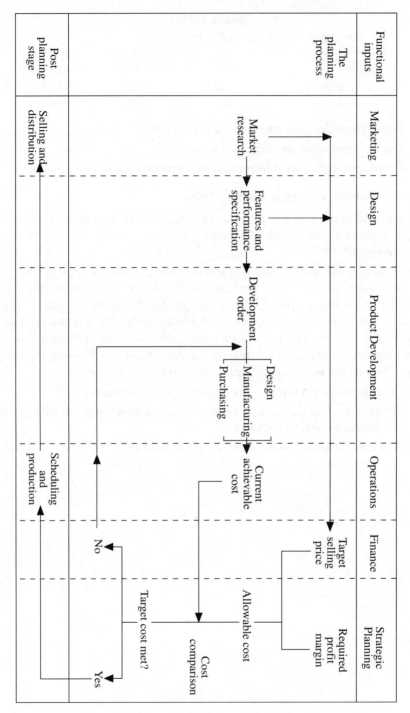

Figure MC1 Setting a target selling price

Mini-Case 3 – Reorganisation of a Service Department

Three years ago, a small customer service unit was set up within a large computing organisation, CSL. Their brief was to contact every customer purchasing computers and software to offer help and advice in setting-up the desk-top systems and tailoring the software to the customer's own specific needs.

The unit had five employees reporting to the head of the unit John Brady. The unit has been very successful and has gained a large amount of business, not only from CSL's own customers but from customers of other computing companies who have been recommended to them.

Now there are 25 people in the unit with everyone working long hours using little of their holiday entitlement. Morale however is high. Everyone really enjoys the challenge and the varied nature of the work. Each member of the unit helps out other members where necessary and the quality of the work done is extremely high, hence their high reputation. John Brady however knows that there are problems. Some potential customers have not been able to get through to anyone in the unit because everyone was out working. Now a clerical assistant is employed to take the phone calls and look after the paperwork.

Some jobs have taken a lot longer than first thought, meaning others have been left for a time.

Customers are scattered throughout the UK and in order to understand exactly the customer's requirements, each has to be visited several times.

John Brady is a great believer in teamwork and it has worked well until now. However, with 25 staff it is more difficult to ensure that everyone knows what everyone else is doing and team meetings are almost impossible to arrange as people are never in the office at the same time.

John knows something must be done to ensure that their high reputation is kept intact yet is worried that morale and motivation may fall if the unit is organised more formally.

You are asked to assume the role of an independent consultant brought in by John Brady to write a confidential report on how things might be improved.

Your report should deal with:

(a) *organisational problems*

(b) *operational issues*

(c) *management issues you consider to be relevant.*

You should, where appropriate, make recommendations for change.

ACCA

Examination Questions (with Answers)

A1. Your organisation is considering the use of a computer based financial model to enable it to evaluate the financial consequences of different courses of action.

You are required to prepare for presentation to the Treasurer a report which briefly answers the following questions:

(a) What is a model?

(b) What procedures are involved in constructing a model?

(c) What advantages are there in using a computer-based model in comparison with the existing manual budget procedure?

CIPFA

A2. Information can be classified into various categories depending on the purpose intended. Within a typical commercial or industrial organisation one possible scheme provides for three-way classification: planning information – operating information – control information. Studies in such organisations show that there are many difficulties associated with the production and use of information, particularly that relating to planning and control, and that in extreme cases the information produced by formal management information systems is virtually ignored by managers.

You are required to:

(a) describe the characteristics of each of the three information classifications given above.

(b) discuss the difficulties associated with the production and use of planning and control information.

CIMA

A3. Why is it necessary for companies to establish and periodically review their objectives. What objectives should a business aim to achieve?

CIM

A4. The processes of corporate appraisal, corporate planning and strategic management require specific inputs of information in order to be effective.

What information inputs are needed for the purposes of corporate appraisal, corporate planning and strategic management? Illustrate your answer with appropriate examples.

ACCA

A5. A major function of an information system is to provide the people within an organisation with information to assist the decision making process.

Discuss the theoretical foundation of each of the following three factors which should be taken into account when designing an information system.

(a) Timeliness of information.

(b) Retrieval and presentation of information.

(c) Centralised and decentralised information stores.

CIPFA

A6. It is conventionally assumed that there are three levels in the organisation at which decision making takes place.

You are required to:

(a) define briefly the three levels;

(b) describe the characteristics of decision making at the different levels;

(c) give an example, for each level, of the type of assistance or information a computer-based management information system could supply to aid decision making.

CIMA

A7. A company operates a stock control procedure which has the essential feature of a closed-loop system, comprising:

i. stores, dealing with the physical receipt, holding and issue of materials.

ii. a stock control office which:
- is supplied with copies of goods received notes, requisitions and return to stores notes;
- maintains stock records;
- establishes parameters for stock and re-order levels, incorporating future usage data from the production control department;
- originates purchase requisitions as required;

iii. a purchasing department

You are required to draw an outline flow chart of the system described, showing the necessary major information flows and linkages. Identify on your chart the three points in the system which function as sensor, comparator and effector.

CIMA

A8. In organisations where a computer-based MIS is being introduced the natural human tendency to resist change can result in dysfunctional behaviour.

(a) In what ways might such dysfunctional behaviour manifest itself?

(b) How can the systems analyst try to overcome such behaviour?

CIMA

A9. The management process depends upon the effective operations of a variety of different controls.

What are the principles upon which any management control system or procedure is based? Illustrate your answer with appropriate examples.

ACCA

A10. Describe and compare Theories X, Y and Z as styles of management. To what contingencies may the choice of management style be subject?

ACCA

A11. The planning department of the L company has identified environmental changes which will affect the L company during its next planning cycle as follows:
- Barriers on transfer of goods and services across national boundaries within the EC will be removed.
- As a result, the L company's competitors will be doubled from four to eight.
- The L company's market will be tripled in size.
- Consumers will have a greater choice.
- Changes in consumer demand will be more frequent and rapid.
- Customers and regulatory agencies will be using languages other than English.
- Sex discrimination on pensions and retirement will be prohibited.

You are required to describe the impact these environmental changes will have

(a) on the managers;

(b) on the staff.

CIMA

A12. A work colleague has been asked to give a presentation on the differences between strategic, tactical and operational planning. You have been asked to help as your colleague knows very little about planning. Write briefing notes for your colleague explaining what each type of planning involves, giving *one* example of each.

ACCA

A13. Your new manager knows that you are studying organisations. She would like to know more about some of the theories on job satisfaction. Write her a set of briefing notes on the main factors associated with job satisfaction.

ACCA

Examination Questions (without Answers)

B1. Discuss how the corporate objectives of a local authority differ from those of a typical commercial organisation?

B2. Indicate the ways in which the process of long-term planning and policy making could be considered to be analogous to the application of general systems theory. Your answer should include definitions of 'long-term planning and policy making' and 'general systems theory'.

B3. 'You can't forecast the future so corporate planning is a waste of time'. Discuss.

B4. Identify the stages by which an 'objectively rational' person would make a decision. Critically examine the assumptions on which this model of decision making is based.

B5. It is generally accepted that effective management is impossible without information. You are required to:
   (a) define information;
   (b) discuss the characteristics of information that assists the key management functions of planning, control and decision making; and
   (c) describe how to assess whether it is worthwhile producing more information for use in a particular decision.

CIMA

B6. In defining the basic principles of management, textbooks often list planning and control as two separate and distinct functions. How far can they be regarded as independent of one another?

CIB

B7. Describe the basic principles by which the enterprise can monitor and control its operational performance. Illustrate your answer with appropriate applications of these principles.

ACCA

B8. Martin is a team leader who has been trained in the concept of Professor Adair's Action-centred Leadership.

He has been very successful in creating a well-integrated, highly-motivated team by devoting most of his management effort to team building and to ensuring that the team is clear about its goals. He has sheltered the team from adverse outside influence, promoted its image, encouraged open communication and established regular meetings and other group events.

The team is now faced with an unexpected task. This not only has to be completed to a tight dead-line, but also involves certain skills which none of the team members possesses, although some have the background to enable them to acquire these skills quickly.

You are required

(a) to describe briefly action-centred leadership;

(b) to recommend how Martin should change his leadership behaviour to cope with the new situation.

CIMA

B9. The over-riding feature of information for decision making is that it should be relevant for the decision being taken. However, decision making varies considerably, at different levels within an organisation, thus posing particular difficulties for the management accountant.

You are required

(a) to describe the characteristics of decision making at different levels within an organisation;

(b) to explain how the management accountant must tailor the information provided for the various levels;

(c) to give an example of a typical management decision, state at what level this would normally be taken and what specific information should be supplied to the decision maker.

CIMA

B10. (a) Define and distinguish between:

(i) structured, semi-structured and unstructured decisions

(ii) operational, tactical and strategic control.

(b) Suggest a classification by type of decision and type of control for each of the following information systems:

(i) accounts receivable

(ii) warehouse location

(iii) budget preparation

(iv) new plant construction

(v) inventory control

(vi) loan approval

(vii) executive recruitment

(viii) research and development planning

(ix) short-term forecasting.

(c) A decision support system has been implemented by a landscape and garden maintenance company. Part of the system is designed to report on unusual problems reported by the various work crews. Some problems, such as a dying tree, may be important and require attention as soon as possible. This may mean reassignment of crews and extra expenses in terms of equipment, chemicals, etc.

(i) Briefly describe the three phases which are commonly considered to make up the decision-making process and identify which phase in the part of the decision support system referred to above is being supported.

(ii) Explain how the decision support system described might support the two phases of decision-making that you did not identify in part (c)(i) above. State any assumptions necessary about the company.

ACCA

B11. In the second half of this century, the classical Approach to management has, in some industries and many organisations, been replaced by the Human Relations Approach. Other parts of society, and other organisations, have not adopted the Human Relations Approach, or have been reverted to the earlier concepts.

(a) Compare the contrast Classical and Human Relations Approaches to management.

(b) Give reasons why some organisations may use one or the other approach in present-day conditions.

CIMA

B12. The work in business organisations is often broken down into functional area such as marketing, production and finance.

(a) What are the main activities of each of these functions?

(b) What are the merits to the organisation of dividing into functional areas? Can you see any problems of these divisions?

ACCA

Additional Reading

1. Davis and Olson, *Management Information Systems*, McGraw Hill

2. Anthony, *Planning and Control Systems*, Harvard UP

3. Simon, *The New Science of Management Decision*, Harper and Row

4. Lucey, *Quantitative Techniques*, Letts Educational (formerly published by DP Publications)

5. Lucey, *Management Accounting*, Letts Educational (formerly published by DP Publications)

6. Beer, *Decisions and Control*, Wiley

7. Parker and Case, *Management Information Systems*, McGraw Hill

8. Peters, *Thriving on Chaos*, Macmillan

9. Avison, *Information Systems Development*, Blackwell

14 Information Technology and MIS

Objectives

After you have studied this chapter you will:

- be able to define Information Technology (IT).
- know the major applications of IT for information systems.
- understand the key features of Office Support Systems.
- know the features of text handling, telecommunications and data transmission.
- understand the main steps in defining information systems that are to be computerised.
- know how to draw Data Flow Diagrams.

What is Information Technology?

There are few aspects of life nowadays which are unaffected by IT. In the office, factory or at home, visiting a bank, supermarket or garage and in many other places IT is used to carry out transactions, provide information, record data, make decisions and perform an every increasing range of tasks.

A useful definition of IT is given by the Department of Trade and Industry:

> 'the acquisition, processing, storage and dissemination of vocal, pictorial, textual and numeric information by a micro-electronics based combination of computing and telecommunications'.

Because this book is about management information systems in organisations, emphasis will be given to the administrative use of computers and telecommunications. This means that some major and important applications of IT are outside the scope of this manual. Examples include; robotics, industrial process control, computer aided design and manufacture (CAD/CAM) and scientific uses of IT.

Background Computer Knowledge

This chapter is about the use of computers in information systems and is not about computers themselves. Accordingly there will be no attempt to explain what computers are, the ways that they work, the nature of their component parts or how they process and store data.

It is assumed that readers will be familiar with the more common terms associated with computers. Examples include; hardware, software, files, VDU, disk storage, terminal, program, packages, printers, on-line. Readers unfamiliar with these terms or who wish to study computers in more detail are advised to study a comprehensive book on the subject, for example, 'Data Processing and Information Technology' by CS French, DP Publications Ltd.

Are Computers Essential for MIS?

The short answer to this questions is, not essential but they can be very useful. The study of MIS is not about the use of computers, it is about the provision and use of information relevant to the user. Computers are one – albeit important – means of producing information and concentration on the means of production rather than the needs of the user can lead to expensive mistakes. There is undoubtedly an important and growing role for computers and IT in MIS but the technology must be used with discretion. As economist Robert Solon has pointed out we see computers everywhere but in the productivity statistics. This point is emphasised by Nobel Prize winner James Tobin who shows that productivity growth actually slowed in the developed world around 1973 and has not recovered despite the subsequent massive investment in information technology.

Computers are good at rapid and accurate calculations, manipulation, storage and retrieval but less good at unexpected or qualitative work or where genuine judgement is required. It has been suggested that computers can be used to best advantage for processing information which has the following characteristics:

(a) a number of interacting variables

(b) speed is an important factor

(c) there are reasonably accurate values

(d) accuracy of output is important

(e) operations are repetitive

(f) large amounts of data exist

These characterisitics can be related to the needs of the various management levels as shown in Figure 14/1.

Information Characteristics	Presence in Management Information		
	Operational Level	Tactical Level	Strategic Level
Interacting Variables	Frequent ⟶		Always
Speed Important	Usually ⟶		Rarely
Data Accuracy	High ⟶		Low
Output Accuracy	Always ⟶		Rarely
Repetition	Usually ⟶		Rarely
Data Volume	High ⟶		Low

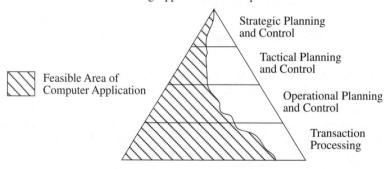

Resulting Application of Computers

Feasible Area of Computer Application

Strategic Planning and Control

Tactical Planning and Control

Operational Planning and Control

Transaction Processing

Figure 14/1 Feasibility of computer application by management level

The unshaded area of Figure 14/1 represents unstructured problems and decisions where human involvement is essential. The division between computer and human tasks is constantly changing. As software and hardware develops and organisations gain more skill in using computers, tasks previously requiring managerial expertise and judgement become worthwhile computer jobs.

An example is the now widespread use of 'credit scoring' in banks. An applicant for a loan fills in a detailed questionnaire and the answers are input into a computer. The program carries out a series of checks and tests and decides whether or not the loan should be granted. Previously all loan applications required a managerial decision which is now needed only for unusual requests, large loans or industrial applications.

Despite some well publicised success stories it remains true that IT has had the greatest impact at operational and tactical levels. A survey by PA Management Consultants on New Information Technology (NIT) found:

> ... firms largely ignoring NIT other than at operational levels e.g. 45% reported that NIT had made little or no impact on their activities and that 39% had no defined strategy for innovation or application of NIT in the next 5 years.

When contemplating the introduction of IT the reactions of users and the people affected by the system must be considered. In general people dislike change and can feel threatened by new systems especially those that use technology with which they are unfamiliar. There is inertia and consequently a slower rate of acceptance of new IT based systems than system designers of IT manufacturers like to acknowledge. For example there have been repeated forecasts that the use of credit and debit cards, 'smart' cards and 'electronic purses' will bring about a cash-less society. However a research study in 1993 by Girobank and Research Surveys of Great Britain found that the everyday use of cash had actually increased over the past few years and that over 85% of payments in retail outlets were made in cash with over £19 billion of cash in circulation. Furthermore over 80% of those polled predicted that there would be little or no change to their personal use of cash over the next 5 years.

IT and Information Systems

Although the boundaries between them are blurred it is possible to distinguish three major areas of application of IT in information systems. These are

1. Office Support Systems
2. Data Processing (or transaction processing)
3. End User computing

These categories overlap and inter-relate and are summarised in Figure 14/2 and developed in the chapters which follow.

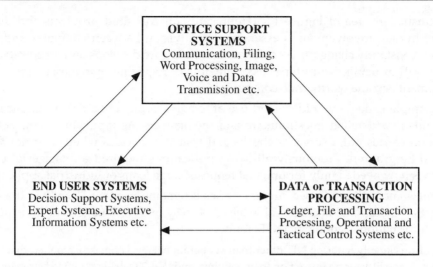

Figure 14/2 IT and information systems

Office Support Systems

Micro-electronics and telecommunications are in the process of transforming office work. In turn this is influencing the availability and type of information that managers use.

Figure 14/3 provides an overview of the main developments in Office Support Systems which are then briefly outlined in the paragraphs which follow.

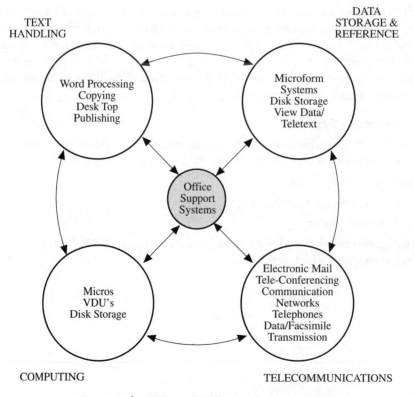

Figure 14/3 IT based office support systems

Although sub-divided into areas for instructional purposes there is no real dividing line between the systems. For example, several micro-computers may be linked through a communication network which allows access from numerous points to the organisation's records maintained on disk storage and so on.

Text Handling

Word processors are now a common feature in most offices. A word processor can either be a stand-alone or dedicated word processor or a general purpose micro-computer utilising a word processing program. In either case the software enables the typed input to be displayed on the VDU, altered or manipulated at will and then transferred to the printer any number of times or stored on disk for future use. Word processors are invaluable for producing 'individualised' standard letters or for lengthy reports which require extensive editing and revision, but less necessary for short one-off letters. They can improve productivity dramatically whilst at the same time improving quality. More modern systems have numerous editing, indexing and referencing features and can be linked with the organisation's computer system.

Photocopiers have become more flexible and in addition to the routine copying of office paperwork, the more modern machines have become miniature printing systems whereby high quality reports and booklets, including colour and graphics, can be produced within the office.

Developments in software and laser printers have enabled the growth of *Desk-Top Publishing (DTP)*. DTP systems are versatile word processors with extensive layout and graphic facilities which enable good camera ready copy to be produced using high definition laser printers. Traditional type setting is thus eliminated. This means that professional quality sales literature, reports, books and other documentation can be produced 'in-house'.

DTP Systems combine text and graphics from other programs. The finished page can be made to resemble any magazine, book or brochure with rulings, boxes and frames emphasising blocks of text. DTP systems require high quality graphics software, the use of a mouse for ease of relocating text and diagrams round a page and a good quality laser printer. An essential element is WYSIWYG (What you see is what you get). This means that what appears on the VDU screen should exactly represent the page being made up.

Data Storage and Referencing

The ability to store and access vast volumes of data is an undoubted benefit of IT in organisations. Routinely the organisation's files, maintained on disk backing storage, are accessed using desk top VDUs and terminals. This facility is invaluable for current operations and for internal information, but where there is the need for repeated reference to information in a visual form then either computer output on microform (COM) or Document Image Processing can be used.

Computer Output on Microform (COM)

Microforms are photographically reduced information on files of which there are two main types:

(a) microfilm – 16mm roll film

(b) microfiche – sheet film

Computer output on tape or disk is fed into a machine called a microform recorder which reads the tape or disk and copies the data onto microforms. The information can subsequently be seen using a viewer which projects the contents of the microform onto a screen. Full size copies can be printed if desired. Reference and archive material is ideally suited to COM; examples being the systems used in libraries, garages and stores.

Document Image Processing (DIP)

DIP is a form of electronic filing. A document is passed through a scanner, translated into digital form and a digitised image is then stored electronically, perhaps on an optical disk. Some DIP systems allow the stored documents to be used in other office systems. The main advantages of DIP systems include:

- space saving
- faster retrieval
- greater security
- multiple simultaneous use via terminals

A typical DIP system can store up to 60,000 pages of A4 on one optical disk.

Teletext/Viewdata

Teletext is a system for supplying commercial and other information through existing television networks. It is a form of electronic reference manual whereby 'pages' of information can be called onto the screen. There are two systems in the UK – CEEFAX (BBC) and *Teletext on Three* (previously called Oracle) provided by the independent television companies.. The systems contain largely general interest material of little value within organisations.

Viewdata is somewhat similar to teletext in that it provides electronic reference to material but there are two main differences. Firstly, it is available to subscribers only and secondly it is interactive. This means that users can interrogate the data held in the system and also supply information to it. The information contained in the system is more specific and relevant to commercial users and the system uses a combination of telephones, computers, television and communication networks.

British Telecom operate a viewdata service known as PRESTEL and there are a growing number of private systems i.e. specific to a particular group. One example of a private viewdata system is that operated by Rover who have a system whereby their dealers can find a car of a required specification if held by another dealer. The dealers can access the system and also input changes to the information contained, for example, when a particular car is sold. Another example is the information provided by airlines which can be accessed by travel agents to check flight times and availabilities and to book seats.

In the UK there are currently over 60,000 PRESTEL users many of whom are associated with the Stock Exchange and the travel and insurance industries.

The take-up of Prestel has been limited in the UK but elsewhere similar systems have achieved spectacular success.

A viewdata system called Minitel was launched in France in the early 1980s. Today there are 6.5 million Minitel terminals in French homes and offices and over 15,000 enterprises selling services on Minitel. These include electronic banking, travel and holiday reservations, permanent news access, games, shopping and access to databases. The success of the system is largely due to two early marketing decisions; to present it as a logical extension of the telephone (its original use was France Telecom's directory enquiries service) and initially to distribute thousands of Minitel terminals free to telephone subscribers. A fourth generation system called Télétel Vitesse Rapide (TVR) is now being installed which will run eight times faster than the original version. Apart from the facilities available to individual users, which include the use of the terminals as a fax machine, a key strategic advantage for the French is the widespread increase in computer literacy within the population. Whilst most countries are still discussing information superhighways the French have had a version working for over 12 years.

Telecommunications

The power and flexibility of IT in organisations derives from a combination of the capabilities of the individual machine and from the ways that machines are linked and combined. Some of the more important facilities which can be classed under the general heading of telecommunications are; electronic mail, voice mail, networks, tele-conferencing, data/facsimile transmission and electronic data interchange (EDI).

Electronic Mail (E-Mail)

This is a system in which messages are communicated by electronic means rather than by paper based communication. Messages are displayed on a desk top terminal and incoming and outgoing messages are filed electronically, if required. Obviously there is a considerable time saving and there is the inherent safeguard of certain delivery. A form of electronic mailing, the telex, has existed for many years but is less flexible than the newer systems for internal purposes. Electronic mail facilities are increasingly being combined with computing, word processing and telephone capabilities in one integrated work station.

A development of *e-mail* is where the sender transmits the message over the telephone network to a central computer which allocates disk storage to act as an electronic mail box for each user. Using a password for security purposes the user can then collect the message when required. British Telecom market a public service of this nature called *Telecom Gold* whereby a message is stored electronically by BT and is accessed by the subscriber using a microcomputer and a telephone. A similar service is offered by Mercury called Link 7500.

Voice Mail

These systems enable the caller's spoken message to be recorded in a 'voice mail box'. This can then be accessed by telephone by the user, say a representative or service engineer in the field. The main advantage is cheapness but the system does not allow two-way conversations which are, of course, possible using mobile telephones or radio links.

Networks

Networks are communication systems which link together computers, storage devices, word processors, printers and even the telephone system of the firm. Within the one organisation, especially on one site, networks are known as Local Area Networks (LAN) and these networks allow interconnections between numbers of micro/mini-computers or between micro/mini-computers and the main processor. LANs form the vital links which allows distributed processing to take place whilst at the same time allowing users to share resources such as disks, printers and files. Network connections are essential if electronic mailing is to be used.

The key feature of a LAN is that the systems are linked by direct cables rather than by general telecommunication lines. In consequence LANs do not need *modems*. A modem is a device to convert digital signals, as used in computers, to analogue or wave form signals used in the telephone network.

When networks are extended they are known as Wide Area Networks (WANs). WANs are usually larger than LANs, cover a wider geographic area and use the general telecommunications network. They thus require modems between the terminals and computers and the telephone lines.

Finally, mention should be made of Internet, the embryonic global information network sometimes called the 'information superhighway'. With suitably powerful work stations information complete with sound and video pictures can be accessed.

At a more basic level anyone with a personal computer, a modem and a subscription to one of the many subscription services can access an enormous range of social, current affairs and reference information available on Internet and can use the world-wide E-mail facility. Although Internet is still largely an American phenomenon more and more UK material is being made available. For example, the Treasury is making Press Releases, Budget speeches and other monetary information available, Edinburgh District Council have introduced a pilot information project, Newcastle University have started Britain's first purely electronic law journal and national newspapers are making more and more information available electronically.

The most important part of the Internet as far as most business users are concerned is called the *World Wide Web*. The Web is the multi-media publishing side of the Internet. Web sites are interactive documents or 'pages' which can be called up on a computer screen and can utilise print, pictures, graphics, sound and moving images. By accessing the unique web address, users can find information about companies, products, services and even individuals. It is becoming common for advertisements, company literature and promotions to feature the Web address for people wishing further information, for example:

http://www/rac/co.uk (the Web address for the RAC)

http://www.j-sainsbury.co.uk (the Web address for J Sainsbury's)

http://www.lib.utexas.edu/Libs/HRC/WATCH (Writers and their copyright holders register)

Value Added Network Services (VANS)

VANS is a term used for the range of computer services provided by commercial companies which are used in conjunction with the telephone network or private communication networks. Examples include:

(a) viewdata services such as Prestel

(b) electronic mail (Telecom Gold, Link 7500 etc.)

(c) database systems

(d) financial information services; share prices, exchange and interest rates etc.

Tele-conferencing and Video-conferencing

An extension of conventional one-to-one telephone conversation has been the development of tele-conferencing facilities. These systems allow numerous people to be simultaneously connected so that discussion can take place even though they do not meet. This can take place either within the organisation or externally and even on an international basis. The importance of discussion and informal contact, especially for senior management, has been stressed earlier in the manual so that these newer telephone facilities could have a significant impact on management's ability to gather and assess information.

Sound only conferencing is inexpensive but has limitations e.g. identification of speakers. Video-conferencing overcomes these problems but is far more expensive and with present levels of technology requires specialist studio equipment.

In the USA over 80% of the Fortune 500 companies (i.e. the 500 largest) have or are planning to install tele and video conferencing and there is little doubt that this will become an increasingly important aspect of office automation.

Data Transmission

In the UK most data transmitted between different locations is transmitted over ordinary telegraph and telephone circuits which are capable of carrying data as well as speech. Data can be transmitted over the ordinary public telephone circuits or a private line can be hired.

Transmission is possible in three modes:

1.9 SIMPLEX – transmission is possible in one direction only.

2.9 HALF DUPLEX – transmission is possible in both directions but not simultaneously.

3.9 DUPLEX – transmission is possible in both directions simultaneously.

Where the telephone circuits are used a MODEM (MODulator/DEModulator) is required to convert digital signals (used by computers) into analogue signals (used for transmission) at each end of the line.

Facsimile Transmission or Fax

Fax allows the transmission of an exact copy of an original document including diagrams, pictures and text. It can be thought of as long distance photo-copying. Fax is a reliable, speedy method of sending duplicates and is widely used in business, government and the professions.

There have been a number of problems with Fax systems including their speed and use of special paper. Newer systems are much faster and produce high definition copies on plain paper. *PC fax* systems do not require a hard copy input to the sender's fax machine. The computer communicates directly with the receiving fax machine.

As with most IT products fax machines are being constantly developed and improved. The latest development, pioneered by Hewlett-Packard and called *Omnishare*, is for an interactive fax machine that transmits voice and data simultaneously. The machine allows people in two locations to examine a document, make corrections that are instantly transmitted as they talk and to negotiate changes over the voice link. The machine can be plugged into any telephone line and is now widely available.

Electronic Data Interchange (EDI)

EDI is computer-to-computer data interchange and so is a form of electronic mail. An important application is direct communication between the computers of different companies thus replacing traditional paper based communication via orders, invoices and so on. EDI is widely used in retailing e.g. Marks and Spencers use the Tradanet system. The use of EDI will increase especially in finance, banking and retailing.

A specialised application of EDI called Electronic Funds Transfer (EFT) is well established. EFT means that the computer user sends electronic data to his bank giving instructions to make payments or to transfer funds between accounts. EFT is used for paying suppliers, paying salaries and so on. There is an international funds transfer system known as SWIFT (Society for Worldwide Interbank Financial Telecommunications) and within the UK, interbank settlements are also made by EFT using CHAPS (Clearing House Automated Payment System).

The greater use of IT and of data transmission is affecting not only *how* work is done but *where* it is done. In America it is estimated that over 8m people now work at home using computers and data links. Alvin Tofler has coined the phrase 'electronic cottage industries' to describe this trend. In the UK, the most common term for this is Teleworking.

Teleworking

Traditionally all office work was carried out in the organisation's own premises either in large, centralised offices or dispersed throughout the organisation. This is still largely true but developments in information technology and communication networks mean that an increasing number of people are able to work from home at least for part of the week. The use of faxes, E-mail and personalised telephone numbers which enable a subscriber to be tracked down anywhere in the world mean that, with the right facilities, a person can always be in two-way contact. Teleworking is defined by British Telecom (BT) as

'working in a location that is remote from an employer or from the normally expected place of work either on full-time or part-time basis. The work generally involves the electronic processing of information, the results of which are communicated remotely to the employer, usually by a telecommunication link'.

As yet teleworking affects only a tiny minority of office workers although some fore-casters think that the numbers will increase dramatically. In reality, progress is slow and there is considerable resistance from staff who miss the personal interactions and social aspects of working with other people.

An Illustration of IT in Practice

Properly selected IT systems and computers can improve the efficiency of single admin-istrative tasks. However, even greater gains can be made when there is integration of various aspects of IT, data transmission and computing.

As an illustration of such integration consider the 1991 Population Census in Britain. A Census is conducted every 10 years and has been done since 1801. Twenty three million forms were completed on 21st April 1991 with two types of answers 'Tick Box' answers for items such as sex and marital status and statement answers for less defined information.

Figure 14/4 provides an overview of the census operation.

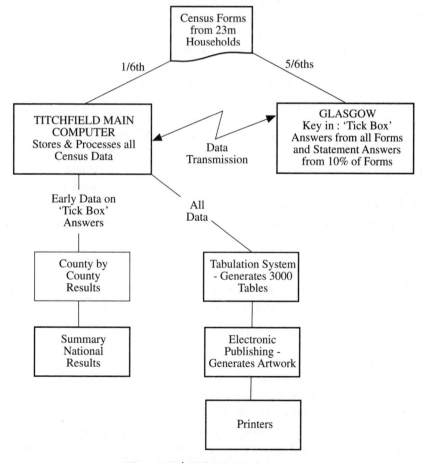

Figure 14/4 The British census

The system used electronic data transmission via the Government's own data network enabling data entered in Glasgow to be transmitted directly to the large, powerful mainframe computer at Titchfield. This process is speedier and more secure than the system used for the 1981 census which involved the transfer of magnetic discs. However, the main time saving came from the technology used to speed up publication of the 3000 tables the census generated. The table layouts were programmed well in advance and only awaited the entry of the census data. The artwork for the tables was prepared directly using electronic publishing so that high quality, camera ready copy was able to be sent straight to the printers.

Overall the system integrated numerous aspects of IT, computing, electronic publishing and data transmission to deal with a massive operation efficiently and speedily.

Computers and MIS

The previous paragraphs have outlined the role of IT in Office Support systems. It is now time to examine in more detail the use of computers in organisations.

The mere fact of using a computer does not of itself mean that work is done more efficiently or that better information is produced. Too often computers are introduced in an attempt to solve a technical problem when the real problem is one concerned with management, or lack of clear objectives, or poor coordination, or one caused by environmental change or some other factor. To gain the maximum advantage from using computers it is essential that problems are clearly identified *before* a computer system is introduced.

This means that there must be considerable investigation into management's requirements, problems, information needs and so on before there is any attempt to design a computer system. If this procedure is not followed, at best there will be additional problems during development, at worst, total disaster. An example of the latter was the cancellation in 1992 of the TAURUS system for computerising share transactions and settlement in the Stock Exchange. From the start the Taurus system suffered from bad planning, inadequate systems investigation and changing requirements culminating in total cancellation of the project at a cost of some £400 million.

In an attempt to increase the possibility of success the next few paragraphs outline the procedures necessary to develop effective information systems.

Defining Information Systems

Before deciding what computer system will be used or even whether a computer is needed it is first necessary to find out what the system must do.

The passive view says; 'We have a system, it needs improvement: lets see how this can be done'. The more radical view says; 'Never mind how we do it now, let's sort out what we want to do and see if we can develop a system to do it. Too often an existing manual system is transferred on to a computer without sufficient thought being given to its real purpose. This approach tends to produce information systems which perpetuate existing deficiencies and which swamp managers with reports which they rarely use.

The preferred approach recognises that an information system is part of a wider management system. It must provide support and assistance to management for planning, control, decision making and other functions. The preferred approach is a top down one concentrating on *what* first, then *how*, and moving to successive levels of detail. The development of an information system can be likened to the stages by which an architect designs a building.

Firstly, he receives a design brief which spells out *what* the building is expected to do. He then considers *how* to fulfil the objectives and produces a high level plan showing the overall perspective of the building. Lower level plans are then drawn each giving progressively more detail. This is a hierarchically structured approach which is also used for the design of information systems.

The overall cycle of information design is summarised on Figure 14/5 which should be read in conjunction with the notes.

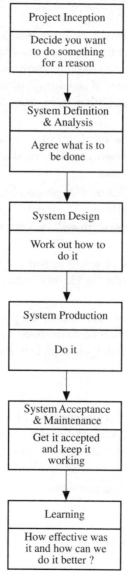

Figure 14/5 Information system development

Notes:

- *Project inception.* This is recognition and identification of a problem. It may be that an existing manual system cannot cope with processing loads, it may be that management recognised that they lack vital information or some other difficulty. This stage is firmly rooted in a management problem which the information system is intended to support. The output from this stage is a high level requirements specification.

- *System definition and analysis:* having regard to the identified management problem this stage produces an overall picture of what the required system should be. This is expressed in terms of what information is needed on files, what data will be needed for processing and what the processing must do. (Techniques such as Data Flow diagrams, dealt with later, are useful here).

- *System design:* this stage considers how best to produce the required results. Remember, the best system is the simplest one that produces the required results. It may be done by using either a manual or computer system. If a computer system, it is normal to sub-divide the overall task into linked modules. These are defined using flowcharts, decision tables and other techniques, at progressively lower levels with increasing detail.

- *System production:* this is the production of a working system which meets the requirements. If computer based it will consist of working programs, documentation, training support and so on.

- *System acceptance and maintenance:* this phase obtains agreement from the user that the system produced actually does what the user defined earlier in the cycle. Maintenance means that the system will be kept up to a desired standard i.e. it is a control mechanism.

- *Learning:* all systems become obsolete in time. When this happens the experiences, successes and failures should be closely examined so that the next time is an improvement.

The above steps provide a general overview of the process of developing an information system. In practice, especially when computerised systems are to be used, a procedure known as Structured Systems Analysis and Design Methodology (SSADM) is often followed.

SSADM

SSADM seeks to create a detailed description of a new system without the need to consider hardware or software. A logical system is developed on the basis of specific objectives which enables the system designer to determine what is required before specifying how it will be achieved. The main stages are:

- Analysis of current systems and problems
- Specification of requirement
- Selection of Technical option
- Logical design
- Physical design

It will be seen that these stages are broadly similar to Figure 14/2 except that there is less emphasis on the critical early stages of problem definition. SSADM is widely used and on the whole is better suited to tactical and operational problems i.e. those that are largely structured with well defined objectives.

One of the techniques used in SSADM, called a Data Flow Diagram, is a useful method of representing information flows and is described below.

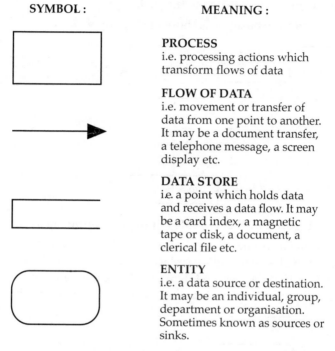

SYMBOL :	MEANING :
	PROCESS i.e. processing actions which transform flows of data
	FLOW OF DATA i.e. movement or transfer of data from one point to another. It may be a document transfer, a telephone message, a screen display etc.
	DATA STORE i.e. a point which holds data and receives a data flow. It may be a card index, a magnetic tape or disk, a document, a clerical file etc.
	ENTITY i.e. a data source or destination. It may be an individual, group, department or organisation. Sometimes known as sources or sinks.

Figure 14/6 NCC data flow diagram symbols

Data Flow Diagrams (DFDs)

DFDs represent the flows of information through a system and between the system and its environment together with the functions that must be performed. They are an effective way of defining data needs and help to clarify flows and highlight anomalies.

The advantage of DFDs is that they are independent of the method of processing and can thus be used to describe either computer based or manual systems. They use only four symbols, shown in Figure 14/6, and it is normal to commence with a high level diagram which is supported by separate diagrams each having linkages to the senior diagram and showing progressively more detail.

DFDs can also be separated into *physical* and *logical* data flow diagrams. The physical DFD is usually drawn first and is a description of how the system operates at the moment. The diagram contains physical details e.g. names of forms and individuals. When this has been done the physical details are removed to depict the logical movements. To really understand the system there must be concentration on the logical flow of information not on irrelevant details such as which form is used at present or who is currently employed in a particular post.

DFD Example

The following example will be used to show how DFDs are drawn and how lower level DFDs relate to the high level or overall DFD.

A warehouse operates a mail order business. Customers send an order, stock and credit is checked and the goods despatched to the customer.

The overview DFD for the business is shown in Figure 14/7.

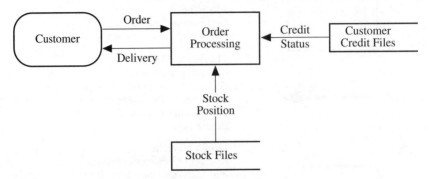

Figure 14/7 Level 1 DFD of mail order business

The next level of detail is shown in Figure 14/8. This shows the process of checking stock. If the item is available the order is placed in a 'To be despatched' file which is used by the warehouse to find the required items, pack and despatch them. At the same time the warehouse will notify accounts that the items have been despatched.

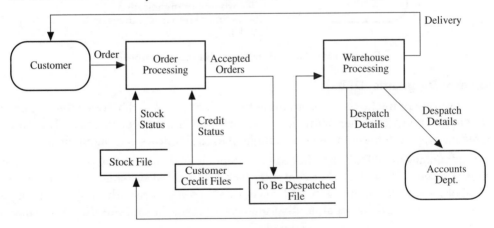

Figure 14/8 Level 2 DFD of mail order business

Figure 14/9 includes the reorder logic when an item is at or below reorder level and brings in another process (reordering) and another destination (the supplier).

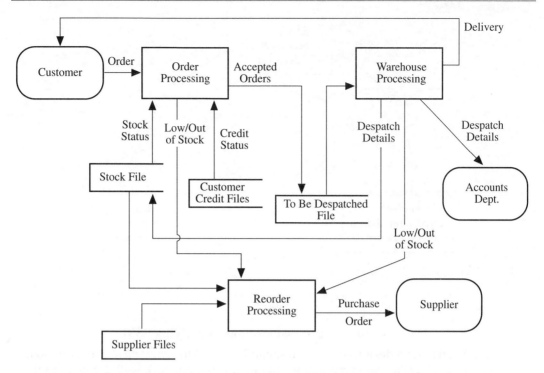

Figure 14/9 Level 3 DFD of mail order business

The process could be continued but to avoid the diagrams becoming cluttered it is normal to take each process and treat it as a sub-system for further expansion. In the above example this could be done for the warehouse processing and the reorder processing.

A variant of DFDs is what are called Decision Information Flow Diagrams. These use similar symbols but show individual decisions and the data flows which they require. This has the advantage of relating information flows to specific decisions but these types of diagram are less useful for showing how information flows around the organisation.

DFDs and their variants are useful devices for clarifying information flows and information requirement and are the best suited to structured operational and tactical decisions. They are less useful where soft issues are involved and for unstructured decisions where the information requirements are less well defined. Assistance with these aspects of systems can be provided by using Soft Systems Methodology (SSM) mentioned previously in Chapter 4.

Soft Systems Methodology (SSM)

SSM is an example of user-driven methodology developed by Checkland. It is a way of analysing unstructured and poorly defined problems in the real world. SSM recognises that change is constant and that there is no objectively verifiable 'real world'. The real world consists of an individual's derived experienced-based view which, of course, changes as actions are taken and new experiences are gained. The underlying assumptions of SSM can be depicted as shown in Fig 14/10.

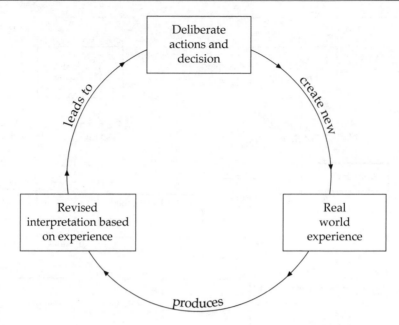

Figure 14/10 Cycle of assumptions underlying SSM

Conventional system design concentrates mainly on *how* to complete a given, previously defined task. However there are many situations where the task is ill-defined or where there are conflicting views of what task is to be done. SSM helps to resolve these problems and particularly to highlight or expose differences between individual viewpoints.

Stages in SSM

In outline the main stages in SSM are shown in figure 14/11.

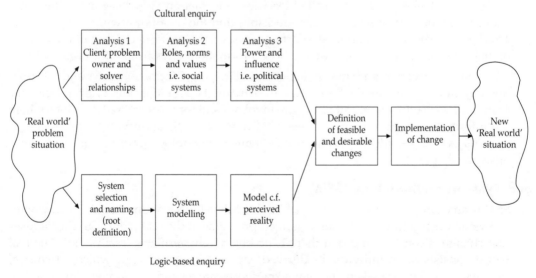

Figure 14/11 Outline of stages in SSM

The 'logic-based' path starts from the selection of a 'relevant system'. This is a subjective choice as it is never possible to identify a particular human activity system as automatically relevant to a given problem. Once the system is selected it is named by developing its *root definition*.

Root Definition

The root definition is a concise, verbal description of a system which captures its essential nature and core purpose. In forming root definitions it is necessary to ensure that six characteristics are present i.e. *who* is doing *what* for *whom*, to whom are they *answerable*, what *assumptions* are being made and in what *environment* is this happening.

A convenient way of remembering these six characteristics is to remember the mnemonic CATWOE thus:

Customer is the 'whom' i.e. the people who benefit or suffer from the system

Actor is the 'who' i.e. those that will carry out the transformation process

Transformation is the 'what' i.e. the conversion of input to output

Weltanschauung (or world view) is the assumptions behind the root definition

Owner is the answerable i.e. the people who could stop the transformation

Environment (or environmental constraints) i.e. the fixed elements outside the system

Root definitions are useful for exposing the differing views of the various people who are affected by the system. As an example the viewpoints of an habitual criminal and a prison governor would be dramatically different if asked to prepare root definitions for a prison.

The prisoner's root definition might be:

Customer	: Me
Actors	: Other prisoners
Transformation	: Improve knowledge of criminal methods and opportunities
Weltanschauung	: Crime is the only way to make a living
Owners	: Prison warders and police
Environment	: The legal system

The governor's root definition might be:

Customer	: The prisoners
Actors	: Me and the warders
Transformation	: Training and counselling
Weltanschauung	: Offenders can be rehabilitated into society
Owners	: Home Office and politicians
Environment	: Financial, political and legal pressures

The above hypothetical example obviously represents extreme positions. In practice some differences will arise and an attempt would be made to encompass one or more of the viewpoints.

After the root definition, a model of the relevant system is created. The model is an account of the activities which the system will perform. It is process oriented and seeks to ensure that the required outputs are produced efficiently and that long-term objectives are met. The model is compared with the real world not merely to establish the correctness, or otherwise, of the model but to stimulate debate as to whether changes should be made in the problem situation.

The cultural stages of enquiry studies the roles and relationships of the groups involved, the norms, values and the political (power) dimension. A tool used in this part of SSM is the *rich picture*. This is a pictorial caricature of the organisation showing such things as; the individuals and groups in the organisation, relationships, resources, conflicts, worries and constraints.

Key Point Summary

- Information technology is increasingly being used in the factory, shop, home and office.
- Computers are not essential for MIS but properly used they can be invaluable.
- Jobs best suited to computerisation are those with the following characteristics: accuracy and speed important, high data volumes, and a degree of repetition.
- The main areas of IT application are: data processing, office support systems and decision support systems.
- Office support systems cover a variety of aids including: word processing, electronic mail, data transmission, computer output on microfilm, document image processing.
- Data transmission by electronics is supplementing traditional paper based communication.
- There are Local Area Networks (LANs) and Wide Area Networks (WANs).
- Electronic Data Interchange (EDI) is computer-to-computer interchange of data.
- The purpose and objectives of an information system must be clear before designing a computer system. 'What before how'.
- Structured Systems Analysis and Design (SSADM) is a systematic method of developing a logical system.
- Data Flow Diagrams (DFDs) represent the flows of information through a system.
- Soft Systems Methodology is a way of analysing unstructured and poorly defined systems.

Self Review Questions

1. Define IT.
2. What are the features of information processing which makes computer use feasible?
3. What are the three main areas of IT application in information systems?
4. What main developments could be described as office support systems?
5. What are word processors?
6. What are the two types of COM?
7. Distinguish between teletext and viewdata.
8. What are electronic mail and voice mail?

9. What is a LAN?

10. What are simplex and duplex transmission?

11. What is EDI?

12. What is the preferred approach in developing an information system?

13. What is teleworking?

14. What is the advantage of a 'top-down' approach?

15. What is SSADM?

16. What is a DFD?

17. What are the advantages of using DFDs?

18. Describe the purpose of SSM.

19. What are the characteristics of a root definition?

15 Computers and MIS

Objectives

After you have studied this chapter you will:

- understand the role of computers in organisations.
- know the characteristics of data processing systems.
- be able to define a data base and know its characteristics.
- know the functions and importance of Data Base Management Systems.
- know what is meant by end-user computing.
- be able to describe the features of Decision Support Systems (DSS).
- know the main characteristics of DSS.
- be able to describe Expert Systems.
- know what is meant by an Executive Information System.
- understand what aids are available to assist End User Computing.
- know the ways technology influences organisations.

Computers and MIS

We now turn to the use of computers in organisation. Although in practice there is no clear cut dividing line between the areas of application, for clarity, the use of computers will be outlined in two broad categories:

- the routine processing of day-to-day transactions, known as *data processing* or *transaction processing*.
- the use of computers *by the end-users* themselves. The end-users include; managers, accountants, office staff, sales people, executives and others.

Both data processing and end-user computing produce management information. The key difference is that data processing systems supply pre-determined outputs and reports so there is less flexibility. This means that great care must be taken in analysing and determining management's real information needs before the system is designed.

On the other hand with end-user computing there is more flexibility and interaction so that the emphasis becomes one of supporting the end user rather than the production of a specified report.

Data Processing Systems

These systems perform the essential role of collecting and processing the daily transactions of the organisation, hence the alternative term, *transaction processing*. Typically these include; all forms of ledger keeping, accounts receivable and payable, invoicing, credit control, rate demands and stock movements.

These types of systems were the first to harness the power of the computer and originally were based on centralised mainframe computers. In many cases this still applies, especially for large volume repetitive jobs, but the availability of micro and mini computers has made distributed data processing feasible and popular. *Distributed data processing* has many variations but in essence means that data handling and processing are carried out at or near the point of use rather than in one centralised location.

Transaction processing is substantially more significant in terms of processing time, volume of input and output than say, information production for tactical and strategic planning. Transaction processing is essential to keep the operations of the organisation running smoothly and provides the base for all other internal information support. This is shown in Figure 15/1.

Figure 15/1 Transaction processing as a base for MIS

Characteristics of Data Processing Systems

These systems are 'pre-specified'; that is their functions, decision rules and output formats cannot usually be changed by the end user. These systems are related directly to the structure of the organisation's data. Any change in the data they process or the functions they perform usually requires the intervention of information system specialists such as system analysts and programmers.

Some data processing systems have to cope with huge volumes and a wide range of data types and output formats. As examples consider the Electricity and Gas Board Billing and Payment Handling systems, the Clearing Bank's current Accounting systems and the Motor Policy handling systems of a large insurer. The systems and programming work required for these systems represents a major investment. For example the development of a large scale billing system for a public utility represents something like 100 man years of effort.

Of course, data processing also takes place on a more modest scale and the ready availability of application packages – i.e. software to deal with a particular administrative or commercial task – means that small scale users have professionally written and tested programs to deal with their routine data processing. The better packages provide for some flexibility and the user can specify – within limits – variations in output formats, data types and decision rules.

Scope of Transaction Processing

Transaction processing is necessary to ensure that the day-to-day activities of the organisation are processed, recorded and acted upon. Files are maintained which provide both the current data for transactions; for example the amount invoiced and cash received during the month for statement preparation, and which also serve as a basis for operational and tactical control and for answering enquiries.

Transaction processing can be sub-divided into:

(a) Current activity processing

(b) Report processing

(c) Inquiry processing

Figure 15/2 shows in outline these sub-divisions with examples of the various processing types drawn from inventory and materials processing.

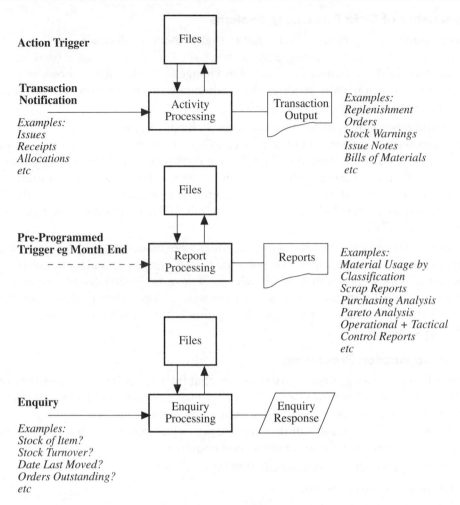

Action Trigger

Transaction Notification

Examples:
Issues
Receipts
Allocations
etc

Files

Activity Processing

Transaction Output

Examples:
Replenishment
Orders
Stock Warnings
Issue Notes
Bills of Materials
etc

Files

Pre-Programmed Trigger eg Month End

Report Processing

Reports

Examples:
Material Usage by
Classification
Scrap Reports
Purchasing Analysis
Pareto Analysis
Operational + Tactical
Control Reports
etc

Files

Enquiry

Examples:
Stock of Item?
Stock Turnover?
Date Last Moved?
Orders Outstanding?
etc

Enquiry Processing

Enquiry Response

Figure 15/2 Sub-division of transaction processing
(with inventory control examples)

A routine data processing system is not in itself an MIS because it does not support all the management functions of the organisation nor does it have the decision focus which previously has been said to be a primary objective of MIS. Nevertheless it should be apparent by now that routine transaction processing is essential for day-to-day activities and provides the indispensable foundation upon which the organisation's MIS is built.

Two illustrations follow of transaction processing. They are in outline only and show the main system flowcharts, the main files and outputs produced.

Illustration of Sales Order Processing

Central Spares Ltd. are based in Birmingham and supply shops and workshops with a range of spare parts for televisions, video recorders and domestic appliances. A range of approximately 2000 items is stocked and there are approximately 500 customers. Virtually all orders are received by telephone or fax and the company prides itself on its 24 hour delivery service. In general orders are processed and accumulated during the day and a twilight shift makes up the orders which are delivered the next day if the items requested are in stock.

The company uses a mini-computer, disk storage and VDUs.

The System

Figure 15/3 shows the Order Handling System

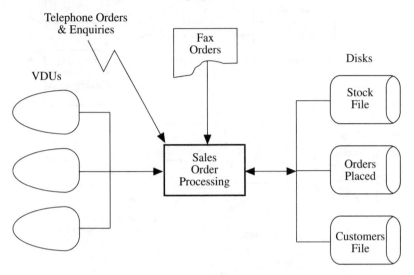

Figure 15/3 Central Spares: order handling

An order clerk calls up information on the screen and, interacting with the customer, processes the order as follows:

Screen information	Customer
Customers name and address and account number	Confirms
Delivery address	Confirms
Order number	Supplies
Credit position	Makes payment arrangements
Product name, stock number and quantity	Orders
Price and any delivery charge	Accepts/Rejects
Alternative products and promotions	Considers
Stock position	Advised of shortages
Expected delivery date	Accepts/Rejects

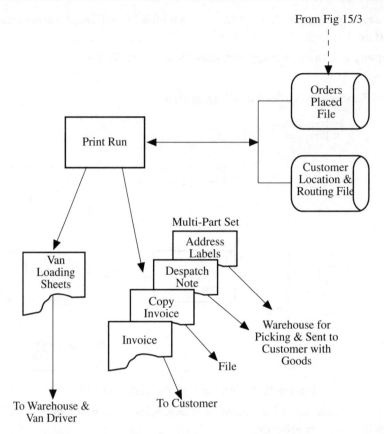

Figure 15/4 Central Spares: despatching process

Assuming that the customer's credit position is satisfactory and the customer accepts the price/delivery/alternatives offered the order is accepted and the customer, orders placed and stock files are updated.

Figure 15/4 shows the Invoice/Despatch Note printing. A multi part set, including address labels, is printed in bin number sequence on a printer located in the warehouse.

After the close of order taking for the day the computer prints out a load sheet for each delivery van.

The load sheet takes account of delivery addresses and economic journeys and is used to obtain delivery signatures from customers.

Finally there is an Accounting Run, shown on Figure 15/5, which deals with despatched orders, shortages, cash received and so on.

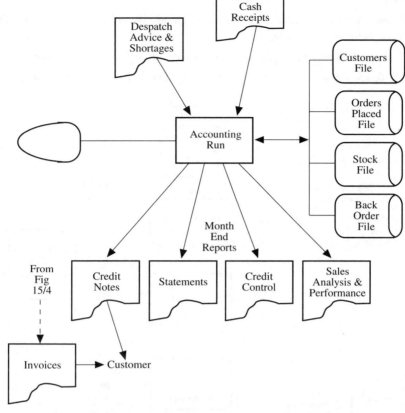

Figure 15/5 Central Spares: daily/monthly accounting

Illustration of Insurance Processing

A medium sized insurance company situated in the City of London specialises in motor insurance. The company deals with approximately 20,000 clients through a network of brokers. All communications with customers are through their broker and the insurance company receives amendments, premiums, new risks, claims and all other information by post or fax from the brokers.

The company has a mainframe computer with both serial and direct access backing storage.

The data processing system deals with the following main activities:

- *Daily*

  Processing of transactions including; new clients, client and vehicle amendments, payment receipts etc.

  Printing of renewal reminders in client within broker sequence.

- *Weekly*

  Processing of agreed claims, claim payment, claim statistics and so on.

  Printouts in client within broker sequence of overdue payments budget payments, insurance terminations.

- *Monthly*

  Analysis of premiums received and claims made by vehicle category within occupation code within zone code.

  Analysis of new business, commission due or earned for each broker.

Figures 15/6, 15/7 and 15/8 show, in outline, the Daily, Weekly and Monthly processing.

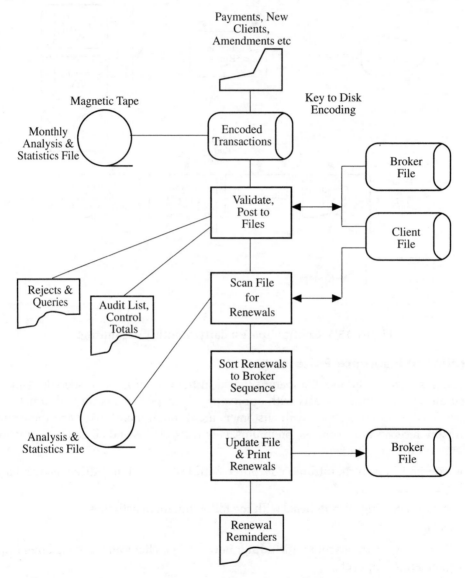

Figure 15/6 Daily insurance process

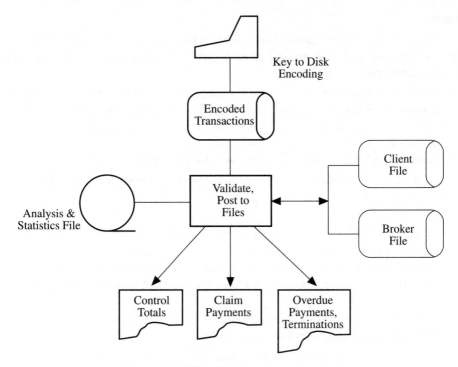

Figure 15/7 Weekly insurance process

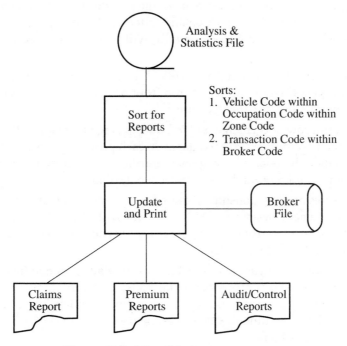

Figure 15/8 Monthly insurance process

Databases

In the early days of computerisation it was normal to maintain specific files for individual applications. Data were processed centrally in batches and there was little or no on-line interrogation of files.

This approach meant that there was duplication of data, inflexibility, concentration on the needs of the computer system rather than the user, and difficulties of accessing files by on-line users. To overcome these problems *data bases* were developed.

A database can be defined in various ways, for example:

A database is a collection of structured data. The structure of the data is independent of any particular application.

British Computer Society

A database is a file of data structured in such a way that it may serve a number of applications without its structure being dictated by any one of those applications, the concept being that programs are written round the database rather than files being structured to meet the needs of particular programs.

CIMA

The important features of a database are:

*   *Date Independence* An item of data is stored for its own sake and not for one specific use. Thus the use of the data is generalised and is independent of the programs which use it.

*   *Data Integrity* means the avoidance of conflicting, duplicated data by only showing one copy. If, for example, a stock balance alters, only one update is needed and all programs which access the stock balance will automatically be given the correct figure.

*   *Flexibility* means that data can be accessed in many different ways and for many different purposes. These can range from routine accesses for transaction processes to one-off queries by the Chief Executive.

The database can grow and change and is built up stage by stage within the organisation. It will actually comprise several databases, each providing the anticipated information for several logically related management information systems where the data can be accessed, retrieved and modified with reasonable flexibility.

The data structures and relationships require highly technical software – known as the Data Base Management System (DBMS) – to deal with them. Fortunately the user is shielded, to a large extent, from the complexity and is able to access the data base with the minimum of technical knowledge.

When the only form of data storage possible was unrelated, unique files for each application, this engendered a narrow, parochial view of information. The reality is that management need information which crosses functions, applications and levels and the flexibility of databases and the linkages possible make the concept a powerful one and essential for end user systems.

Figure 15/9 shows the relationship between the database, transaction processing, end-user systems and the DBMS.

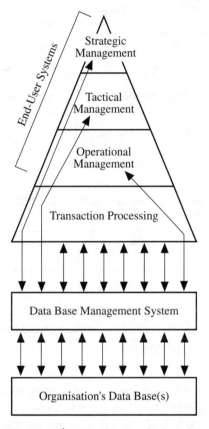

Figure 15/9 Database relationship

An organisation is not confined to its own internal database. There are companies which sell access to databases dealing with matters which an individual organisation would find expensive to collect. Examples of these public databases include those providing; Stock Exchange and financial data, environmental data, legal matters including EU treaties and legislation, consumer research and marketing data. In 1995 over 8000 external databases were available and the numbers are continually growing.

Data Base Management Systems (DBMS)

The DBMS is a complex software system which constructs, expands and maintains the database. It also provides the link, or interface, between the user and the data in the base. Figure 15/10 provides a summary of the three main elements of DBMS – definition, processing and enquiry.

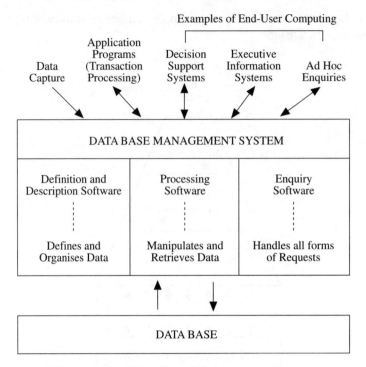

Figure 15/10 Data Base Management System

The three primary categories of DBMS are:

* *Relational*

    Where each type of record is represented as existing in a table or file of like records. For example, there could be customer records, product records, order records and so on. These systems are relatively simple and are suitable for manipulation by non-data processing personnel (as in a DSS) but their technical efficiency may be poor.

* *Hierarchical*

    This is a system having in-built linkages whereby there are 'owner' records which 'own' numerous 'member' records.

* *Network*

    These are further developments of linkage systems with many more record types and linkages.

Both the linkage systems require the user to know what linkages have been established in order to know on what basis data can be retrieved. The linkage systems are technically more efficient but do require greater data processing knowledge so their use tends to be restricted to information specialists.

The ability to store and access vast amounts of data in an efficient manner is being used to refine and improve activities at strategic, tactical and operational levels. For example the UK Clearing Banks use databases in marketing. Previously data were collected on a branch basis mainly relating to current accounts. If a customer had a loan or mortgage this was recorded separately. Now the banks adopt an integrated database approach so that all information about a customer is maintained centrally so that a financial profile of a customer can be derived and used for marketing.

Database marketing in retailing is well developed in America and is being explored in this country. In America it has developed to the point where the detailed buying patterns of individual shoppers are recorded making possible the precise targeting of marketing information, special offers etc.

Although many organisations are accumulating vast quantities of information in data bases it is increasingly being recognised that there are hidden relationships and patterns contained in the data which are difficult to find using conventional query tools. To try to overcome this problem various other techniques are being developed one of which is known as *data mining*. Data mining developed from research into statistical analysis and artificial intelligence and is the process of extracting previously unknown information, patterns and linkages from large databases. The process has been used for credit analysis, fraud detection, targeted marketing, banking, health care and many other applications. As an example, shopping basket analysis utilises Electronic Point of Sale (EPOS) data to analyse combinations of products purchased by individual buyers in order to find relationships which are used for refining purchasing, display and promotional decisions by the store. Commercial data mining products currently available include; Intelligent Miner (IBM), MineSet (Silicon Graphics), Knowledge Seeker (Angoss).

End User Computing

Traditionally, the only people who had direct contact with computers were the systems professionals (programmers, systems analysts etc). The introduction of personal computers, terminals, networks, user-friendly software, databases etc has altered the position dramatically and has led to the growth of end-user computing.

This may be broadly defined as:

> the direct, hands-on approach to computers by users – not indirect use through systems professionals. Users include; managers, office staff, sales people, production workers and others.

End-user computing is a large and growing field and some of the applications are listed below:

- Decision Support Systems
- Expert Systems
- Executive Information Systems
- End-user programming
- Computer based training
- Search and retrieval of information
- Text handling and publishing

Because of our emphasis on management and information this book concentrates on the first three applications shown above i.e. Decision Support Systems, Expert Systems and Executive Information Systems.

Decision Support Systems (DSS)

The objective of DSS is to support managers in their work, especially decision making. DSS tend to overlap both data processing systems and office support systems. They acquire much of their basic data from routine transaction processing and the results of analyses performed on such data may be included in reports prepared by the office support system, for example, on a word processor.

DSS tend to be used in planning, modelling, analysing alternatives and decision making. They generally operate through terminals operated by the user who interacts with the computer system. Using a variety of tools and procedures the manager (i.e., the user) can develop his own systems to help perform his functions more effectively. It is this active involvement and the focus on decision making which distinguishes a DSS from a data processing system. The emphasis is on support for decision making not on automated decision making which is a feature of transaction processing.

DSS are especially useful for semi-structured problems where problem solving is improved by interaction between the manager and the computer system. The emphasis is on small, simple models which can easily be understood and used by the manager rather than complex integrated systems which need information specialists to operate them.

The main characteristics of DSS are:

(a) The computer provides support but does not replace the manager's judgement nor does it provide pre-determined solutions.

(b) DSS are best suited to semi-structured problems where parts of the analysis can be computerised but the decision maker's judgement and insight is needed to control the process.

(c) Where effective problem solving is enhanced by interaction between the computer and the manager.

Where to Apply DSS

DSS are man/machine systems and are suitable for semi-structured problems. The problem must be important to the manager and the decision required must be a key one. In addition, if an interactive computer-based system is to be used then some of the following criteria should be met.

(a) **There should be a large data base.**

A data base is an organised collection of structured data with a minimum duplication of data items. The data base is common to all users of the system but is independent of the programs which use the data. If the data base is too large for manual searching then a computer-supported approach may be worthwhile.

(b) **Large amount of computation or data manipulation.**

Where analysis of the problem requires considerable computation or data manipulation, computing power is likely to be beneficial.

(c) **Complex inter-relationships.**

Where there is a large data base or where there are numerous factors involved it is frequently difficult to assess all the possible inter-relationships without computer assistance.

(d) **Analysis by stages.**

Where the problem is an iterative one with stages for re-examination and re-assessment it becomes more difficult to deal with manually. The computer-based model can answer the questions, 'What if?' quickly and effectively.

(e) **Judgement required.**

In complex situations judgement is required to determine problem and solution. Unaided, no computer system can provide this.

(f) **Communication.**

Where several people are involved in the problem solving process, each contributing some special expertise, then the co-ordinating power of the computer can be of assistance.

It follows from the above criteria that DSS are inappropriate for unstructured problems and unnecessary for completely structured problems because these can be dealt with wholly by the computer and man/machine interaction is unnecessary.

In outline DSS require a database, the software to handle the database and decision support programs including, for example, modelling, spread sheet and analysis packages, expert systems etc.

Types of DSS

In an extensive study of DSS used in organisations Alter found that they fell into 7 main groups. These are shown on Figure 15/11 together with examples of DSS applications within each group.

DSS Classification	Type of Operation	Examples and Comments
File Drawer Systems	Access of data items	Data oriented systems. Basically on-line computerised versions of manual filing systems e.g. account balance, stock position queries, monitoring loads and capacities.
Data Analysis Systems	Ad hoc analysis of data files	Data oriented systems. Used to analyse files containing current or historical data e.g. analysing files for overdue account, bad payers.
Analysis Information Systems	Ad hoc analysis using databases and small models	Data oriented systems. Extension of data analysis systems to include internal and external databases with limited modelling e.g. a marketing support DSS could include internal sales data, customer data and market research data.
Accounting Models	Estimating future results using accounting rules	Model oriented systems. Typically these generate estimates of cash, income, costs etc based on accounting relationships and rules e.g. cash and expenditure budgeting, balance sheet projections.
Representational Models	Estimating results, consequences where risk exists	Model oriented systems. These generate results using probability based simulation models e.g. risk analysis for new project, traffic simulation with variable flows
Optimisation Models	Calculating optimal results where constraints exist	Model oriented systems. These are used for structured decisions where constraints exist and there is a clear objective e.g. machine loading, material usage, production planning.
Suggestion Models	Producing suggested results where decision rules are known	Model oriented systems. These compute suggested decisions for semi-structured problems. Expert systems are one of the tools e.g. credit authorisations, insurance rate calculations.

Figure 15/11 Alter's DSS Classifications

Decision Support Packages

The existence of the database and a DBMS to handle it means that the manager can interrogate and access a mass of data at will. He then needs to be able to use this data in exploring alternatives and making decisions. To do this there is an enormous range of packages available. These include packages for:

(a) Modelling and simulation

(b) Spread sheets

(c) Forecasting

(e) Non-Linear and Linear Programming

(f) Regression modelling

(h) Sensitivity and risk analysis

(i) Expert systems

It is clearly beyond the scope of this book to describe all these types of packages in detail but two of the more relevant ones are briefly described below, namely, spread sheets and expert systems.

Spread Sheet Packages

A general outline of modelling and simulation has already been given earlier together with an explanation of how modelling can help the manager in planning and decision making. One useful practical way is for the manager to use a spread sheet package to show the results of different actions.

The basis of a spread sheet package is an electronic worksheet whereby data can be stored and manipulated at will. The spread sheet is a matrix of locations which can contain values, formulae and relationships. The key feature is that all elements in the matrix are changed automatically when one or more of the key assumptions are changed.

For example, a series of interlocking departmental operating statements culminating in an overall projected profit and loss account may have been prepared on the spread sheet. If one or more of the variables (rates of pay, output levels, sales, absorption rates and so on) needs to be altered then the new value needs only to be entered once and the whole of the matrix is recalculated virtually instantaneously with all relationships, sub-totals and totals automatically catered for. This facility allows a series of outcomes to be explored, providing answers to the 'what if' questions which are so essential to the manager. For example, what would be the effect on profit of a change in inflation rate/cost per unit/contribution margin/scrap rates or whatever factor need to be explored. Used in this way spread sheet packages perform a modelling function and this facility is greatly expanded in the latest spread sheet packages.

Spread Sheets and Budgeting

One of the important tasks of tactical level management is concerned with budgeting. Spread sheets can be of great assistance in exploring the effect on a budget of different values and assumptions so that the manager can make more effective decisions. As one example, consider the Credit Controller dealing with cash budgeting.

Cash budgets are examples of routine but highly essential reports which need frequent updating to reflect current and forecast conditions, changes in credit behaviour, anticipated gains or expenditures and so on. Each period (weekly, monthly, quarterly, as required) changes and up-to-date information are input and, in combination with the brought forward file data, the cash budget will be automatically projected forward by the spread sheet program with highlighted surpluses and/or deficiencies, balances carried forward from one period to another and all the usual contents of a cash budget. The budget could be shown in both an abbreviated and detailed format and could also be displayed in a graphical form.

Figure 15/12 shows the possible output of a Summary Cash Budget and a corresponding graphical display, the facility for which is increasingly being included in modern spread sheet packages such as Lotus 1-2-3.

Summary Cash Budget (Ref Detail Budgets A–E)									
	Jan £'000	Feb £'000	Mar £'000	Apr £'000	May £'000	Jun £'000	Jul £'000	Aug £'000	Sep £'000
Opening Balance	−2850	−2900	−2925	−2850	−3100	−3450	−3375	−3425	−3625
Add Total Receipts	3250	2900	2700	3100	3300	3200	2900	2700	2650
Less Total Payments	3300	2925	2975	3350	3650	3125	2950	2900	2450
Closing Cash Balance C/F	−2900	−2925	−2850	−3100	−3450	−3375	−3425	−3625	−3425
Current Overdraft Limit	3000	3000	3000	3000	3500	3500	3500	3500	3500
Warning Indicator				☆				☆	

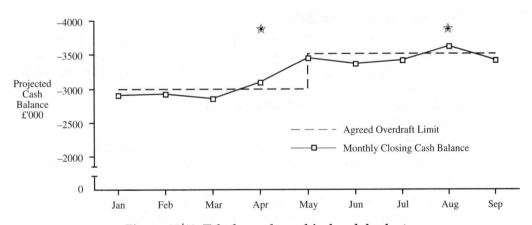

Figure 15/12 Tabular and graphical cash budget

Expert Systems

At the present time, Expert Systems represent the most advanced stage of decision support systems. An Expert System is a computer system which embodies some of the experience and specialised knowledge of an expert or experts. An Expert System enables a non-expert to achieve comparable performance to an expert in the field. It uses a reasoning process which bears some resemblance to human thought.

The unique feature of an Expert System is the *knowledge base*, which is a network of rules which represents the human expertise. These rules and linkages are derived from discussions with experts and analysis of their decision making behaviour. Attempts are made to include the effects of uncertainty and judgement and clearly such an approach is likely to be costly and time consuming. Expert Systems are much more sophisticated and powerful that simply automating a typical structured decision but conversely, they are very much more difficult to implement.

As an example a doctor might supply a Medical Diagnosis Expert System with a particular set of symptoms. The program searches its knowledge base of symptoms and possible causes then, at certain stages, begins an interactive exchange with the doctor to find out more information or to suggest further tests that might be carried out. Thus, the user is not surrendering his judgement but is using the system to enhance his judgement and improve his decisions.

Expert Systems have been developed in a number of fields of which the following are examples:

- Medical diagnosis (e.g. MYCIN)
- Personal tax planning
- Product pricing
- Selection of selling methods
- Statutory Sick Pay Entitlement and Claims
- Credit approval in banking
- Air crew scheduling
- Geological Exploration (e.g. PROSPECTOR)

Executive Information Systems (EIS)

These are forms of data retrieval systems that provide selected and summarised information for senior executives. They assist top management by providing information on critical areas of the organisation's activities drawn from both internal and external databases. EIS are becoming, more widely available and organisations such as British Airways, ICI, BP, Glaxo and others are enthusiastic users.

The key features of an EIS are:

- Easy to use. The system must be fast and extremely simple to use as it will be used by busy executives. The use of touch screens, mice and icons, pop-up menus etc. is normal.
- Access to data. There must be unhindered rapid access to data permitting vertical and horizontal exploration. This is known as *drilling down the data*.
- Data analysis. Having obtained the data the EIS should provide facilities for such things as; ratio and trend calculations, data integration, forecasts.
- Quality presentation. The system should provide interesting and understandable formats using colour, graphs, diagrams.

A typical way that an EIS works is by exception reporting and *drilling down* to investigate the causes. For example a director may be alerted that a particular department is well over budget. (An exception to budget or target is known as a '*hot-spot*' and would be highlighted by the EIS). The manager would then drill down the data by pursuing lower and lower levels of detail. He might first seek a breakdown of the departmental budget and actual expenditure into broad categories such as; Material, Labour and Overheads. If he discovered that the major overspend was in overheads he would access the detailed expenditure on the various items of overhead cost such as; Salaries, Depreciation, Telephones and Insurance. In this way the executive can explore at will and is thus provided with better assistance in planning and controlling.

EIS are used personally by managers and it is thus essential that the system reflects their requirements. The managers must be involved in the development and implementation of the system. There have been several developments aimed at encouraging users to become more involved in developing their own systems. Typical of these are; Fourth Generation Languages, Prototyping and Information Centres, which are dealt with below.

Fourth Generation Languages (4GLs)

4GLs are very high level programming languages designed so that system development becomes easier and users can become more involved. A 4GL has an English-like set of commands and readily understandable control structures in which general data processing and numerical operations can be specified. Normally the 4GL programs are then translated by the computer into a conventional 3rd generation language such as COBOL and thence to machine code.

Compared to 3rd generation languages, 4GLs are quicker and easier to write, require less lines of code and are designed for interactive use. They have good help facilities (especially useful for users who are not IT specialists) and produce their own documentation. Typical examples of 4GL systems are ORACLE, MANTIS and SQL. The main advantages and disadvantages of these languages are:

Advantages

- make it easier for users to develop their own programs easing the load on analysts/programmers
- taps user creativity and helps to diffuse IT proficiency throughout the organisation
- greatly increases programmer productivity
- enable progam/system changes to be made more easily.

Disadvantages

- 4GL programs make less efficient use of processing power and memory
- overuse may overload hardware facilities.

Prototyping

Prototyping is based on the simple idea that people can express more easily what they like or do not like about an actual working system rather than specify what they would like to see in an imagined, future system.

Prototyping consists of four steps:

1. Identify the user's basic requirements.
2. Develop an initial prototype. This is a live, working system to meet the users basic requirements. It is usually programmed using a very high level 4GL language. The

emphasis is on speed of development rather than completeness and efficiency. Programming may be by a specialist or the user.

3.   The user works with the prototype. Using real data and problems the user works with the prototype. He thus gains hands-on experience, finds problems, sharpens his requirements, tests assumptions and so gains deeper insight. Normally the user finds problems and omissions in the initial prototype and feeds back his reactions to the systems designer for revisions. It is thus the user who controls the process and defines the system.

4.   Revise the prototype. Based on the feedback from step 3 the prototype is revised and enhanced. Steps 3 and 4 are repeated until an acceptable working system is developed.

Prototyping is useful for most interactive applications especially where the user is more concerned with the format and layout of VDU screens for data entry, output and error messages than the underlying processes of the system.

Information Centres (IC)

In essence ICs are support departments which provide assistance to people within the organisation who use computers. They also provide help to users who wish to develop their own programs and act as a go-between or link between computer users and the organisation's own DP department or external software and hardware suppliers. ICs are of particular value where distributed data processing is used or where microcomputers are spread throughout the organisation. In such circumstances many non computer-technical people are in charge of files, software and hardware and thus need technical support and advice from time to time.

Typical of the services ICs provide are the following:

*   to identify areas where IT could usefully be employed
*   to provide technical advice on existing and new hardware: capabilities, limitations speeds etc.
*   to show users how to deal with all types of software: application packages, operating systems, programming languages etc.
*   to encourage good practice throughout the organisation e.g. system/program documentation, back-up procedures, quality checks etc.
*   to help avoid over-laps, duplication of effort
*   to provide general IT training and specialist training on new developments, equipment, software
*   to provide assistance and guidance to users developing their own systems
*   to provide a telephone 'hot-line' service and a 'drop-in' advice centre

Properly staffed information centres provide a valuable service to the organisation and to individual users.

The Impact of Technology on Organisations

Technology, which includes IT, influences organisations in a variety of ways. In summary, technology alters the skills requirements for individuals, it changes jobs and the way they are done. It can also alter relationships between individuals and departments within the organisation and may affect some relationships outside the organisation e.g. with customers and suppliers. It is likely to be a major factor in determining the type of information available and how the information is used and consequently how the organisation operates.

In addition there is some evidence that technology, in its broadest sense, has a significant effect on the structure of the organisation. Developments in technology may cause some jobs to disappear, for example traditional newspaper typesetters, but it can also open up new business opportunities which create jobs, for example the growth in telephone banking and insurance which rely heavily on advanced computing and communication facilities. Some of the more important elements outlined are developed below.

Technology and Job Changes

Technology simplifies and reduces tasks needing manual skills and strength especially in factories and all forms of production. Properly applied, it can increase productivity. The use of re-programmable robots for such things as welding, spraying, materials handling help to eliminate dirty or hazardous and repetitive work. Robots and computer aided manufacturing (CAM) as well as reducing costs improve quality and the consistency of finished products.

The use of technology requires more problem solving skills and the ability to interpret data and is thus likely to lead to a widening gulf between skilled and unskilled workers. Routine tasks requiring a low level of skill are disappearing fast. As an example the copy typist has all but disappeared from many offices. The availability of word-processors, flexible printers and photo-copiers have effectively eliminated copy typing.

Computers, VDU screens and communication equipment have made it possible to combine jobs which were previously carried out separately. In the process it has also enabled the tasks to be carried out by lower-level staff – known as *empowering*. As an example, consider the range of tasks now carried out by a British Telecom tele-assistant. Dealing directly with a customer by telephone and having the customer's account and service details displayed on the computer screen the assistant can deal with such matters as; settling account queries, initiating new services required by the customer, taking orders for new equipment, changing payment methods, deleting services no longer required and so on. Previously such tasks were carried by separately by manual methods and there were inevitable delays. Nowadays they are dealt with immediately by one person.

Technology and Operational Changes

The use of appropriate technology in properly planned systems can have dramatic effects on operations. There are numerous examples; travel and holiday agents are all linked by networks directly to the databases maintained by airlines, railways and holiday companies making possible virtually instantaneous booking, computing cash tills and bar-code readers in supermarkets are linked to computers and form part of an integrated stock control, ordering and sales analysis system without which modern supermarkets could not function.

Technology can also influence the way organisations interact with customers, suppliers and competitors. Sometimes, because of the investment required and the mutual benefit competitors collaborate over technology. For example the banks exchange clearing information in compatible form and allow other banks' customers to use their cashpoint machines. Sometimes suppliers supply free hardware and software to customers in order to make switching more difficult and costly. Pharmaceutical companies, airlines and holiday providers frequently do this. The increased use of JIT systems in manufacturing means that much closer liaison is required between suppliers of components and final assemblers. As a consequence, stock control and ordering systems are frequently shared and there are often direct computer to computer links. It is worth noting that as well as increasing efficiency the close linkage means that a major assembler of, say, cars or domestic appliances, can exert considerable influence on their suppliers.

Technology and the Organisation Structure

Research over many years has confirmed the influence of technology on organisational structures and on the way they operate. For example; Woodward found that when organisations were classified in order of the technological complexity of their production systems each production system was found to be associated with a characteristic pattern of organisation. Typically it was found that the number of levels of management increased with technical complexity leading to 'tall' organisations whilst simpler technologies were able to operate with flatter structures. The span of control of supervisors was at its highest in mass production and decreased in process industries.

Information technology is also having effects on structures. Because of the easier and speedier communications and the increasing sophistication of automatic decision making by computers, middle management is tending to disappear in many organisations. Organisations are becoming flatter and leaner because top management are able to monitor operations more directly and computers are now taking many decisions previously taken by middle management. Examples include; computerised stock and production control in manufacturing, automatic credit scoring and loan authorisations in banks. IT is also changing the nature of the debate about centralisation versus decentralisation. Properly planned IT systems with distributed data processing enable both more centralisation of standards, performance targets and policies and more decentralisation of operations through more immediate and speedier service to customers.

It is also causing the worth of traditional departmental structures to be questioned. These developed when work was done manually and was passed from department to department with each carrying out a particular function. Nowadays much of this work is carried out by computer and it is realised that work should be divided into processes rather than traditional functions. For example dealing with a sale from the receipt of the customer's order through manufacture, despatch, invoicing and accounting was traditionally handled by several administrative departments although it is all one process. Businesses are increasingly being reorganised into processes rather than functions. This is known as *process re-engineering* and means that firms must identify their core processes and design them so that delays, confusion and demarcations are reduced or eliminated.

Key Point Summary

- Transaction processing systems are pre-specified and changes require the intervention of system specialists.
- Transaction processing comprises: activity processing, report processing and enquiry processing.

- A database is a collection of data, available to all, which is independent of individual programs.
- A Data Base Management System is the software which controls the database and which acts as a link between the users and the database.
- A DBMS comprises software for organising data, retrieving data and handling enquiries.
- Decision support systems are operated by the end user and supplement human judgement in semi-structured decision making.
- Decision support packages include: modelling, spread sheets, forecasting, linear programming, statistical analysis, expert systems and so on.
- Spread sheet packages can be used for transaction processing and for modelling in decision support systems.
- Expert Systems aim to incorporate human judgement and experience into a knowledge base.
- Executive Information Systems are easy to use data retrieval systems in which the executive can drill down for data.
- Prototyping means obtaining experience from using a prototype which is refined to produce a working system.
- Information centres provide a support and advisory service
- Technology, including IT, influences jobs, relationships, and organisation structures.

Self Review Questions

1. Describe data processing systems and their characteristics.
2. What are the sub-divisions of transaction processing?
3. What is a database?
4. What is a DBMS?
5. What is end-user computing?
6. What are DSS?
7. Where should DSS be applied?
8. What are the main types of DSS?
9. What types of packages can be of assistance in support of decision making?
10. What is a spread sheet package and how can it be used?
11. What are expert systems?
12. What are the features of Executive Information Systems?
13. How does prototyping work?
14. What services do Information Centres provide?
15. How does technology influence organisations and jobs?

16 Influences on MIS Design

Objectives

After you have studied this chapter you will:

- understand the main factors which influences MIS design.
- know that management must be directly involved with MIS design.
- understand the key MIS design features at strategic, tactical and operational levels.
- be able to give examples of MIS at the three levels.
- understand the importance of environmental scanning at the strategic level.
- know the key provisions of the Data Protection and Computer Misuse Acts.

Influences on MIS Design

There are numerous factors which influence the structure and scope of an organisation's MIS which are summarised in Figure 16/1 and developed below.

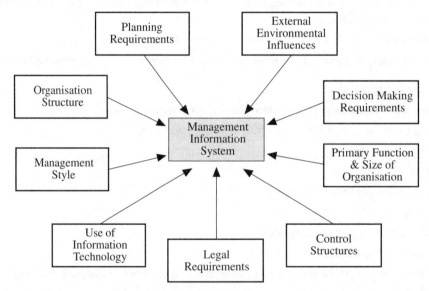

Figure 16/1 Major influences on the organisation's MIS

(a) *The primary function of the organisation.* Is it a manufacturing or service company, a wholesaler, a local authority, a public utility, a hospital? Are there numerous functions? What linkages exist between them? Are they complementary or disparate? What type of technology is used?

(b) *The structure and levels of the organisation.* Is the organisation composed of numerous sections and levels? What degree of autonomy have the section/ departments?

(c) *The degree of centralisation or decentralisation.* Is the organisation tightly controlled at the centre? What decisions/actions are the sections allowed to take? What is the committee structure?

(d) *Interaction with environment.* To what extent is external information of importance? In what ways does the organisation need to communicate with its environment – to customers, suppliers, trade unions, government departments etc? What is the legislative framework? To what extent, if any, does the Data Protection Act apply?

(e) *What decisions need to be taken.* What is the extent of programmed and non-programmed decision making? What levels take the decisions? What is the urgency surrounding the decision making process? What is the time scale of decisions?

(f) *The scale of operation.* How many employees? How many branches/departments/sections? What is the volume of orders, invoices, bills, enquiries, transactions etc?

(g) *The management style.* Is it an authoritarian or participative style? Are procedures and operations routine and closely prescribed? Is management by exception practised? What is the control structure?

(h) *Use of information technology.* What is the extent and type of IT usage? What degree of expertise exists throughout the organisations – not just the IT specialists? What is the availability of equipment?

(i) *To what extent is planning formalised?* What time scales are involved? What is the extent of participation in planning? How is planning monitored? How are plans implemented?

Categories of Information

Within a MIS various categories of information can be distinguished which determine the urgency and way that it produces or handles the information concerned. The main categories are:

- **Demand/Response**

    A demand is a request for information which is essential for the task in hand and a response is the answer to a demand. In general the time scale is short and immediate response may be required. All MIS must be able to deal with these categories which can occur at any level. For example, at one level an order clerk will need to know the stock position and credit standing of the customer before accepting an order, whilst at a higher level the Marketing Manager will need to know the buying pattern over a period before negotiating a long term contract.

- **Deposit/Reference**

    A deposit is an item of information which is stored for possible future use and a reference is a request for information which may or may not be available. The MIS designer must constantly be examining management's information needs in order to be able to store information likely to be relevant in the future. Not all information can be stored and the major problem with databases is deciding what is relevant and irrelevant. Note the distinction between the essential nature of the demand/response category and the useful but supplementary characteristics of reference information.

- **Internal/External**

    Internal information originates within the organisation and flows horizontally and vertically around it. External information is about the environment and should be obtained by a continuous scanning and intelligence gathering process. Although often nebulous and imprecise, environmental intelligence is of great strategic importance and cannot be ignored, especially by organisations operating in a turbulent and competitive environment.

Management's Involvement with MIS Design

It was pointed out at the beginning of this book that worthwhile MIS have a decision focus, that is, their rationale is to improve decision making. This cannot be done unless the manager is intimately involved with the selection of issues and problems the system addresses, the information content of reports and files, the nature of the models used, the structure of any automated decision making and the dividing line between programmed and non-programmed decision making.

In many practical situations the manager is the main source of data. He knows the problem and has been given the responsibility to solve it. Accordingly he must play a key role in devising a system which will help to generate a solution. This not only ensures the validity and practical nature of the system but will also increase the manager's confidence in it. The design of many planning and control information systems requires management participation at several levels in the organisation. Both senior and subordinate management must agree on what factors are to be controlled, how performance will be judged, what are realistic reporting periods and so on before any information system can be designed.

Formal and Informal Systems

Informal information systems complement formal systems. They are more spontaneous and provide for flexibility and adaptation yet they may themselves suffer from bias and noise. The key design decision is where to draw the line between the formal and informal and continually to monitor the dividing line. This may mean, on occasions, 'adopting' an unofficial system and formalising it, or ceasing to produce information which becomes inappropriate.

Some of the questions which can be asked are:

(a) What information produced by the formal system is not used? Why?

(b) How is formal information used?

(c) Does the MIS encourage short-run behaviour?

(d) Is formal information accepted too slavishly?

(e) Is the formal information essential for the decision making process or is it merely confirmatory?

(f) Do managers manage their reports rather than real operations?

(g) How reliable is the data on which formal information is based? Does it include 'fiddles' or bias?

(h) What informal or private information is used? How does it differ from formal information? Is it more effective?

If such a review finds that private files are kept and informal information is widely used then formalisation should be considered. There is a prima facie case for formalisation if the informal information overloads the user and would be improved by more analysis/aggregation or some other form of filtering. Especially at strategic levels, informal information gathering will always have a key role however sophisticated or technologically advanced the organisation's formal MIS.

MIS Characteristics and Management Levels

Figures 16/2 and 16/3 show an outline of the characteristics of MIS related to the three management levels. Subsequent paragraphs deal with some of the important design features of MIS at the operational, tactical and strategic levels.

Figure 16/2 MIS and management levels

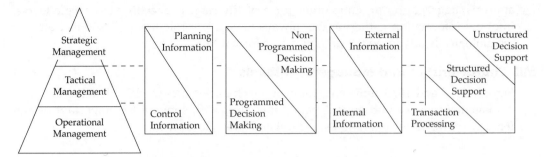

Figure 16/3 MIS and management levels

MIS at the Operational Level

Operational management are concerned with the implementation and control of the day-to-day activities of the organisation. Their activities are highly dependent on formal MIS dealing almost exclusively with internal information. Effective and efficient information processing is essential since controls are numerous, monitoring is constant, data volumes are often high and response is needed rapidly, often in real time. Hence many operational information systems are computer based.

At the operational level many decisions are structured and are frequently incorporated into computer based systems. Because the circumstances are well defined, optimising techniques such as linear programming are frequently used. Linear programming (LP) is probably the most used optimising model and LP packages are widely available for all computer systems.

LP is used where it is required to optimise the value of a single objective (e.g. maximise contribution) where the factors involved (e.g. labour hours, machine capacity etc.) are subject to some constraint or limitation. It can be used to solve problems which:

(a) can be stated in numeric terms

(b) all factors have linear relationships

(c) permit a choice between alternatives

(d) have one or more restrictions on the factors involved.

LP is used for numerous problems including: production planning, least cost mix problems in food, fertilisers and so on. It will be apparent that the closely defined requirements for the use of LP and other optimising techniques are more likely to be found at the operational level, less so at the tactical level and not at all at the strategic level where uncertainties abound.

Processing Operational Level MIS

MIS at the operational level, whether manual or computerised, are file processing systems. Their input comprises the data from operational transactions and their outputs are reports (for example, variance analyses for labour cost control), action documents (for example, a purchase order for materials), and enquiry handling (for example, what is the balance on Jones account?) MIS at this level fulfil most of the tests of computability mentioned earlier so that most are computer based. A major design question which thus arises is the selection of the mode of computer processing. Should this be batch processing or real-time processing?

Most MIS at the operational level have traditionally been batch processing systems. This form of processing will continue to be appropriate when:

(a) data volumes are high

(b) there are large files

(c) data processing efficiency is important

(d) periodic reporting/action is sufficient to meet operational demands.

In addition, on-line enquiry and data entry facilities can be combined with batch processing so providing a degree of immediacy.

However, operational activities may require an immediate or rapid response in which case real-time computing may be necessary. The following conditions indicate a need for real-time computer systems.

(a) On demand service required.
    e.g. hotel reservations, travel agencies, theatre bookings.

(b) Short action time span.
    e.g. stock exchange transactions, foreign exchange dealings.

(c) Immediate data validation critical.
    e.g. factory floor data collection.

(d) Immediate reference/updating critical.
    e.g. telephone sales, stock issuing, production planning and scheduling.

(e) Short activity life-cycle.
    e.g. newspaper distribution, handling of perishables.

(f) Continuous process operations.
    e.g. refineries, chemical works, steel rolling mill control.

Real-time processing needs careful design. Being transaction driven the system must be reliable and cope with all contingencies and conditions. There must be inbuilt recovery procedures so that files can be reconstructed and that transactions cannot be 'lost'. Also the system must respond swiftly even under pressure otherwise it will be discredited and cease to make a positive contribution to efficiency.

MIS at the Tactical Level

Tactical or middle level management is the broadest spectrum of management. Managers at this level face complexity and uncertainty and require judgement, insight and much inter-personal skill to carry out their tasks. Both formal and informal information flows are essential and there is much less reliance on computer dominated systems although computer based decision support systems can provide invaluable assistance.

Unlike MIS at the operational level, there is no one best design for tactical level MIS. The environment is so diverse, there are numerous variables and there are so many behavioural and personal factors that off the shelf solutions are rarely applicable. Optimising models, such as LP, are of limited value because managerial judgement plays a large part in tactical decision making, although these models can be of value for review purposes.

In broad terms, tactical level management implement strategic objectives and monitor operations. Control systems with information feedback are essential to carry out the monitoring role and it is this level which administers most of the well known conventional control systems. These include: budgetary control, production control, inventory control and so on. To avoid rigidity it is important that the MIS incorporates more than one level of feedback thus:

(a) conventional feedback used for routine reporting which initiates corrective action if deviations occur.

(b) adaptive feedback causes the amendment of short term plans or budgets where the MIS indicates that conditions have changed sufficiently for small scale corrections to be inappropriate.

(c) 'crisis' feedback which is a response to substantial or uncontrollable deviations from plans which may indicate changes to long term plans.

Types of Tactical Level MIS

Much of the information used by middle management comes from informal sources and is gathered, assessed, analysed and judged by the manager personally. In addition, the manager is supported by formal MIS which are increasingly computer based. Four types of formal MIS can be identified:

1. Control systems which monitor and report on the organisation's activities. Most of the information used comes from internal sources but key external factors must also be scanned, for example, competitors' actions, raw material prices, new legislation and industrial relation trends.

2. Database systems which process and store internal and external information in order to provide the organisation's 'memory'.

3. Enquiry systems which allow planned and ad-hoc interrogations of databases. These may be internal to the organisation or commercially available external databases which are often useful as the background to forecasting.

4. Decision support systems. These provide computer based support for semi-structured decision making. Facilities include: modelling and simulation, statistical analyses, forecasting, investment appraisal models and so on.

Examples of MIS at the Tactical Level

Middle management are largely concerned with specific functions in the organisation, e.g. personnel, marketing and so on. Examples follow of typical MIS support within functional areas. The examples explain the scope, reports produced, inputs handled, major relationships and the boundaries between the systems. The examples chosen are drawn from a typical manufacturing firm and are by no means exhaustive and many different types of MIS exist in manufacturing and other types of organisation.

Marketing and Sales

(a) **Scope**

MIS in the area to help to provide information to enable Marketing and Sales Management to control and monitor current operations (orders, enquiries, sales campaigns, representatives, distribution etc.) and to provide a basis for policy development on pricing and discounts, patterns of promotions and distribution, changes in product mix, changes in product design etc.

(b) **Typical Reports Produced**

Trend of orders
Order position by product/area
Order progress
Customer analyses and profiles
Product Profitability
Market Surveys
Finished Stock positions and forecasts
Selling Costs by product/area/representative
Distribution costs by product/area/representative
Discount Forecasts by area/product

(c) **Typical Inputs Handled**

  i. **Internal**
    Sales orders
    Despatch notes
    Goods inwards
    Returns
    Representative returns
    Cost data etc.

  ii. **External**
    Market Research data
    Economic statistics
    Trade and Industry data etc.

  iii. **Major relationships** The marketing and sales MIS has major relationships with other systems as follows:

    Financial Accounting   (e.g. for Credit control)
    Cost Accounting   (e.g. for distribution cost data)
    Production control   (e.g. for order progress)

(d) **Boundaries of system.** The exact extent of any MIS depends largely on the structure and organisation of a particular firm but some decisions must be taken on the boundaries between systems. For example; is credit control a sales or accounting responsibility, is invoicing a sales or accounting responsibility, is order handling and documentation a sales or production control responsibility?

Personnel

(a) **Scope**

MIS in this area provide information to help Personnel and other Management in the selection, recruitment and training of personnel, wages and salaries, administration, and promotion and grading. In addition, information must be provided for the development and operation of policies on Welfare, Health and Safety, Conditions of Employment, and Industrial Relations.

(b) **Typical Reports Produced**

Wages and Salary analyses
Labour Turnover Statistics
Accident and Absentee reports
Training Returns
Job Descriptions
Joint consultation reports and minutes
Pension analyses and projections
Job Evaluation reports
Manpower planning reports and projections etc.

(c) **Typical Inputs Handled**

i. **Internal**
Time cards and production data
Application forms
Interview summaries
Staff review data
Factory review data
Factory level trade union data
Training summaries etc.

ii. **External**
College/University reports
National Trade Union Agreements and proposals
Government legislation (Factories Acts, Labour Law etc.)
Wage and salary comparative data
Relevant economics statistics, e.g. employment trends
Pension fund performance etc.

iii. **Major relationships** Personnel must, of necessity, have close relationships with all functional areas to provide them with services and data on all aspects of staffing but it also has specific operational links with a number of functions including:
Accounting   (e.g. for Wages and Salary payment)
Production   (e.g. for absentee and attendance data)

(d) **Boundaries** The boundaries of a Personnel system vary considerably from one organisation to another. For example, does the Personnel Department actually engage an employee or does it provide the services necessary to produce a short list of suitable candidates for the appropriate functional manager to make the final decision? Does the personnel department arrange for the putting up and payment of wages or is this considered to be part of the Accounting Function? Does Production Management carry out negotiations with Trades Unions or is this a function of the Personnel Department. These and numerous other boundaries have to be resolved in designing any system.

Management Accounting

(a) **Scope**

MIS in this area provide management in all functional areas with cost and budget data, control data, contribution and profitability analyses to guide and control current operations. In addition, investment appraisals, special investigations, comparative profitability and contribution data etc. provide background material for strategic and tactical planning and decision making.

(b) **Typical Reports Produced**
Operating Statement
Budget Statements
Standard Costs and Variance returns
Cost investigations
Project Investment appraisals
Expenditure analyses
Profit forecasts
Cash flow statements and forecasts

(c) **Typical Inputs Handled**

i. **Internal**
Labour bookings
Material usage
Stores issues
Standards
Product data
Output details
Asset data etc.

ii. **External**
Market projections
Comparative Cost Data on national/industry basis
Government legislation etc.

iii. **Major relationships.** Management Accounting departments supply control and planning data to all areas, functions and levels. Specific operational links include:
Financial Accounting   (e.g. for taxation purposes)
Production   (e.g. for output and performance data)
Material Control   (e.g. for material usage and issue)

(d) **Boundaries.** The dividing line between Management Accounting and Financial Accounting varies considerably from firm to firm but typically Financial Accounting would deal with such matters as Taxation, Financing, preparation of Annual statements etc. i.e. more exclusively with the external financial affairs whereas management accounting would be concerned with the internal financial control and planning. Another boundary decision relates to the extent to which detailed day-to-day costing matters (e.g. production cost data, material usage etc.) would be dealt with centrally or under the control of Production management.

Management by Exception

A major task of middle management is to monitor and control operations. Typically the operational tasks are well defined yet for the manager to monitor and control each individual activity would be a lengthy job and, as most will proceed according to plan, a largely unproductive task. Because of this problem, most routine control systems are designed to highlight the exceptions rather than the normal adherence to the plan. This is known as management by exception which can be said to exist (a) when a subordinate is given a prescribed and defined role to perform with the necessary authority to satisfactorily perform the role, (b) where the role definition includes a clear statement of what constitutes normal performance and (c) where matters which are not proceeding to plan are reported upon so that the superior may take corrective action.

A common example of management by exception is the accounting technique of budgetary control whereby a subordinate, after consultation, is given a budget showing what constitutes normal planned performance and significant variances are reported to his superior.

Management by exception is more than a method of reporting – it is a style of management. It has the advantage that subordinates are given clearly defined objectives and the authority to carry them out. They can see what they are required to do and feel that they are trusted to carry out a meaningful task. Their superiors have the advantage that they need not concern themselves with the majority of items which, it is hoped, are proceeding according to plan whereas the items which may require attention are brought to their notice through the reporting system. Wherever possible, MIS should be built round management by exception principles. Management by exception is a closely controlled form of delegation and it is clear that the types of decisions that are suitable for delegation within management by exception systems are 'programmed' or structured decisions which frequently occur at the operational level.

MIS and Strategic Management

Because much of strategy making is novel and unstructured, formal MIS have a limited role especially in the processing of information. However, there is a need for MIS to obtain information about the environment by a scanning and information gathering process in order to identify potential threats and opportunities.

The characteristics of useful strategic information are as follows:

(a) Largely external

Although some internal information will always be required, the critical and most difficult strategic problems concern the external environment. For example: competitor's performance and actions, economic trends, technology changes, market changes, political factors and so on.

(b) Largely concerned with the future.

Strategic planning is concerned with the medium to long term future so trends, forecasts and assessments are vital. Information on past performance – so vital to middle management – is of secondary importance.

(c) Qualitative as well as quantitative.

Much strategic planning and decision making requires quantative information but in addition qualitative opinions, judgements, insights and observations are often vitally important, especially for political and social factors.

(d) Largely informal

Systematic information processing has a place in strategic planning but this must not be at the expense of informal processes which are more effective and sensitive to environmental disturbances. Research has shown that over-formal systems at the strategic level make the organisation less adaptable and responsive. Too narrow a view of strategic MIS stifles initiative and creativity and bias preferences towards the status quo.

(e) Boundary free.

Lower level information tends to be confined to a specific functional area or activity. At the strategic level there must be no artificial boundaries and information must be broad ranging and reflect a holistic view of the organisation.

(f) Multi-dimensional

Strategic management must take an all-embracing view of problems, so needs to consider all facets which may be relevant. For example personnel, production, marketing, financial, engineering, research and other view points must be explicitly taken into account. The wider view should be contrasted with the much narrower functional or activity view common at tactical and operational levels.

Environmental Scanning

A key difference between MIS for strategic management and MIS for other levels is the emphasis on the environment. Strategic planning and decision making is essentially about understanding the environment and predicting key changes, trends and influences on the organisation in the future. The process by which information is gathered about the environment, whether by formal or informal means, is known as *scanning*.

Four types of scanning can be identified.

1. *Undirected scanning.*

Where the manager explores generally with no specific purpose in mind.

2. *Conditioned scanning.*

Where the manager, influenced by experience or some trigger, recognises certain events or items of information, but as they are encountered rather than by specific search.

3. *Informal directed scanning.*

Where the manager actively looks for specific information or information for a specific purpose but in an informal and unstructured fashion.

4. *Formal scanning.*

Where specially designed procedures or systems seek specific information or information about a specific problem.

Types of Environmental Information

It has been suggested that there are nine areas into which environmental information may be grouped:

1. *Economic and financial data* e.g. growth rates, interest rates, tax and interest rates, GDP forecasts, financing and banking projections

2. *Competitive data* e.g. threats from new products, competitors, substitutes. New pricing and marketing strategies from competitors

3. *Political data* e.g. government policies and influences, industrial and trade policies

4. *Legal data* e.g. implications of recent/proposed legislation, legal restraints on trade/marketing/products

5. *Social data* e.g. changing attitudes, culture, educational standards. Buying patterns, population changes, family patterns, availability of labour.

6. *Technological data* e.g. technological changes and developments and their implications for the organisation, availability and effectiveness of equipment, software and expertise.

7. *Geographical data* e.g. marketing and consumer data analysed to region and country.

8. *Materials and energy data* e.g. availability and likely costs of raw materials and energy.

9. *Stakeholder data* e.g. changes in stakeholder requirements (e.g. greater say over executive salaries), group influences.

Sources of Environmental Information

Of necessity, much scanning is done outside the organisation but internal sources are also important and should not be ignored. The following list are examples of possible sources of information about the environment.

(a) *The organisation's employees*

Contacts with customers and suppliers
Social contacts
Membership of professional associations
Attendance at courses and conferences
All forms of professional and industrial contacts

(b) *The organisation's contacts*

Trade and commerce associations
Local and central government departments
Customers and suppliers
Bankers

(c) *Published material.*

Books
Business periodicals and magazines
Local and national press
Reference services, directories, etc.

Government reports and statistics
Trade and Professional Association publications
Annual reports
Stockbroker and investment reports
Computer/satellite based databases
Television
Correspondence

(d) *Organised meetings*

Conferences
Seminars
Committees
'Think-tanks'

(e) *Commissioned sources*

Consultants
Academics
Special surveys
Market research

It should be emphasised that strategic planning is not only about economic and financial factors but it also is concerned with political, social, demographic and ecological influences. As an example in the 1990s no organisation can afford to ignore environmental factors. This may be a Local Authority considering the habitat destruction involved in a new development, it may be Sainsbury's acknowledging the consumer's growing awareness of environmental matters, it may be Audi advertising that all their cars are fitted with catalytic converters as standard and so on.

Data Protection Act (DPA)

Another important influence on the design and operation of computer based system is the need to conform to the DPA of 1984. The DPA was passed to prevent the misuse of personal data in computer systems and to allow individuals to know what data are held concerning them. All data users and computer bureaux must be registered with the *Data Protection Registrar* before they can hold personal data on computer files (manual files are not covered by the DPA.)

The DPA in the UK follows closely similar legislation introduced in other countries. Its main provisions include:

- personal data shall only be held for one or more specified (i.e. registered) and lawful purposes
- the information to be contained in personal data shall be obtained and processed fairly and lawfully
- personal data held for any purpose(s) shall not be used or disclosed in any manner not compatible with that purpose(s)
- personal data shall be adequate, relevant and not excessive in relation to the specified purpose(s)
- personal data shall be accurate and, where necessary, kept up to date
- personal data shall not be kept for longer than is necessary for the purpose(s) held

- an individual shall be entitled to:
  - (a) at reasonable intervals and without undue delay or expense to be informed by a data user whether he holds personal data on that individual and to have access to the data
  - (b) where appropriate to have such data corrected or erased
- appropriate security measures shall be taken to prevent unauthorised access to personal data and against accidental loss or destruction of such data.

Computer Misuse Act (1990)

Unlike the DPA the CMA does not impose additional requirements on legitimate computer users but introduces powers to prosecute those who deliberately and without authority misuse computer systems.

The Act defines three offences:

- *Unauthorised access*

  This covers access to the computer system without authorisation. This includes hacking and also authorised users that deliberately exceed their authority.

- *Ulterior intent*

  This refers to unauthorised access to a computer system with the intention of carrying out a serious crime. This could be fraud, or accessing personal information with the intention to commit blackmail.

- *Unauthorised modification*

  This covers unauthorised modification of any form, including computer viruses, which are intended to impair use of the computer system.

Ulterior intent and unauthorised modification are regarded as the more serious crimes and can be punished by up to five years imprisonment or an unlimited fine, or both.

A Postscript

Readers who have conscientiously worked through this book should be in a better position to design or use information systems. They will understand that information is not an end in itself. Its value comes from improvements in decision making, planning or control made possible by having good information. In effect the whole book has been about defining and producing good information and ensuring that it is used.

Finally, readers would do well to remember the advice of Joseph Pulitzer:

'Put it to them briefly, so that they will read it; clearly, so that they will appreciate it; picturesquely, so that they will remember it; and above all, accurately, so they will be guided by its light'.

Key Point Summary

- The major determinants of MIS design are: the organisation characteristics, planning, control and decision making requirements, external factors and the use of IT.
- Information may be demand/response, deposit/reference, internal/external.
- Managers must be actively involved in MIS design.

- Both formal and informal MIS are required.
- Operational level MIS are formal, structured and usually computer based.
- Tactical level management face uncertainty and complexity and require MIS support.
- Control systems incorporating multi-level feedback are a major feature of tactical level MIS.
- Four types of formal MIS are: control systems, database systems, enquiry systems and decision support systems.
- Management by exception is more than a reporting method, it is a style of management.
- Although informal systems are probably more important at the strategic level, formal systems have a part to play especially in environmental scanning and information gathering.
- Information specialists should avoid the temptation of implementing standardised solutions and systems to meet management's information needs. There are many superficial attractions in this approach but there is the genuine possibility that a standard solution is being applied to a non-standard problem.
- The Data Protection Act 1984 offers a measure of protection to individuals regarding data held about them by data users and computer bureaux who must be registered under the Act.
- The Computer Misuse Act introduced three computer related offences.

Self Review Questions

1. What are the main factors which determine the organisation's MIS?
2. What categories of information does an MIS deal with?
3. What is the relationship of formal and informal systems?
4. What are the characteristics of MIS at the operational level?
5. What factors determine whether an operational level MIS should be a batch or real time processing system?
6. How do tactical level MIS differ from those at the operational level?
7. What types of formal MIS can be identified at the tactical level?
8. What is Management by Exception and why is it used?
9. What are the characteristics of information likely to be useful at the strategic level?
10. What is environmental scanning and why is it so important at the strategic level?
11. What are some possible sources of information about the environment?
12. What are the key provisions of the Data Protection Act?
13. What are the three main offences defined in the Computer Misuse Act?

Assessment and revision section

Assignments

1. Virtually all products sold in Supermarkets have a Bar Code recorded on them. Find out what the Codes are used for and the basis of the Code. Try to find out the complete system in which the Codes are used.

2. Select an item of office equipment (e.g. a photocopier or a word processor, or a fax machine) and obtain details from various manufacturers about their machines. Do a comparative analysis of the key features offered by the various manufacturers. Which would you choose?

3. Draw a Data Flow Diagram of the data, processes and flows of a real office or department.

4. Find an application (not already computerised) that you think a spreadsheet package could be used on. What features make it a suitable application? What would be the advantages? What are the problems?

5. Prepare a report to management advocating why an organisation should consider using a Data Base and DBMS. (Use in your report features and details of one of the DBMS available commercially. You can obtain details from the suppliers.)

6. For a restaurant, a local authority and a paint manufacturer identify:

    (a) a strategic decision;

    (b) a tactical decision;

    (c) an operational decision.

    What information support is required for each of the decisions?

7. For the Insurance Transaction Processing illustration described in Chapter 15 define the contents of the Broker and Client files.

8. Automatic Teller Machines (ATM) are now a common feature outside nearly all banks. Investigate these machines thoroughly. What facilities do they offer? What input and output devices do they use?

9. Draw up a comparative table showing features, advantages and disadvantages of the following types of printer; daisy wheel, laser, ink-jet.

Mini-Case 1 – Information Flows in a Mail Order Business

Gratwoods is a large mail order business selling through a network of Agents. The Agents sell on commission and also receive a discount from the Catalogue price for personal purchases. Goods are normally paid for in 20 weekly instalments and the Agents are responsible for collecting the amounts due and paying the money to Gratwoods through the bank giro system. The Agent sends the receipted paying in slip and an analysis of payments to Gratwoods weekly.

The Agent completes an order form for all goods required containing the quantity,catalogue code, price, customer name and delivery address. On receipt at Gratwoods the order form is checked and then used as direct data entry for the on-line order processing system. The system generates a multi part set which includes an acknowledgement to the Agent, Invoice copies, and a warehouse copy for despatch. Goods are supplied on a sale-or-return basis. If not required, the Agent returns the goods using a Returns Form which is input to credit the Agents account. Each week the computer system produces a payments schedule for each Agent. This shows payments due, balances, overdue accounts and so on.

Gratwoods use a multi-access computer with disks.

Task 1 Flowchart the main information flows in the system.

Task 2 Draw a Systems Flowchart showing the computer system.

Task 3 Define the likely contents of the following files

- Agents file
- Stock file
- Suppliers file

Task 4 What information, additional to the items mentioned in the case, will the management of Gratwoods need to operate and control their business?

Mini-Case 2 – Communication and Control

Acme Mutual Life are a life assurance and pensions company based in Birmingham. There are 40 sales representatives housed in the company headquarters in the city centre. The company is concerned at the costs of operating from a city centre site and are contemplating a change in policy whereby the representatives work from their homes. Although the company recognises that there will be space and cost savings at Headquarters it is concerned about possible communication and control problems.

Task 1 List the main communications with which the representatives will have to deal.

Task 2 Decide what equipment should be supplied to the representatives and give the functions which will be performed.

Task 3 Discuss what control problems might arise and how these could be overcome.

Mini-Case 3 – Centralisation of Purchasing

ABC plc is a medium sized manufacturing company, with separate departments for the major activities of the business. Each department is currently responsible for its own purchase ordering and goods received system, covering raw materials, consumables and small items of office equipment. Invoices are received by the accounts department for recording, checking and subsequent payment.

A new system of purchase ordering and goods received is proposed, whereby goods are requisitioned by the user departments, but are ordered centrally. Items which are common to several departments, e.g. stationery, will also be stored and issued centrally.

The new purchasing department will obtain quotations from suppliers and raise purchase orders. One copy of the order will be sent to the supplier, a second copy sent to the requisitioner, and a third copy retained in a purchase order file. When the goods are delivered to the central warehouse, the accompanying delivery note will be checked against the goods, and a goods received note (GRN) raised. A copy of the GRN will be sent to the purchasing department for comparison with the copy order. Matched GRNs and copy orders are filed together, and any queries placed on a queries file. When the invoice arrives in the purchasing department, it will be compared to the order and GRN. If approved, the invoice is passed to the accounts department for recording and payment, and the GRN and copy order are filed in a 'completed orders' file. If it is not approved, the documents are placed on the queries file.

It is envisaged that the new procedures will be incorporated into the company's existing centralised computer system in due course, and will be integrated with other accounting systems.

You are required

(a) *to draw a Data Flow Diagram of the proposed purchase ordering and goods received system as described above. You may use any symbols with which you are familiar provided that you define what they stand for;*

(b) *to identify five problems which are likely to exist in ABC plc's current purchase ordering and goods received system and explain how they may be alleviated by the proposed centralised purchase ordering and goods received system;*

(c) *to evaluate three benefits which could arise from the integration of the purchase ordering and goods received system with the existing computerised accounting systems of ABC plc;*

(d) *to describe four advantages of a centralised computer system over one which offers distributed processing facilities.*

CIMA

Examination Questions (with Answers)

A1. Management Information Systems should facilitate decision-making at all levels of management; each level requires information with different characteristics, and with differing degrees of probability.

You are required

(a) to compare briefly the characteristics of information used in strategic planning with those required for operational control;

(b) to discuss the features of deterministic, probabilistic and adaptive systems. Give a practical example of each type of system.

CIMA

A2. A 1992 survey by the National Computer Centre found that more than 1 in 8 firms now use some form of teleworking, and a third of these are planning to extend it.

(a) Define teleworking with reference to an example, and draw a simple diagram to illustrate the type of network which would be required.

(b) Explain the advantage of teleworking to:

(i) The employer

(ii) The employee

IAM

A3. (a) Explain how the use of information technology can bring about improvements in productivity within a business organisation.

(b) Explain how the use of information technology may sometimes harm a business's performance.

CIMA

A4. The general manager of a large organisation has asked you to draw up a document identifying no more than 10 important system characteristics against which managers can evaluate the success of an information system, together with a brief explanation of each.

What would your document contain?

ACCA

A5. AB plc is a national freight distribution company with a head office, five regional offices and a hundred local depots spread throughout the country. It is planning a major computerisation project. The options which are being considered are as follows:

- a central mainframe system with terminals at each depot.
- distributed minicomputers at each regional office.

You are required to draft a report to the board of AB plc describing the ways in which each of the options would suit the company's structure and explaining two advantages and two disadvantages of each.

CIMA

A6. The context dataflow diagram below shows a system used to process orders in a manufacturing company in its most generalised form:

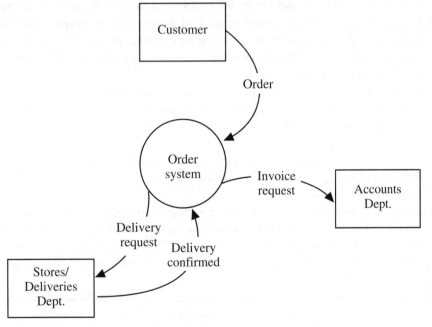

(a) (i) Produce a possible Level 1 dataflow diagram which 'explodes' this process order system, whilst still retaining a Level 1 symbol labelled 'process order'.

(ii) Produce a Level 2 'explosion' of the Process Order process.

(b) What process specification tools might you now need to use to further expand on the logic of the system?

ACCA

A7. (a) What are the technical and organisational advantages of a database management system (DBMS) when compared with conventional file organisation methods?

(b) What are the functions of a data dictionary?

ACCA

A8. (a) In the light of the three categories of management information – strategic, tactical and operational; and three types of decision – structured, semi-structured and unstructured, briefly define and describe the differences between:
- a transaction processing system
- a management information system
- a decision support system
- and executive information system
- an expert system.

(b) Suggest ONE application of each of the system types listed in part (a) above for each of the following functional areas of business:
- sales and marketing
- finance.

ACCA

A9. (a) An Executive Information System (EIS) has been defined as *'a computer-based system under the direct control of the executive, which provides the executive with current status information on conditions internal and external to the organisation'*.

Clearly explain the characteristics of an EIS, identifying why these characteristics discriminate such a system from other information systems used by management.

(b) During the information-gathering stage of the systems analyst's work, the analyst will expect to spend some time with the executive and his staff to try and determine the information requirements of the executive so that the EIS can be designed to meet these requirements.

Describe the different methods that a systems analyst may use to assess the information requirements of an executive for inclusion within an EIS, noting briefly any shortcomings of the methods.

CIMA

A10. A company which designs and manufactures marine engines regards customer service, i.e. the ability to respond effectively and in a timely fashion to service calls, as critical to its well-being.

Initially field engineers inspect faulty machines. Currently three quarters of faulty engines are referred to the repair centre, to be mended by repair centre engineers, resulting in a turnaround time of up to 10 days. The company has decided to investigate the possibility of carrying out more field repairs, with the aid of a portable expert system, in order to reduce the turnaround time.

The prototyping approach was used, and evaluation of the final prototype made it clear that an expert system, used in conjunction with laptop microcomputers would improve the situation to the extent that only 10% of engines would need to be returned to the repair centre, with the majority of repairs being carried out at the customers' premises by the field engineers.

(a) Define what is meant by an expert system, and explain how it might be of use in this context;

(b) Define what is meant by prototyping, briefly comment on the advantages and disadvantages and explain how and why this approach is used;

(c) Discuss the changes that would take place if the expert systems was implemented in terms of the position, status, tasks and responsibilities of engineers at the organisation's repair centre and in the field.

ACCA

A11. (a) Explain what is meant by negative feedback. Give an example of how this principle could be used in a business information system.

(b) Spreadsheets are often constructed and used by managers to help them make tactical decisions. Explain why spreadsheets are so appropriate for assisting managers to make this type of decision.

(c) Describe two possible problems that might arise in an organisation where end-users are extensively using spreadsheets for model building.

ACCA

Examination Questions (without Answers)

B1. It is not uncommon for system designers involved in the introduction of computer based data processing to encounter resentment and opposition from existing employees.

For what reasons may employees react in this manner? What steps can the system designer take to reduce this resistance?

CIMA

B2. It has been stated that quality is the paramount consideration in regard to management information provided by a computer system.

What does 'quality' mean in this context?

CIPFA

B3. Typically information within an organisation can be classified into three levels.

Using a typical manufacturing company as background define the three levels and give examples of the information which would be provided at each level. In what ways does the destination level influence the presentation of the information?

CIMA

B4. One of the pitfalls a system designer must avoid is that of sub-optimality.

(a) Define what is meant by sub-optimality and explain how it might be avoided.

(b) Give a practical example of sub-optimality.

CIMA

B5. What is the role and purpose of a Management Information System?

Compare the costs and benefits of computerising the MIS.

ACCA

B6. (a) State three advantages of the use of additional microcomputers as terminals as opposed to the use of VDUs.

(b) Describe how electronic mail might be implemented and used to advantage.

(c) Describe eight functions which may be carried out with word processing software, illustrating the advantages over conventional typing.

CIMA

B7. Dr Bentley in Defining Management's Information Needs (CIMA MIS Series) says that the information systems designer should not:

(i) Just ask the manager what he wants.

(ii) Tell the manager what he needs.

259

(iii) Give the manager what is available.

You are required:

(a) to explain why the systems designer is recommended to avoid the three steps mentioned above;

(b) to describe how management's information needs could be defined;

(c) to describe the characteristics that information should possess for it to have value.

CIMA

B8. (a) What do you understand by the term 'decision support system?'

(b) The fundamental components of a decision support system are:

- dialogue management
- data management
- model management

Briefly describe the functions of each.

(c) Give an example of the use of a decision support system.

ACCA

B9. 'Teleworking is performed away from direct supervision of employers and delivered to, and received from, workers by IT based communications systems.' Review the reasons why an organisation might be attracted to teleworking.

IAM

B10. (a) Explain what a DBMS is and what it does.

(b) Describe three advantages of the DBMS approach to data processing.

(c) An application requires that information is held about orders and customers, where a customer places many orders, but an order can only be placed by one particular customer. Each customer is identified by a unique account-number and each order has a unique order-number. List the likely content of the order and customer tables in a relational DBMS and explain how particular orders are linked to the customer who placed that order.

B11. The following passage has been adapted from a newspaper article:

ABG, an aircraft manufacturing company, has been addressing a problem familiar to many businesses - a growing awareness that the company's computer system, far from supporting the business, may even be holding it back. Over many years, ABG had put together a centralised, mainframe computer system operating a large number of individual software applications serving each functional requirement of the business. The system was generally very unwieldy and reinforced the vertical divisions between business functions and departments in ABG's pyramid-shaped organisation structure. ABG has now adopted a new computer system which involves PC-based local area network systems rather than mainframe computers. By devolving responsibilities, simplifying processes and giving 'decision making' back to each unit within the factory, the new computer system is contributing significantly to the reorganisation of the business. The new approach has also avoided a frequent mistake made by industry in its use of computers, which is to assume that all parts of the production process would benefit from computerisation. Under the new system, ABG has computerised the planning of production, but actual execution of the plan is handled by a non-computerised 'just-in-time' production system.

With the mainframe computer system, any significant change to an order meant that ABG had to spend several days reorganising manufacturing processes. But with the new PC-based system, changes can be made immediately. Within only a few weeks, inventories have been reduced by £200,000 and lead times have been cut. Important gains have also been made in controlling the order book. Before the PC-based system was introduced, the production unit would often have to re-make a part if a customer claimed not to have received it. Now a member of the production team can check all the documentation, and convey accurate information back to the customer about when the part had been sent. Invariably, the 'missing' part turns up in the customer's stores.

(a) Explain the following terms mentioned in the passage: mainframe computer system; local area network systems; 'just-in-time' production system.

(b) Describe *two* examples (other than those mentioned in the passage) of a company's computer system holding back rather than supporting the growth of the business.

(c) Discuss how the changes in ABG's IT system mentioned in the passage could affect the company's organisation structure and also the company's relations with external suppliers and customers

CIMA

B12. It is often said that the application of information technology (IT) is leading to *flatter* organisation structures.

(a) Explain the differences between a *flat* and a *tall* organisation structure and describe how information technology is leading to *flatter* organisation structures.

(b) Discuss the advantages and disadvantages of a *flatter* organisation structure for a business.

CIMA

Additional Reading

1. French, *Data Processing and Information Technology*, Letts Educational (formerly published by DP Publications)

2. Davis and Olsen, *Management Information Systems*, McGraw Hill

3. Finlay, *Decision Support Systems*, NCC Blackwell

4. Clifton and Sutclife, *Business Information Systems*, Prentice Hall

5. Schoderbek, Schoderbek and Kefalas, *Management Systems*, Business Publications

6. Martin and Powell, *Information Systems – A Management Perspective*, McGraw Hill

7. Doswell, *Office Automation – Context, Experience and Future*, Wiley

8. Sprague & McNurlin, *Information Systems: Management in Practice*, Butterworth.

Answers to Examination Questions

Assessment – Chapters 1–4

A1. (a) This can be taken directly from the book.

(b) These characteristics can be summarised as shown in Figure A1/1.

	Planning Information	Control Information	Decision Making Information
Coverage	Not segregated by function or department. Transcends organisational divisions.	Follows organisation divisions. Related to specific functions, departments and managers.	All matters that could change as a result of taking the decision.
Time Scale	Covers relatively long time periods and seeks to show trends.	Covers short time periods, shifts, days, weeks and months.	Related to decision being taken. Approximate information speedily prepared often most valuable.
Amount of Detail	Patterns and trends more important than fine detail particularly for long range planning.	Detail and precision important but trends also of importance.	All relevant matters. Therefore may be detailed or in broad terms.
Orientation	Objective is to provide insight into the future.	Shows past results and activities and relates these to targets, standards and budgets.	Decision making is entirely concerned with future changes. The past is irrelevant except as a guide to the future.

Fig A1/1 Characteristics of Planning, Control and Decision Making

(c) The theoretical answer is that the costs of producing extra information should be compared with the additional benefits obtainable by using the additional information. However it is often difficult to assess the incremental benefits, and sometimes the incremental costs. Asking for extra information is a well known ploy used for delaying taking a decision. Used for this purpose, the extra information is not likely to produce extra benefits.

A2. All levels of management require information on which to base decisions, to organise, to plan and to control.

Whilst timing is important, other factors such as completeness, accuracy and relevance are equally important in assessing the value of information to an organisation.

Clearly the quality of management information is directly related to its timing, but this in itself is linked to the particular situation giving rise to the need for such information.

To illustrate, the following examples are given:

(a) provision of historical information – into this category come annual accounts where there is no conflict between speed and accuracy, as time is taken to produce the information required; most companies, however, have a well defined timetable.

(b) provision of information for control purposes as, for example, in production or quality control. Speed and accuracy are important to avoid costly delays or bad production.

(c) provision of information for planning purposes. Here the time scale may well be years and thus there is less pressure on time and no need for a fine degree of accuracy.

It is well to understand that by accuracy is meant an acceptable level dependent on the circumstances. The cost/benefit ratio is something not to be overlooked.

A well designed management information system will provide the various levels of management with appropriate information to enable them to manage. Thus the starting point must always be the uses to which information is to be put.

The following factors will influence the design of such a system:

(i) the organisation structure – including the number of levels through which information must flow. Generally decisions should be taken at the lowest level.

(ii) the data processing cycle – starting with how and where data originates; the preparation and input of data; processing and output of resultant information.

(iii) the form of reports. Very often delay occurs through too much transcription. Techniques such as teleprinters and visual display units can overcome this using on-line or real-time data processing.

The overall consideration, of course, will be the comparison of the costs of producing the information with the benefits to be obtained from having it.

A3. Systems theory is a broad conceptual basis for examining the operations of any system; whether a business, a school, a machine and so on.

The elements which need to be identified include:

- The environment and boundaries. This will include the idea of a hierarchy of systems.
- The inputs to the system.
- The outputs from the system.
- The processes contained within the system. This will include the resources required to operate the procedures.
- The objectives that the system wishes to achieve.

Relating these broad categories to a business system we find that they concern management functions such as planning, control and decision making.

Thus planning deals with setting the objectives and deciding the pattern of operations in both the long and short term. Information is needed from both external and internal sources.

Control deals with the feedback of results to ensure that operations are proceeding according to plan. At lower levels control information is mainly internal but longer term control means adjusting to the environment and relies on external information.

Decision making occurs in planning and control at all levels. It requires relevant, timely and accurate information from both internal and external sources.

A4. A closed system is one which does not interact with its environment where an open one does. In practical terms this means that modern organisations must interact with the environment, must change to suit the environment and must continually adapt so as to keep up to date in order to ward off competitors and to survive!

The environment may be a local one, the national economy or the international scene. As examples of industries which did not react and adapt to the environment (in this case Japanese – market penetration) consider the UK car industry and the UK television industry. The environmental changes may be technological ones for example the traditional Swiss watchmaking industry was decimated by not reacting to micro-chip technology.

However, it should be said that organisations have always had to interact with their environment so it is probably too simplistic a view that traditional organisations were closed systems which implies no interaction whatsoever.

There is considerable evidence to indicate that the organisation which adapts to environmental changes is able to survive and prosper in conditions in which the more traditionally organised and structured organisations contract and founder.

The modern organisation (an open system) must be prepared and organised for change. This implies a second order level of feedback. The first order level feedback provides information regarding the progress of control parameters (stock levels, standard cost etc.) against targets whereas the second order feedback is of a higher level concerning the behaviour of the system itself in coping with operations i.e. does the system need to be altered to suit the changes?

A5. Implicit in the systems approach to solving organisational problems is the recognition of the overall objectives. It is said to be objective-orientated. One would assume that such objectives were determined by the board in this case and that they were clearly understood.

We are told that the production plan was decided upon after 'consideration of all factors' so one would assume that the sub-system (production department) objectives were established with a full knowledge of the overall goals.

However it is clear that sub-optimisation has taken place in the production department. This is the term used to describe the situation that exists where the sub-system goals are pursued to the detriment of those of the system as a whole.

The evidence is in the change of production levels which has taken place without reference to the central authority. Reasons why such sub-optimisation takes place vary but it can be caused by:

(a) *poor communication* – i.e. overall system objectives not clearly identified and subordinate nature of sub-system objectives not properly explained.

(b) *control systems failing* to carry out their monitoring function thus highlighting variances from planned targets.

(c) *a lack of co-ordination* between sub-systems leading to over de-coupling.

If one assumes the original targets to be in the best interests of the company as a whole then the existence of such sub-optimisation is a matter for concern to other sub-systems, e.g. stores, accounts and sales.

Conclusion

General acceptance of the systems approach is required and a clear identification of overall system objectives. This must be followed by an understanding of the way sub-system goals contribute to the achievement of overall goals.

Communication is a key factor with a well thought out management information system.

A6. The question is concerned with the systems approach to solving organisation problems. A prime feature of such an approach is that it is 'objective orientated'. As a first step therefore the correct objectives are set and a system designed for their achievement.

It is important that the overall organisational objectives are well defined before considering those of the particular area being studied. This is the task of top management. Having done this the overall objectives should be unambiguously communicated to those responsible for sub-systems. The sub-systems objectives must be consistent with the achievement of the overall objectives.

There will of course be problems in establishing the relevant objectives in any area under study.

Quantification

It is often difficult to state objectives in quantitative terms. For example a computer may be able to produce 'more and better' information for stock control purposes. However it may be difficult to state precisely what the savings may mean in terms of actual reduction in stock levels as a result of the information provided. Nevertheless the attempt should be made.

Sub Optimisation

Within a company production, sales and finance are frequently in conflict. Sales want as much diversification as possible to satisfy customers' whims with a 'next day' delivery service. Production want long, interruption-free runs of standard products with plenty of time to change planned production (because of stocking, and scheduling problems). Finance wants to minimise the stock holdings and demands early settlement from customers to improve cash flow.

Ideally, each sub-system should work as independently of any other sub-system as possible (be 'de-coupled') in order that reference need not be made to other sub-systems when decisions are made. Hopefully the systems approach will help to avoid such optimism.

> *Conflicting Objectives.* It is quite common to have objectives in all systems which conflict with one another, in which case of course some form of compromise is necessary. As an example, there may well be a conflict of requirements between capital costs, and operating costs and high safety standards.

> *Changing Circumstances.* The objectives may need to be changed due to outside circumstances, e.g. government intervention or competition. For example, it may be necessary to offer a 'same day' service instead of a '48 hours' service because a competitor is doing so (because not do so would mean a loss of business and customers).

A7. (a) An open system is one which interacts with its environment and consequently is affected by changes in the environment and, to a limited extent, affects its environment.

(b) Organisation theory recognises that all organisations, private, social, profit and non-profit seeking must be open systems. They receive inputs from the environment and produce outputs which go into the environment. They must take account of changes in their environment which include; competitive and market changes, social, legal, financial and cultural influences and many others. The ability to adapt to change is a key feature of successful organisations and adaptation can only take place with open systems which are attuned to environmental influences.

A8. (a) Data are events, facts and results which have been recorded. They are the raw materials from which information is produced. Information is data that have been processed in such a way as to be useful to the recipient.

(b) Information properly used, adds value to planning, decision-making and control. Information does not have value in itself, its value derives from the changes in decision behaviour caused by the information being available. Without information most decision making would be simply guess work.

(c) Useful information has the following features

- Relevance for problem/decision being considered
- Communicated in time to the right person
- Accurate and complete enough for the problem
- Understandable by the user.

A9. Three major barriers to good communication in organisations are:

1. Badly designed and badly written reports and statements.

   Messages produced with unexplained technical terminology (jargon) and without considering the precise requirements of the recipient, do not communicate efficiently. Highlighting, concise summaries, clear layouts all help to promote understanding.

2. Organisational structure and protocol.

   Numerous levels in the structure, rigid hierarchies and adherence to formal rules and procedures tend to delay messages and cause poor communications.

3. Information overload.

Too often management are swamped with data (often incorrectly called 'management information') which is routinely produced. this means that vital messages are not read in time or at all. A key result of many surveys is that management do not need *more* information, they need *better* information.

Assessment – Chapters 5 to 9

A1.   In answering a question of this type it would be necessary first to identify the members of the Classical School. These include, Taylor, Gilbreth, Fayol, Urwick, Brech, Weber and so on.

The scientific managers (Taylor et al) concentrated on the factory floor and by specialisation and work organisation greatly improved the efficiency of production. Their approach was a mechanistic one which was the forerunner of modern work study.

The classical theorists (Fayol et al) were concerned with the organisation as a whole and particularly with its structure and with the development of management principles which were thought to be universally applicable. These included span of control, the principle of authority, functionalism and so on. Weber and others demonstrated the apparent inevitability of hierarchical structures in organisations and the group as a whole showed how important it was to consider structure (departments, relationships and hierarchies) as an essential part of the development of an efficient organisation.

A2.   Decentralised organisations are those where local managers not at the top of the organisation, have the power to make decisions and commit resources, usually within specified limits.

The main advantages and disadvantages are:

Advantages

(a)   Decision making is speedier.

(b)   Decisions are more likely to reflect local conditions.

(c)   Information delays are reduced and local information is likely to be more relevant.

(d)   Motivation of local management is increased and decentralisation provides good training for potential senior management.

(e)   Senior management have more time for strategic matters.

Disadvantages

(a)   Better quality and better trained managers are required,

(b)   Sub-optimal activities can take place.

(c)   First class information and control systems, which may be expensive, are required.

(d)   There may be a lack of overall control/guidance resulting in an inconsistent approach to problems.

A3.   The Hawthorne Studies marked a major shift from the classical/scientific management approach to the consideration of social and psychological factors, especially the influence of the work group and informal cultures. The Human Relations School grew out of these studies and its main principles can be summarised thus.

1.   People should not be treated in 'isolation' but as members of a group. The group exerts strong influence on performance, decision making and so on.

2.   People are motivated by social factors and thus the amount of work is determined by technical/physical factors and social factors.

3.   Leaders will develop in groups and are important in setting group norms and motivating individuals.

The Tavistock Institute of Human Relations extended and modified the results of the original Hawthorne Studies. The work of Trist and Bamforth in the Durham coal mines concluded that effective work was a result of the interdependence of technological and operational factors (equipment, layout etc.) and the social needs of the employees in the working group. It was discovered that there were clear benefits from allowing people to complete a whole task rather than specialised fragments.

The findings have become known as the Socio-technical approach.

A4. *Main points*

    (a) Economic security, reputation/standing, recognition of achievements, social contacts, interesting work. In general although money is a motivator it appears not to be a lasting motivator. Factors associated with the work and self-esteem appear to be stronger motivators for most people.

    (b) This is clearly an important part of every manager's job and a key to improving efficiency. Because motivation is a personal matter the conditions which motivate vary from person to person. However the following list provides the main factors:

- provide support and feedback
- make the job as complete and challenging as possible
- provide good training
- arrange for career development
- encourage group and team working
- good working conditions
- promote good communications
- be frank and fair
- provide adequate pay.

A5. Line authority is the direct authority exercised in the chain of command. Every manager has line authority over his subordinates.

Functional authority is the power to exercise command or influence over specialised functions e.g. personnel, accounting. This means that, within their area of expertise, a functional specialist may give instructions to a line manager.

Staff authority is restricted to the provision of advice or service. It is usually exercised by people who are 'assistants' to others.

It is normal for the accounting function to have functional authority over accounting and finance matters throughout the organisation. To an extent this is a dilution of the authority of line managers but with the complexity of modern organisations this is probably inevitable.

A6. Flexible organisations are those which are capable of adapting to changing circumstances. Their features include;

- use of networks of control authority and communication rather than formal hierarchies.
- emphasis on the use of specialist knowledge.
- commitment to task and progress rather than to a particular organisation.
- adjustment and redefinition of tasks is continuous.
- emphasis on advice rather than instruction and lateral rather than vertical communication.

Flexible organisations have many advantages but may exert pressures on individuals thus;

- the lack of clear authority may be a source of ambiguity, conflict and tension
- uneven work demands and the need to learn new skills may cause anxiety
- continual re-adjustments may mean difficulties in developing groups loyalties
- flexible structures may make it more difficult for individuals to see their career patterns and thus cause discontent
- constant changes favours those with political skills and may cause less fortunate people to become frustrated.

A7.   Conflict develops when there are recognisable entities (groups, sections, department, teams and so on) which perceive they are in competition for some scarce resource (for example, money, facilities, awards, status).

The main way of avoiding conflict is by setting over-riding goals. These are goals which are attractive to both groups but which require co-operation for their achievement. Wherever possible conflict should be avoided by management emphasising the need for co-operation and interdependence and by not creating circumstances in which undue competition occurs.

A8.   (a) The main principles and explanations can be taken from the text. The principles include: span of control, definition of objectives and duties, the scalar principle, specialisation and division of labour, and the principle of correspondence.

(b) The main criticisms of the Classical Approach are:
- There was undue emphasis on structures, formal authority and control.
- The behaviour and needs of the people in organisations was largely ignored.
- The approach was prescriptive with only limited analysis of actual behaviour.

The contributions of the classical theorists provided a foundation upon which later researchers could build and they made the study of management respectable in an intellectual sense.

A9.   This can be taken directly from the text.

A10. The reasons for the decline in morale and productivity may be a single factor or a combination of numerous factors. Some possible factors are listed below:

(a) *Resentment.*
All or the most senior subordinate may feel resentment at the appointment of an 'outsider'.

(b) *Resistance to change.*
The new manager may introduce new practices and methods which are resisted.

(c) *Style of management.*
Almost inevitably there will be a new style of management which may cause problems. Whichever way the style develops – greater or lesser control – difficulties may occur.

(d) *Incompetence of new manager.*
The new manager may not have the requisite technical, managerial or organisational skills to cope with the demands of the job.

(e) *Job changes.*
The new manager may have introduced new methods, or swapped jobs around in the department causing inefficiencies and reducing commitment. If the jobs are less satisfying, motivation will be reduced and personnel alienated.

A11. Stakeholders can be defined as those people or organisations that have a financial or other form of interest in the organisation. Typically these include:
- the owners or shareholders
- the staff, including management
- the customers and suppliers of the organisation
- trades unions, trade organisations
- the firms bankers
- environmental groups
- the government especially the Department of Trade and Industry, Inland Revenue and Customs and Excise.

A12. (a) A functionally-based business is described in the text, the usual functions being; Production, Marketing, Purchasing etc.

Other ways of organising structures are; product-based, geographically or regionally based, market based structure e.g. as in banking.

(b) Traditionally, especially in manufacturing, functionally-based organisations have been popular. The advantages of such structures include; expertise is concentrated and enhanced, authority for particular functions is clearly recognised, common standards and approaches throughout the organisation are encouraged. The disadvantages include; conflicts with line managers, focused functional expertise may not recognise other important interactions, difficult information flows across and between functions, slower reaction to changing conditions.

Assessment – Chapters 10 to 13

A1. *Report on computer Based Financial Model*

To: Treasurer

From: A.N. Other

As requested I give below the answers to the questions you posed.

(a) What is a model? A model is any representation of reality. It may be a physical model (e.g. an architectural model of a town layout) or an abstract model. These are representations of reality in numeric, algebraic, symbolic or graphical form. For example a Balance Sheet is a model which depicts the relationship between a firm's assets and liabilities at a given point in time. A Balance Sheet is essentially a static model and a model which permits analysis and projections can be considerably more useful. Such a model is a computer based financial model which is essentially a linked series of equations and formulae (expressed in computer instructions) which enable projections, forecasts, statements etc. to be prepared.

(b) What procedures are involved in constructing a model? To construct a useful and appropriate model is a complex task requiring much detailed investigation and a thorough technical knowledge of the area involved (e.g. budgeting, loans fund, financial forecasts etc.). It is essentially an iterative process as it is extremely unlikely that a perfect model will be produced first time. The major steps in producing a computer based financial model are as follows:

1. *Establish the objectives of the model.* This is a management task and involves answering many questions such as: what results/calculations/forecasts are required from this model? What will be the frequency of use? What will be the required input data? What format will be required? etc.

2. *Define the logic of the model.* Management having specified the objectives it is usual to work backwards from the model's objectives identifying the relationships between the variables and eventually specifying all data that must be input to the model. It is at this stage that identification of the critical variables becomes of crucial importance. All models are a simplification of reality and the real skill in model building comes from identifying the important variables and disregarding the unimportant ones.

3. *Code of model.* Once the logic has been defined and expressed in the forms of flowcharts and/or equations and/or decision tables, the logic is coded into a series of instructions.

4. *Test model.* After coding and compilation where appropriate, the model (as any other program) is tested using sample input data.

5. *Model revision.* Almost inevitably the model will not meet the exact requirements or changed circumstances so that some revision will be necessary.

(c) Advantages of using a computer-based model. Although there are many problems involved in establishing a comprehensive model a number of significant advantages accrue. These include:

(i) ability to handle large volumes of data speedily.

(ii) ability to carry out long series of calculations without error.

(iii) ability to test various possible circumstances and see the results which would be virtually impossible manually e.g. to test out effects on budget calculations of 10%, 12%, 15% etc. inflation rates; various wage cost increases and so on.

(iv) inclusion in a comprehensive modelling package of a whole range of facilities including investment appraisal, cash flow forecasting etc.

A2. (a) Information characteristics:

Planning information

Is future orientated and often covers a relatively long time period. Trends and patterns are more important than fine detail. Often there is wide coverage involving both internal and external sources. Considerable use is made of forecasting techniques.

Control information

Shows past results and activities and often relates the results to a target, standard or budget. Often very detailed and is usually concerned with specific functions, operations, departments or personnel.

Operating information

This is information about the essential day-to-day activities of the business e.g. the information on a customer's order, information on stocks, production figures and so on. There is a huge range and volume of operating information which is often in great detail. The information is specific and, consolidated and summarised, provides a prime input for the provision of planning and control information.

(b) The main problems associated with the production and use of planning and control information include the following:

Planning information

Planning always relates to the future and the only certain thing abut the future is that it is unknown. This is the key problem regarding planning information for which there is no complete solution. There are difficulties with forecasting in uncertain conditions and often great difficulty in obtaining essential information from external sources, even if it is known what factors will be important over the planning period involved which, of course, is not always the case. The user of planning information has to exercise judgement or flair in deciding whether or not to accept the forecasts presented. If conditions change, or unknown factors arise – which is likely to happen – forecasts based on past results are unlikely to be of much value.

Control information

The effectiveness of control information relates to the speed at which it is gathered and processed ready for use. The information must be directed at the appropriate level in the organisation for maximum effectiveness. Surveys have shown that control information is often not used, mainly because of the following reasons:

(i) It arrived too late.

(ii) The subjects covered were outside the manager's control.

(iii) It was insufficiently detailed or thought to be inaccurate or in a form which could not be understood.

A3. It is necessary for companies to establish and periodically review their objectives for the following reasons:

(a) An up-to-date statement of objectives sets a framework for the organisation's activities and serves as a focal point for management's efforts.

(b) The objectives provide the supporting detail to the broad, overall goals of the organisation.

(c) Objectives help to clarify how the organisation intends to develop over the short, medium and long term.

(d) Periodic reviews of objectives ensure that relevant objectives are being pursued, provide a structure for debates about the organisation's activities and provide an important formal reason for examining the environment.

Objectives are specific to each organisation and must reflect the purpose of the organisation, whether a manuracturing concern, a charity, a college, a bank and so on.

Drucker suggests that there are eight areas in which objectives of performance and results have to be set for a typical commercial organisation, namely:

- Market Standing
- Innovation
- Productivity
- Physical and Financial Resources
- Profitability
- Manager performance and development
- Worker performance and attitude
- Public responsibility

A4. This can be largely answered from the text. Note particularly the importance of external information and forecasts relating to; the market and consumers, demographic trends, economic and financial trends, social and political factors and others.

A5. The three factors, Timeliness, Retrieval and Presentation, Centralised-decentralised are critical factors to consider when designing information systems.

(a) *Timeliness of information.* Research studies indicate that a major source of dissatisfaction with information systems is the arrival of information too late to be able to be used effectively. The more formal the information system the greater the care which needs to be taken to ensure timely arrival. With information systems involving feedback and control processes timing is the critical factor. The late arrival of information may cause control action to be totally inappropriate for current conditions; at the level of the organisation, stock levels may have already begun to rise of their own accord when belated control information indicating low stock levels is acted upon causing stock levels to be increased sharply; at the level of the economy, information on demand management is often 3-6 months behind current events making effective fiscal control action more difficult and likely to be less appropriate. The whole process of gathering raw data, processing, information production and communication must be minutely scrutinised to cut out delays and reduce the time lag between event and information about that event being given to the user. With systems where there are fluctuating values, (stocks, cash flows, production etc.) the late arrival of control information causes a change from negative to positive feedback with a consequently greater chance of system instability.

(b) *Retrieval and Presentation.* The accessibility of information i.e. the ease of retrieval is an important factor in all information systems. Undue difficulties e.g. complicated request forms, delays, complex coding systems etc. make retrieval by the manager more difficult and cumbersome and makes it more likely that the manager will avoid using the formal information systems and substitute his own, perhaps less efficient and objective system. At the technical level manufacturers have paid considerable attention to the problems of information retrieval e.g. direct access storage media, database management systems, microfiche, key-word – in context (KWIC) systems etc.

Another powerful reason for the less efficient use of information systems is the problem of information presentation. Research indicates that managers consider a substantial amount of information they receive to be badly presented. The following factors should be carefully considered by system designers:

- Are the layout, heading, captions etc. of the report clear?
- Would a graphical/pictorial representation be preferable to tabular format?
- Is the report too detailed, not detailed enough?
- Are trends, exceptions, comparisons clearly shown?
- Is technical terminology kept to an unavoidable minimum and adequately explained?
- Above all has the manager been consulted about the presentation?

(c) *Centralised and decentralised information stores.* In general as information systems become more formal and mechanised there is, or has been until very recently, a strong tendency for the information processing to become more centralised. This has some advantages for example, greater control, possible financial savings, standardised systems/coding etc. easier to implement.

Of course there are several disadvantages of centralised systems for example, remoteness, delays, slowness to react to change, lack of immediacy, possible resentment by departments serviced by the central system, possible lack of relevance etc.

The reference above to recent developments is of course to such things as terminals, VDUs, micro processors etc. Such developments blur the distinction between centralised and decentralised information stores because of the immediacy of response and interrogation at the point of information need coupled with a centralised information stores. The advent of the silicon chip and associated micro processor will enable more decentralisation of information processing and storage because of its cheapness, power and availability.

A6. (a) Typically the three levels are described as:

Strategic or top management. This level of management co-ordinates the activities of the business as a whole and is concerned with establishing overall objectives for the organisation and developing and implementing appropriate policies in order to achieve objectives.

Tactical or middle management. This level of management's task is to implement top management policy and to direct the operations and functions of the organisation.

Operational or lower management. This level is concerned with the day-to-day processes of supervision and direction of the routine activities of the organisation.

(b) Characteristics of decision making at the three levels.

Strategic. An open system perspective is necessary because of the unstructured, long term nature of decision making (non-programmed as defined by Simon). This decision making is largely concerned with external factors and trends and is judgmental.

Middle. Characterised by medium to short term decisions with a greater – but not exclusive emphasis – on internal factors. Co-ordination and control activities form the basis of much decision making at this level.

Lower. Decision making is highly structured (programmed as defined by Simon) and operates according to well defined rules. Often the decisions are quantitatively based and are invariably short term.

(c) Examples of assistance provided by computer based information systems for the three organisational levels.

Strategic level – 'decision-support' systems involving modelling, information retrieval.

Middle level – analysis and exception reporting systems, spreadsheets for modelling, budgeting and similar control systems.

Lower level – essentially automated decision making used in accordance with pre-determined criteria e.g. stock control and re-ordering systems, aspects of production control.

A7. See Figure A3/7 on the next page.

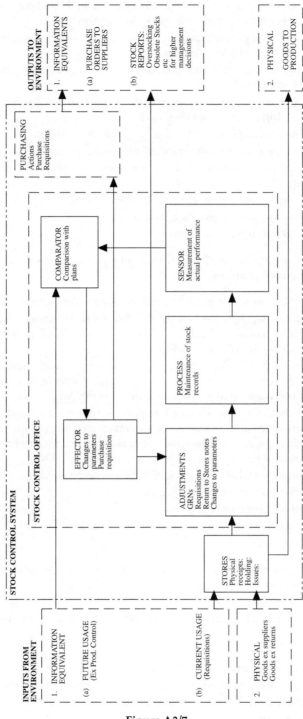

Figure A3/7

A8. (a) Dysfunctional behaviour is behaviour which produces organisation inefficiency. With an obvious target such as a computer such behaviour is quite common and manifests itself in numerous ways including; projection, avoidance, and aggression.

Projection means that people blame the new system for all problems even where they previously existed and are unconnected with the new system.

Avoidance means that people especially in managerial positions ignore the new system and persist with older, less efficient systems.

Aggression can take many forms including miscoding, delaying tactics, even physical damage to the equipment.

(b) Dysfunctional behaviour tends to occur with change that is not sympathetically managed. Ways of minimising adverse reaction include:

(i) Full and genuine participation in the design of new systems.

(ii) Open dialogue and frank communications before any changes are made.

(iii) Where appropriate safeguards should be given regarding status or job changes, redundancies etc.

(iv) Full training before, during and after implementation.

(v) Reasonable, mutually agreed targets and norms.

(vi) Full managerial support for change.

A9. This can be largely answered from the text. Make sure you are aware of the importance of information flows in the control process.

A10. The key features of Theories X, Y and Z as styles of management include:

Theory X assumes workers are lazy and dislike work avoiding it wherever possible. In consequence there would be clearly laid down plans, schedules and directions. There would be centralised decision making and close control.

Theory Y assumes that workers find work natural and desirable and accordingly management seek to release the personal potential of staff. Subordinates are involved in setting objectives and encouraged to participate in decision making.

Theory Z extends Theory Y by seeking a high degree of consensus and trust. A consensus of values throughout the organisation is sought and employee commitment is rewarded. There is an emphasis on open and democratic relationships and on consensus decision-making. Ideally there should be long-term employment and career paths.

Some of the contingencies which may affect the choice of management style include:

- the nature of the work and technology used
- the ability and education level of employees
- employee expectations and traditional norms of behaviour
- national and cultural factors.

A11. The items listed in the question represent major changes in the company's environment which are likely to have significant impacts, especially on management.

Possible impacts on management:

- increased pressure to maintain market share/profitability in the face of increased competition.
- less security
- more travel and need to learn other languages
- need to change management style to deal with new conditions and legislation.

Overall, managers are likely to have to be more aggressive and flexible.

Possible impacts on staff:

- more job insecurity
- greater pressure for performance
- need for more flexibility.

A12. The key features of strategic tactical and operational planning can be taken from the text. The key features are that strategic planning is concerned with the long-term future of the organisation, tactical planning allocates and schedules resources to fulfil the strategic plan and operational planning deals with the day to day running of the organisation.

A13. The main theories on Job Satisfaction were developed by Maslow and Herzberg which are covered in some detail in the text. Apart from the listing of the main factors (ranging from pay to recognition) it is necessary to stress that Job Satisfaction needs constant re-enforcement. It is not a once-off task.

Assessment – Chapters 14 to 16

A1. (a) This can be taken largely from the text. Key points include; planning information is long term, often external, without great detail, future looking. On the other hand, control information is mainly internal, often detailed and is essentially a monitoring exercise on past transactions.

(b) Deterministic Systems: these are totally predictable with outputs known with certainty given a particular input. Computer programs are an example.

Probabilistic systems: these are systems which contain uncertainty so that outputs are not exactly predictable. A stock control system cannot predict the exact stock level in the future although the average level can usually be predicted.

Adaptive systems: these are systems which change and adapt to suit changes in conditions and data input. There is an element of learning in such systems. Organisations as a whole are adaptive systems.

A2. The answer can be taken from the text.

A3. Productivity is usually defined as the output per worker. Machinery of all types, materials handling, IT and various forms of capital equipment all contribute to improvements in productivity.

(a) The special features of IT that can improve productivity include:
- faster access to information and records
- automatic processing and decision-making
- wider range of information availability through files and databases
- electronic communications of all types
- automatic monitoring of balances, stock levels, debtors etc.
- reduction of errors caused by human processing
- ability to use simulations, modelling and operational techniques.

(b) The use of IT can harm performance in various ways:
- where IT use is uncontrolled, files and data may be lost or corrupted
- competitors may be able to access confidential files through networks
- unauthorised amendments to programs and files may be made for fraudulent purposes
- computer viruses may cause disastrous problems.

A4. Ten important characteristics to evaluate information systems.

Effectiveness i.e. does system accomplish its objectives?

Quality i.e. what errors are produced, what are delays and service performance?

Costs i.e. are initial and running costs acceptable?

Efficiency i.e. are objectives achieved in a cost-effective manner?

Flexibility i.e. is system capable of responding to change?

Acceptability i.e. is system acceptable to, and relied upon by, users?

Complexity i.e. is system simple enough to manage and use or is it over-complex?
Controllability i.e. is system controllable and capable of being adapted by the users?
Capacity i.e. is system capable of handling the tasks it is asked to perform?
Reliability i.e. what is the amount of down time?

A5. Key points in report.
Central system
Advantages
Central control
Consistent standards in development and operations
Central database open to all
Disadvantages
Cost of communications
Remoteness of users
Single system vulnerable to breakdown
Distributed systems
Advantages
Regions directly involved
Lower communication costs
Faster response
Less impact caused by breakdown
Disadvantages
Control over development standards etc. more difficult
Hardware costs likely to be higher
More staff in total required

A6. (a) Possible Level 1 dataflow diagram.

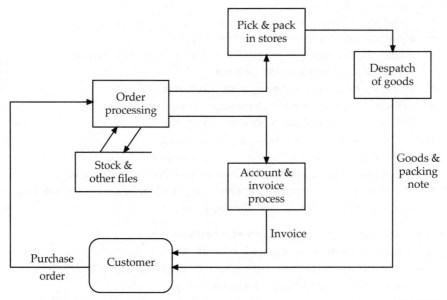

(b) Possible Level 2 'explosion' of order processing

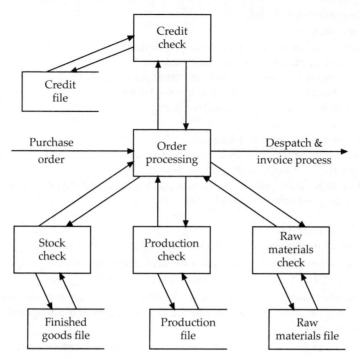

(c) Other process specification tools are:
- Structured English
- 4th Generation program languages
- Decision tables
- Decision trees.

A7. (a) This part can be taken from the text.

(b) *Data Dictionary*: this is defined by the British Computer Society as 'An index of data held in a database used to assist in maintenance and any other access to the data'.

It is thus a list or record of each data store and each data flow in the system. It is a form of technical documentation to ensure that everyone in the organisation defines and uses data consistently.

A8. (a) The key elements of the five categories given can be taken from the text. The main points are:
- transaction processing are the routine structured systems which process operational information
- management information systems, in this context, are those that produce management reports, based on transaction processing, for routine management purposes for planning, control and decision making
- decision support systems support management decision making in an interactive manner in semi-structured situations
- executive information systems provide flexible access to all types of corporate information. They use the database developed by transaction processing and are typically used by senior management
- expert systems are linked suites of programs which capture the special knowledge of experts and makes this more widely available

(b) Possible applications include:

Sales and marketing:
Transaction processing systems: invoice production.
Management information system: sales analyses.
Decision support systems: modelling effects of price changes.
Executive information systems: access to sales trends.
Expert systems: developing competitive strategies.

Finance:
Transaction processing: ledger keeping.
Management information system: credit control report.
Decision support system: project appraisal using DCF.
Executive information system: access to departmental operating performance.
Expert system: assessing loan applications in banks.

A9. (a) Can be taken from the text

(b) Typical of the methods the Systems Analyst may use are the following:

- Detailed interviews with staff and executive. These help to clarify requirements but care must be taken to avoid concentration on current problems only.

- Case observation and analysis of work being done and types of decisions made. Again care must be taken to consider future developments and infrequently occurring, but critical, work.

- Analysis of the key performance indicators require to measure success. Typically these are targets with a financial bias e.g. cash flow, profitability, return on capital employed but other factors need attention for long-run success. Examples include; quality, customer relations, staff training and so on.

- Prototyping. Details can be taken from the text.

- Modelling the system. Details can be taken from the text.

A10. (a) Details of Expert Systems can be taken from the text.

(b) Can be taken from the text.

(c) Typical changes that might occur if an expert system was implemented include:

- Workload and status of Repair Centre Engineers is likely to be diminished.

- Possible redundancies at the Repair Centre.

- Communication and co-ordination between Field Engineers and the Repair Centre may become more difficult.

- Because the new system is more decentralised both financial and quality control may become more difficult.

- Job responsibilities will need to be re-defined.

A11. (a) Details of negative feedback can be taken from the text.

(b) Spreadsheets enable simple but effective models to be developed so that various options can be examined using the 'What if' facility. This makes them useful for tactical decision making which uses mainly internal data which can easily be incorporated into the spreadsheet calculations.

(c) Typical problems which may occur are:

- lack of clear documentation making it difficult for other staff to use the models

- lack of audit trails

- unsystematic use and development due to poor training.

Index